PARALEGAL
CAREER STARTER

PARALEGAL CAREER STARTER

by Jo Lynn Southard

LearningExpress ◆ New York

Library of Congress Cataloging-in-Publication Data

Southard, Jo Lynn
    Paralegal career starter/Jo Lynn Southard.
        p.   cm.
    ISBN   1–57685–098–6
    1. Legal assistants—Vocational guidance—United States.
I. Title.
KF320.L4S68   1998
340'.023'73—dc21   98–10846
                                                                    CIP

Printed in the United States of America
9 8 7 6 5 4 3 2 1
First Edition

Regarding the Information in this Book
Every effort has been made to ensure accuracy of directory information up until press time. However, phone numbers and/or addresses are subject to change. Please contact the respective organization for the most recent information.

For Further Information
For information on LearningExpress, other LearningExpress products, or bulk sales, please call or write to us at:
    LearningExpress™
    900 Broadway
    Suite 604
    New York, NY 10003
    212-995-2566

LearningExpress is an affiliated company of Random House, Inc.

ISBN 1-57685-098-6

CONTENTS

ACKNOWLEDGMENTS

I'd like to thank all of the paralegals, educators, students, and attorneys who shared with me their thoughts about and experiences with the paralegal profession. Most of all, thanks to Claire G. Andrews, Audrey M. Casey, Kevin Huntington, Gayle Lund, and Ann Tompkins. My thanks also to Leigh Anderson, Christina Buffamonte, James Gish, and Shirley Tarbell at LearningExpress.

ABOUT THE AUTHOR

Jo Lynn Southard has Juris Doctor and master of laws degrees from the University of Iowa. She is an adjunct professor in the Andover College Paralegal Studies Department and a freelance writer living in Portland, Maine.

INTRODUCTION

> Paralegals, also known as legal assistants, interview and communicate with clients; locate and depose witnesses; compose letters and pleadings; assist with depositions and hearings; and conduct will executions and real estate closings. Indeed, paralegals do any kind of legal work that is not the actual practice of law. This book gives you the information you need to join the ranks of this exciting and ever-growing career.

WHY ENTER THE PARALEGAL FIELD?

Recently, I mentioned to a friend from law school that I was writing a career guide for paralegals. She sighed and said, "I probably should have been a paralegal." What she meant was that paralegals do all of the things she enjoys the most about working in a law office—such as research, writing, and interviewing clients and witnesses. The paralegal profession is growing faster than other professions because it is an exciting and important occupation, and you can prepare for it with a reasonable and manageable commitment of resources.

The first thing to know is that a paralegal and a legal assistant are exactly the same thing. Sometimes, situations such as local court rules that allow a "legal assistant" to sit at the counsel table in a courtroom determine which term is used. "Paralegal" seems to be growing in popularity and is the term generally used in this book.

But what *is* a paralegal? Basically, as mentioned above, paralegals do a lot of the same things lawyers do, except presenting arguments to a court and giving legal advice. Throughout this book, you'll find details on the kinds of work that paralegals do as a matter of course. If the law interests you, but you don't particularly care if you get to argue in court, and you enjoy attending to detailed work, you might prefer being a paralegal to being an attorney. It certainly doesn't usually take as long to get your training.

This guide contains an extensive discussion of how you go about getting paralegal training. There are hundreds of different paralegal training programs in the U.S., representing a variety of perspectives of the profession. You'll find out how to distill all this information to find the right program for you. To get you started on—and probably complete—your search for a paralegal program, this book includes a state-by-state list of over 900 paralegal programs, as well as information that will help you find and apply for financial aid to help pay for your schooling.

To help you land your first job after you complete your training, there's information on job search strategies, resume preparation, writing cover letters, handling job interviews, and networking as a means of job hunting, as well as tips for making the most of your first job as a paralegal. Think of this book as a road map; if you follow it, you'll end up in an interesting and rewarding profession that is growing every year and shows no signs of slowing down. Here's a preview of some of the things you'll see and do along the way:

Step 1: Investigate What Paralegals Do

Paralegals work under the direct supervision of an attorney. One way of looking at the role of the paralegal is that paralegals do the legal background work. This means paralegals do a lot of research, both "book research," in a library or on an online service, and client and witness interviews. A good lawyer knows that preparation is the key to success, and many lawyers rely on paralegals to perform a lot of that preparation. Paralegals also keep track of client files, making sure they are complete and that things are done on time. They often write the first draft of a memo or brief; in many instances, paralegals send out correspondence under their own names.

Some paralegals, who work for solo practitioners or in small offices, are generalists, who may perform their duties under the rubric of criminal law one day, real estate law another, and torts the next day. On the other hand, paralegals who work for the government or in very large law firms specialize in particular areas of the law. Paralegals who work in the legal department of a corporation specialize in the area of the law appropriate to the company, for example, insurance law, and also in employment and corporation law. See chapter one for more discussion of the duties and specializations of paralegals.

Step 2: Decide on Your Training

At a minimum, you will need a high school diploma or General Educational Development (GED) Diploma in order to attend a paralegal program; in some cases, you'll need a bachelor's degree. There are just under 1,000 paralegal training programs in the U.S., ranging in length from a few months to four years. Some programs provide a general paralegal education, and some allow you to specialize in various ways. You'll have to decide, based on a variety of factors, what kind of paralegal education you want. Chapter two helps you analyze your talents, background, and interests in order to make this decision.

This chapter also gives you information about the various programs and what you can expect from them. It includes sample curricula from paralegal programs and information about accreditation that you can use to help you determine which program is right for you.

Step 3: Find and Pay for Your Training

Chapter three offers a list of over 900 paralegal programs; chances are you can find one that meets your needs. There are also pointers for finding other schools in your area.

Chapter four details the possibilities for financing your education, including loans, scholarships, and grants. You'll find out what forms you need, where to get them, how to fill them out, and where to send them, and get some tips for surviving this arduous process.

Step 4: Attend a Paralegal Program and Get the Most Out of Your Classes

Once you begin attending a program you want to make sure you get the most you can out of it. Chapter two offers pointers on succeeding in your classes; some of these are things I picked up as a law student, some in teaching paralegal classes. You'll also find note-taking abbreviations that will not only help you in school, but will also help you communicate with attorneys once you begin working.

Step 5: Conduct a Job Search

While you're still in school, you should begin thinking about job hunting. In chapter two you'll learn how an internship can lead to your first job, and in chapter five you'll find information on using other resources of your school to help you find your first job and to help you succeed on it.

Chapter five also includes some other effective methods for finding a good job once you finish your training. The information in this chapter helps you research the job market, write effective and attention-getting resumes and cover letters, and nail the scariest part of job hunting—the interview. It also covers networking, a way in which more and more people find a position. Job hunting is rarely a painless procedure, but the hints in this chapter will ease your anxiety and allow you to come through the whole process intact and with a good job.

Step 6: Succeed In Your New Profession

Chapter six gives you information that you can use to make any paralegal job—especially your first one—go smoothly and successfully. It includes hazards that can appear in the legal workplace and how you can avoid them—or recover from one. This chapter shows you how to fit into your new job and get along with your boss and coworkers. And you will learn the importance of having a mentor and how to go about finding one, and other ways that you can promote yourself.

On occasion, I will relate some of my own experiences in law school, as a practicing attorney and teacher of paralegal students. More important, though, are the thoughts of a variety of paralegals, paralegal students and educators, and lawyers that are sprinkled throughout. They are the people who know the most about the profession.

This book will tell you everything you need to know about becoming a paralegal and direct you to other resources as well. Whether you are just getting ready to graduate from high school or with a bachelor's degree or whether you are in the workplace and want a change of career or are returning to work outside the home, the information in this book can help get you where you want to be. Good luck!

CHAPTER | 1

BECOMING A PARALEGAL

What paralegals do depends on who they work for and where they are in their professional development. Generally, they research the law, prepare documents, conduct investigations, keep track of the status of clients' cases, and interview clients and witnesses; that is, they do almost anything a lawyer does, except actually give legal advice or represent clients in court. In this chapter, we'll look at some of the different places paralegals work and the things they do.

The paralegal profession is one of the fastest growing careers around, and it appears it will continue to grow, as more and more lawyers learn about the value of paralegals. From *Perry Mason* to *L.A. Law* to *The Practice*, television has given us one version of what a lawyer does. The media has never told us much, however, about what paralegals do. It's probably just as well; I never found TV lawyers were much like the lawyers I knew. For one thing, TV lawyers seem to work independently; but real lawyers depend on support from clerical staff and paralegals. *Para* is from the Greek and means "alongside." So a paralegal is one who works alongside a legal professional, or lawyer. Real lawyers, not TV lawyers.

Here are some definitions of "paralegal." According to the 1996 *Occupational Outlook Handbook,* published by the U.S. Bureau of Labor Statistics, "paralegals perform many of the same tasks as lawyers, except for those tasks considered to be the practice of law." The National Federation of Paralegal Associations (NFPA) defines a paralegal as "a person qualified through education, training or work experience to perform substantive legal work that requires knowledge of legal concepts and is customarily, but not exclusively, performed by a lawyer. This person may be retained or employed by a lawyer, law office, governmental agency or other entity or may be authorized by administrative, statutory or court authority to perform this work."

WHY BECOME A PARALEGAL?

There are several reasons to become a paralegal. Read on to find out more about the many benefits of this growing profession.

Job Satisfaction

According to a survey conducted by the NFPA, paralegals find that contact with attorneys and a sense of responsibility are the most satisfying parts of their work. Of course, job satisfaction among paralegals can vary greatly. Once you have received paralegal training, you have a certain flexibility in the kind of work you do. That's even more true when you have a couple of years of experience. So if you do end up in a job that you find is not satisfying, it is fairly easy to change positions. Of course, the market for paralegals varies across the country, but if you have a certain amount of drive, you can find or create a position that is fulfilling.

A potential area for dissatisfaction is the duties you, as a paralegal, are expected to undertake. The profession is still new enough that not all lawyers really understand what a paralegal is, especially as compared to a legal secretary. Many others, in small firms and solo practices, feel that economics keep them from hiring both a legal secretary and a paralegal. As a result, paralegals are often asked to undertake tasks that are clerical in nature. For the most part, a paralegal who works in an environment where everyone—including the attorneys—pitches in as needed probably doesn't mind so much performing the occasional clerical duty. On the other hand, a lawyer who understands and is respectful of your position will realize that while paralegals and legal secretaries both do important and difficult work, the two jobs are not the same. Most people, for example, wouldn't expect someone lacking legal training to conduct research or draft a pleading. Nor should they expect someone trained as a legal assistant to do clerical work. It can be a good idea to ask for a written job description when you apply for a job.

Professional Growth

As you gain experience as a paralegal, opportunities for advancement will present themselves. If the firm or company you work for is fairly large, you will have a chance to advance in-house into supervisory and management positions. However, if you work at a smaller firm or company, you may need to make a lateral transfer to a bigger employer to move on to a managerial position. Certainly, even if you work for a very small employer, you will be given more responsibility and be expected to perform your duties with less supervision as time goes on.

One way to demonstrate that you have continued to grow in your profession and therefore deserve to advance in your career is by receiving certification. Certification is voluntary, and currently few paralegals receive certification, but it may become more important as the field grows.

A Word About Certification

The National Association of Legal Assistants (NALA) administers the certified legal assistant (CLA) exam, the most common method of certification for paralegals. It is important to note that this certification is not the same thing as the certificate you may receive from your paralegal training program (see chapter two). The CLA program is an attempt to recognize national minimum standards of competence for paralegals. According to NALA, there were 8,630 certified legal assistants and 690 certified legal assistant specialists in the U.S. as of May 1997. For comparison purposes, the *Occupational Outlook Handbook,* compiled by the Bureau of Labor Statistics, estimates that in 1994 there were 111,000 paralegals working in the U.S. So less than one-tenth of paralegals have their CLA. Nonetheless, NALA claims that paralegals with CLAs are consistently higher paid than those without.

To take the CLA examination, you must have graduated from a paralegal training program that is ABA approved or that grants an associate or bachelor's degree or a post-baccalaureate certificate, or a program that consists of a minimum of 60 semester hours, of which at least 15 semester hours are substantive legal courses. Or if you have a bachelor's degree in any field plus one year's work experience as a paralegal, or a high school diploma and seven years of experience, you may take the exam. It is unusual for a paralegal to sit for the CLA exam right out of school; in fact, depending on your education, you may have to work for a while before you qualify to take the exam. However, you may want to take it someday, so it is worth keeping its requirements in mind as you make decisions about your education and career.

The CLA is a two-day exam based on federal law and procedure. The exam covers the following topics:

ethics	interviewing methods
legal research	legal terminology
communications	judgment
human relations	analytical ability

It also tests knowledge of substantive law, including the American legal system and four areas of your choice: administrative law, bankruptcy, business organizations/corporations, contracts, family law, criminal law and procedure, litigation, probate and estate planning, and real estate. Upon successful completion of the exam, you may use the designation C.L.A. (a registered trademark) after your name.

NALA also offers you the opportunity to receive advanced certification in one of several specialty areas. After you have passed the CLA, you may take an exam in bankruptcy, civil litigation, corporations/business law, criminal law and procedure, intellectual property, estate planning and probate, or real estate. Successful completion of one of these four-hour tests allows you to designate yourself as a specialist in the particular area.

In 1994, the National Federation of Paralegal Associations decided to begin administering its *own* certification test, called the Paralegal Advanced Competency Exam (PACE). To qualify to take this exam, you must have a minimum of two years of paralegal experience and a bachelor's degree and a certificate from an accredited school or a bachelor's degree in paralegal studies. You also must not have been convicted of a felony or had any kind of license, registration, or certification revoked. Because the test is new, until December 31, 2000, if you do not have a bachelor's degree but have four years of paralegal experience, you may take the exam. If you successfully complete this exam, you may designate yourself PACE registered paralegal or RP. The PACE test also has a specialty component.

A few states have begun providing their own paralegal certification, and more are considering it. Often they give the tests in conjunction with the CLA or the PACE. As of now, certification for paralegals is voluntary. However, it is always possible that it will be required in the future. Either it will be required *de facto* (in fact) because "everybody else" has it, or it will be required *de jure* (by law). Remember that to some extent, attorneys exert influence over the paralegal profession, and the majority of them had to take grueling bar exams in order to practice. They may decide that certification of paralegals is a good idea, too.

Salary and Benefits

The same NFPA survey reported that in 1995 the average paralegal salary was $32,875. However, the earnings of paralegals can vary a great deal, depending on the level of education and experience of the paralegal and the geographic location and size and type of the employer. Throughout the country, paralegal salaries range from about $10,000 to over $80,000. As a rule, if you are in a large urban area and work for a large firm, you will make more than paralegals in smaller cities at smaller firms. The average salary of paralegals employed by the federal government is about $5,000 more than that earned by legal assistants in the private sector, but there are opportunities to make more in the private sector.

Paralegal benefits vary as well. Most paralegals receive vacation, sick leave, life insurance, and medical benefits. Less than half of paralegals have access to a pension plan. Paralegals who received a bonus reported that it averaged over $1,800.

A current issue in the paralegal profession is that of overtime. Most paralegals are nonexempt employees; that is, they must be paid overtime for working over 40 hours a week. Some paralegals would prefer to be exempt employees and be paid a straight salary; they believe that nonexempt employees, because they are paid an hourly wage, are seen as less professional. Gayle Lund, a litigation paralegal in Los Angeles, notes, "The paralegal associations are very involved in the dispute about whether we should be professionals and receive a straight salary or whether we should receive overtime. To me, overtime is unprofessional. You might have to sacrifice for a few years on a straight salary, but if you want to be respected as a professional, you need to be recognized as a professional, and that's one of the ways you do it."

WHAT DO PARALEGALS DO?

The paralegal profession was born in the 1960s, during former President Lyndon Johnson's "War on Poverty," as a way of providing basic legal assistance to the poor. Although unable to give legal advice, a paralegal could help clients fill out forms, prepare them for court appearances, maintain contact with them, and help attorneys prepare their cases. A few attorneys, assisted by paralegals, could provide services to many more people than the lawyers would be able to handle alone. Originally, paralegals worked in public agencies charged with providing legal services to the poor. Over time, corporations and private attorneys began to see the benefit of employing paralegals in their practices as well; now, most paralegals work in large, private law firms. Initially, paralegals were trained on the job; in the 1970s, paralegal training programs began to appear. There are now nearly 1,000 distinct training programs, many of which are listed in chapter three.

Although the term "paralegal" is generally preferred over "legal assistant," tradition and even court rules dictate which term is used in different areas. Paralegals are also distinct from legal secretaries, although many legal secretaries become paralegals. Of course, the size of a legal office can affect this distinction; also, the advent of computers means that almost everyone—even attorneys—does some clerical work. As the Iowa Bar Association puts it, "In general, the legal assistants are performing a number of activities involving client contact, and their activities for the most part are different from, and more demanding than, those normally associated with secretarial or stenographic work."

Typical Duties

Paralegals do a variety of tasks, just as lawyers do. As a paralegal, some of your duties could include:

- **Research:** Library, on-line, public records, medical, scientific
- **Investigation:** Interview clients, witnesses, experts; on-site analysis
- **Writing:** Draft memos, briefs, correspondence, interrogatories, pleadings
- **Administration:** Index documents, digest documents, organize pleadings, organize trial exhibits, monitor tax and corporate filings
- **Docket control:** Prepare discovery requests and responses, schedule depositions, notify clients, witnesses, and attorneys of trial dates, file motions and pleadings

As you look at this list, it becomes apparent that there are a few basic skills you need if you want to be a paralegal. A good legal assistant is bright, personable, literate, organized, and even more organized. Lawyers depend on paralegals to do much of the background work for any given client. This includes getting information from the client, researching the particular area of the law involved, preparing memos that keep the attorney informed of the progress in the case, maintaining the client's file, and making sure that all deadlines are met. Falling short in one of these areas is one of the worst things an attorney can do; if it's up to you to keep the lawyer on track, it becomes your nightmare, too.

Morning Appointments		Afternoon Appointments		Things To Do Today
7:00		1:00		✓ Research motion to quash
7:30	NALA Breakfast	1:30	Eddie Evidence— testimony prep	✓ Prepare quitclaim deed
8:00				✓ Notify Cathy Client of trial date
8:30		2:00		
9:00	Meet w/ Paula Partner	2:30	Deposition of Jerry Justice at Barrister, Counselor, & Solicitor	✓ File pleadings re: Tess Torts
9:30				
10:00	Initial interview with Rex Retainer (2nd OUI)	3:00		
		3:30		
10:30		4:00		
11:00		4:30		
11:30	Arraignment— Miles Misdemeanor— Court B	5:00		
		5:30	Drinks with B. Scheck	
12:00		6:00		

The particulars of any paralegal job will depend on your employer and the firm's clients. Since paralegals work under the supervision of an attorney, it is up to your boss to determine which tasks you will be assigned in any given case. As in any profession, different attorneys have different ways of working. You might find that you have a great deal of autonomy to handle a case, or your boss may prefer a team approach. A mere glance at this "daily planner" wouldn't tell you whether it came off a lawyer's desk or a paralegal's.

What a paralegal cannot do that an attorney does is practice law. Believe it or not, this is a fine line, and it's not always easy to see when it's been crossed. It is imperative that, as a paralegal, every time you communicate with a court, client, witness, or opposing counsel, you make sure you make it clear that you are a paralegal and not an attorney. And never tell someone what to do about a legal matter. For example, paralegals frequently help clients fill out forms, such as tax, corporate, or bankruptcy forms. But as Claire Andrews, director of paralegal programs at Casco Bay College in Portland, Maine, notes, "The dangerous part is [when helping clients with a bankruptcy,] they can easily step over into the unauthorized practice of law. Technically, what they should be doing is helping people fill out the forms. If they do something like help them decide whether they're going to file Chapter 15 or Chapter 11 [bankruptcy], they're practicing law." See the NALA Code of Ethics and Professional Responsibility at the end of this chapter for more information.

No matter what kind of office you work in, there are a few things you can count on if you decide to become a paralegal. First, the work will be interesting. When people come to a lawyer, it is because something has happened—or is going to happen—in their lives that they want help dealing with. For example, the first thing most of us would do if we were arrested is hire an attorney. And it's probably going to be interesting to hear the story behind a person's arrest—and, no doubt, an explanation of why he or she is innocent! Less obvious things can be quite interesting, too—for example, why your client wants to cut someone out of a will or how one company is attempting a hostile takeover of another.

Second, the work will be varied. Even when you specialize in a particular area of the law, your clients will have an assortment of legal issues. In corporate law, for example, you may deal with companies that produce anything from apple cider to zoo enclosures. Third, the work will be satisfying. While it is true that a lawyer can't solve every problem just exactly the way a client wants it solved, in most cases people seem to feel that the attorney helped them through a troubling time. Also, from your perspective, most of the tasks you work on have an end, a solution. Sometimes when you begin researching a legal problem, you feel as if it's brand new and no one ever faced it before. Then you usually find that the law has dealt with it and there is an answer. It can be very gratifying when you are the one who finds that answer.

Finally, as the paralegal profession continues to grow, you will be presented with more and more opportunities for growth within your career. Whether you take on more responsibility within a job or take the plunge and leave your job for a new paralegal position in another area of the law, you will be in charge of your own professional destiny. As the demand for paralegals grows throughout the country, it can even provide you with the opportunity to move to a new area—and almost be guaranteed you'll be able to find a job.

SPECIALIZATION

What area of the law you work in may depend largely on the specialty of the employer. In a small general practice firm, the area of the law pretty much depends on the problems of the clients who come through the door. Was your client arrested? Then you'll be researching criminal law. Does your client want a divorce?

Then you'll bone up on family law. A will? Estate planning and probate. The possi-bilities are almost endless. For many people, that's part of what makes the law interesting; others prefer to become specialists in one or two of these areas.

Common specialty areas include:

administrative law	criminal law and procedure
family law	intellectual property
civil litigation	estate planning
bankruptcy	probate
corporate and business law	real estate law.

Others, such as environmental law, will continue to grow but are currently less common specialties. There are many other areas that are very specialized and limited to rather small numbers of law firms, such as Native American law or education law. The following is information about a few of the most common areas of specialization.

Administrative Law

Administrative law refers to the law that is generated by governmental administra-tive agencies. Although these agencies may fall under the legislative branch of the federal, state, or local government, most of them are under the rubric of the exec-utive (the president, governor, or mayor) branch. The agencies may be in federal or state government and vary from state to state, but they include the Social Secu-rity Administration, the Internal Revenue Service, and, in states, such areas as education and worker's compensation. In addition, more and more cities have human rights boards that deal with discrimination issues within the city. Special-izing in this area may allow paralegals to represent clients in adversarial settings before administrative law judges, because in many cases petitioners may be repre-sented by anyone they choose; it need not be a lawyer.

Family Law

In family law, you will be dealing with divorce, child custody and support, and adoption. This can be a very rewarding area of the law, but it can also be quite stressful. A lot of people I know who specialize in this area have very strong polit-ical beliefs (about the rights of women or of children) that impel them to work in family law, where they feel they can make a difference. For many firms, especially small firms, family law is the real bread-and-butter of the business. As a paralegal, you will draft divorce and child custody petitions and gather financial and asset information and spend a lot of time with clients.

Civil Litigation

Litigation involves lawsuits and the possibility of court battles, although most lawsuits are settled before reaching trial. "Civil" refers to the areas of the law that are not criminal—that is, disagreements between parties that do not involve the police power of the state. By definition, this area deals with disputes, one side trying to prove it is right and the other side is wrong. To be successful in this area, you need to be flexible; you may be on a side you don't personally believe in, but you must represent your client zealously. You also need to be organized and detail oriented. Clients can lose cases because their attorneys failed, for example, to file a response on time. This also opens the offending lawyer up to a malpractice suit. As a litigation paralegal, you will be responsible for, among other things, keeping track of dates and deadlines. You will also conduct investigations and witness interviews. It can be very interesting and varied work. On the other hand, some cases drag on for years!

Bankruptcy

Bankruptcy law used to be about as prestigious as ambulance chasing. Now it is often called debtor-creditor law and is becoming more reputable. It can also be very lucrative. In the last couple of decades, the number of bankruptcies has increased greatly. This used to be tied very much to the economy in general; that is, when the economy was bad, bankruptcies increased. Recently, though, even with a good economy, people seem to continue to get into too much debt, and bankruptcies continue to be a profitable area of the law. As a paralegal, you may work for an attorney who represents debtors, creditors, or trustees. Obviously, debtors are the ones who owe the money, and for them you will gather together financial information, draft the bankruptcy petition, prepare the schedule of assets and liabilities, and file any periodic reports. If you work for the person to whom the money is owed—the creditor—you will draft and file the proof of claim. If you work for a trustee (who may or may not be a lawyer), you will notify all parties who might have claims, track any transfers or payments of assets, and review claims.

Unlike most areas of the law, bankruptcy can be handled by a paralegal from beginning to end, except for the decision to file and the decision about which chapter to file. There is very little "practicing of law" in bankruptcy.

Corporate and Business Law

Although many paralegals work for corporations, not all of them are practicing corporate law. Paralegals who work, for example, for an insurance company and deal with customer claims are working in insurance law. These paralegals are sometimes called corporate but are more appropriately labeled in-house legal department paralegals. On the other hand, corporate law deals with business transactions, incorporations, mergers and acquisitions, and ongoing corporate matters. These include drafting or amending articles of incorporation or bylaws; drafting shareholders' agreements and stock options; and preparing meeting agendas, notifying meeting participants, and taking meeting minutes.

Criminal Law and Procedure

Criminal law involves violations of the rules of society, such as rules not to drive drunk or assault someone. Criminal procedure involves constitutional law, in the form of the Fourth Amendment to the U.S. Constitution, which states, "The right of the people to be secure in their persons, houses, papers, and effects, against unreasonable searches and seizures, shall not be violated, and no warrants shall issue, but upon probable cause, supported by Oath or affirmation, and particularly describing the place to be searched, and the persons or things to be seized." Sometimes you'll hear that a criminal defendant "got off on a technicality." I like to point out that the Fourth Amendment to the Constitution should hardly be considered a technicality!

On occasion, the people and situations you deal with in criminal law and procedure are a bit unsavory, but it is always interesting work. And nothing is more important in our society than protecting individual constitutional rights.

Intellectual Property

The practice area of intellectual property involves protecting the creations, ideas, and inventions of people and businesses. This area of the law deals with trademarks, which protect manufacturers' rights to the identification of their products; patents, which protect inventors' rights to make and market their inventions; copyrights, which protect the products of authors and artists; and trade secrets law, which deals with a company's right to keep secret formulas, designs, and other information that gives them a competitive advantage. Intellectual property deals with the property that results from using one's intellect.

This is a very specialized area of the law; in fact, lawyers who work in this area are members of a distinct bar. The advent of computers and all the software that goes with them have made this a very hot and fast-growing field.

Estate Planning and Probate

Like bankruptcy, many paralegals are attracted to estate planning and probate because it is a field in which they can work quite independently. Estate planning involves helping clients utilize procedures—such as the creation of trusts—that allow them to bequeath their property without having to go through probate. Probate is the legal procedure by which a deceased person's property is located and distributed. If the decedent had a will, it is called a testate proceeding; if there is no will, it is an intestate proceeding, and state law will determine how the person's property is disbursed. Conservatorships and guardianships are also under the purview of the probate courts. A conservator is appointed to care for an adult who is deemed to be incompetent. A guardian does the same thing for a child.

Estate planning in particular requires knowledge of accounting procedures and investments, as well as the law of trusts and estates. For paralegals who have this knowledge, there is a great deal of autonomy in the field; there are even times when you can appear in court on behalf of a client.

Real Estate

Real estate law is another field that allows paralegals to work autonomously. This area involves representing buyers and sellers of residential or commercial property; lenders or borrowers of the financing for these sales; and landlords or tenants. To do this, paralegals deal with titles, the documents that give possession of property to a particular owner, and also with any rights that others may have to the property (through a lien or lease, for example). Titles must be thoroughly searched in order for a sale of real estate to commence.

Once the title is clear and the sale is going through, paralegals are often responsible for seeing that the closing of the sale goes smoothly. This involves drafting any documents needed, such as mortgages, deeds, or bills of sale; estimating what the closing will cost; and managing the documents for the title company. A great deal of this work can be done by a paralegal with only minimal supervision from an attorney.

Other Areas of the Law

If you decide to pursue training and a career as a paralegal, you will no doubt be struck by how the law seems to touch every aspect of our lives. Almost anything can conceivably be a specialty area of the law. In addition to the areas I've already discussed, others you may run across are

AIDS law

agriculture law

alternative dispute mediation (ADR—also known as mediation)

animal rights law

antitrust law

civil rights law

computer and Internet law

elder law

employment law

entertainment law

environmental law

human rights law

immigration law

labor law

legal malpractice law

medical malpractice law

Native American law

personal injury law

private (business) international law

sports law

Almost anything you are interested in, or an expert in, can be a specialty area of the law. Sometimes being a specialist means that you will be highly sought after and, as a result, highly paid. Sometimes you must content yourself with minimal income and the satisfaction that you are doing something that is interesting and important to you. The only thing restricting you is the market; how many people where you are need what you have to offer? I don't, for example, recommend planning on being an agriculture law specialist if you live in Manhattan. You may not find a situation where you can practice your specialty exclusively, but maybe you can join a firm where you can at least do it some of the time. In other cases, if you are determined enough to specialize in a particular area, you may have to create the market.

WHERE DO PARALEGALS WORK?

Most paralegals work in private law firms. However, law firms may be comprised of a few lawyers or several hundred. Paralegals also work for corporations, the government, nonprofit employers, and a variety of other places. Almost every agency of the federal government employs legal assistants; the majority of them are at the Departments of Justice, Treasury, Interior, and Health and Human Services. Many state and local government departments employ paralegals as well. Where you work has a large impact on what kind of work you do. The specialty of the firm or agency will determine your specialty. In addition, different workplaces have different cultures. The local Legal Service Corporation office or environmental action group will no doubt offer a much more casual work atmosphere than a large firm or a court. It's wise to keep in mind some of the different kinds of work settings as you embark on your paralegal career.

The Large Firm

The relative size of a large law firm depends on the city in which it is located. In Chicago, for example, a 100-lawyer firm is probably considered medium-size, while in Springfield, Illinois, that same firm would be large indeed. Baker & McKenzie in Chicago claims to be the world's largest law firm, with over 2,300 lawyers. (But those lawyers are divided among dozens of offices worldwide; the largest is the Chicago office, with over 180 attorneys.) In most places, however, a firm with more than 100 lawyers is considered a large firm. In some large law firms, there will be even more paralegals than lawyers!

Large law firms are generally divided up into departments, such as litigation, probate and estate planning, corporate and business organizations, and international law. This specialization allows the paralegals who work for these firms to specialize as well. A large firm may also contain a structured paralegal "department." This doesn't affect the specialization of the work you do, but rather provides you with a paralegal supervisor and, possibly, paralegal assistants. This structure usually also means that there will be an in-house training program and regular staff meetings. All of this can be very helpful, both in keeping you apprised of the latest developments in the firm and in the law, and in providing you with a intermediary between you and management. This structure also provides you with opportunity for advancement as a paralegal.

The attorneys in large firms will be either partners (although there may be senior and junior partners) or associates. Associates are usually hired right out of law school, although they may have clerked for a judge for a year or two before joining the firm. It used to be that most associates expected to become partners of the firm in about seven years. During the time I was job hunting, though, in the mid-1990s, there was a glut of lawyers on the market, and some were finding themselves unemployed after a few years, rather than gaining the key to the partner restroom. Things have calmed a bit in the last few years, but even very competent associates are not guaranteed partnership.

Generally speaking, paralegal training is more practical than law school. Even as a newly hired paralegal, you may find you know more useful legal information than your recently graduated associate boss! As Audrey Casey, chair of the Paralegal Studies Department at Andover College in Portland, Maine, notes, "I've worked with attorneys who say, 'I know everything there is to know about a complaint, but how do you *do* one?'" On the other hand, at a large law firm, your new boss probably graduated from a prestigious law school and has now been hired by a large, important firm and is no doubt feeling pretty pleased with life. This creates a situation in which your boss may not want to hear that you know something he or she

Sample Job Advertisements

Antitrust Group Coordinator

Great opportunity for senior antitrust/litigation paralegal to utilize years of supervisory experience and advance to a management position. Responsibilities include coordinating work flow and case assignments, interviewing applicants and preparing performance evaluations for the junior paralegals in the antitrust group. Case management and administrative responsibilities. Salary up to $50,000.

Litigation

Immediate need for litigation paralegal with two to five years of experience in insurance and insurance coverage litigation or general litigation. Responsibilities include case management, document review, and trial preparation. Salary negotiable. Work for one of the top group of litigators in the country.

Entry Level

1997 graduate with top credentials, 3.5 GPA, sought for international trade paralegal position. Great firm. Lots of responsibility. Immediate need.

Logging Hours on the Job

Firms of any size generate their income via billable hours. These are the actual hours of work that can be billed to a client, and they include the time that the lawyers and paralegals spent working for that particular client. They don't include things like taking a break or learning how to unjam the copy machine. As a firm paralegal, you'll have to keep track of your time and be accountable for it. In 1995, according to the National Federation of Paralegal Associations, billing for paralegals ranged from $41 to $80 per hour.

In any firm, no matter what the size, the length of your workday will vary. Although it doesn't usually affect paralegals as much as the new associates, when there is a looming court date, it's not unusual to find the lights burning in the law office long into the night. And you can bet it's usually not the senior partners who are losing any sleep!

---

doesn't. This kind of situation can lead to clashes among the personnel of law firms, and when it's a large firm, there are more chances for disputes to arise.

The stereotype of large firms is that they tend to be stuffy. As with many generalizations, this is both true and not true. Traditionally, the largest firms have been considered the slowest to change: the slowest to hire women associates, for example, and the last to consider changing their workplace conditions to meet the needs of their employees. Large firms tend to be more hierarchical and structured; they are places where things are done a certain way because that's how they've always been done. Some people like that; some people prefer more flexibility.

Large firms offer many advantages as well. First of all, the salaries they pay paralegals are among the highest. They also may be more willing to hire new graduates, since there will be other paralegals at the firm who can train and mentor them. Large firms have more resources than smaller firms. Their in-house library will probably be fairly complete, and they will have access to a variety of the latest technology in research. The physical equipment in a large firm—computers and the like—is more apt to be state-of-the-art than in smaller firms. All in all, a large firm can be a very rewarding work environment for a paralegal, particularly one who has recently graduated from school.

The Small to Medium-Size Firm

When you work in a small to medium-size firm, you will have to take on a greater variety of duties than in a large firm. Although some smaller firms, and even solo practitioners, specialize, most are general practitioners. Even if they specialize, they often supplement that work with an extensive general practice. Your work on any given day depends a great deal on who walks through the door. Small firms do a lot of criminal law, usually for more minor offenses such as traffic violations. Family law is also a large component of a small practice. Real estate law and probate and estate planning are two more areas that come up often in small firms.

In addition to a variety in the areas of law practiced, there is also variety in the work assigned to people who work in smaller firms, including the attorneys, paralegals, and secretaries. When there is a lot of business, everyone has to be willing to pitch in to run the copy machine. When it's quieter, everyone can afford to stick to their own job descriptions more closely. As a result, a paralegal in this setting may easily become an important and trusted member of a team rather than just one among many paralegals in a large firm. The environment of smaller firms is usually more relaxed and more open to change than larger firms.

On the down side, smaller firms usually have fewer resources. This means that their law library may be quite small, and you may have to go to the local law school or courthouse to do your research. Computer research possibilities will probably be limited, possibly nonexistent. It is also not unusual for paralegals to be expected to perform some clerical duties in a small firm. As I said, in frantic times,

---

Sample Job Advertisements

Corporate Transactional Paralegal

Enjoy the diversity of a small firm (25 attorneys). If you are a proactive, energetic professional with a desire to expand your areas of expertise, this is an opportunity to consider. At least two years of corporate/transactional experience required. Competitive salary; stable environment.

Entry to Mid-Level Paralegal Position

Mid-size energy, environmental, and civil firm needs paralegal with excellent skills (Bluebook, Shepard's, LEXIS, Westlaw). Must have the ability to conduct research on a wide range of topics. Strong academic background, attention to detail, and good organizational skills essential. Must also be computer proficient (preferably Windows 95, Word). Position provides extensive contact with attorneys, discovery team participation, and high level of responsibility. Please mail or fax resume to: Managing Paralegal.

Entry-Level Litigation Paralegal

Not for the average performer. Integrity and commitment are highly valued in this unique environment. Must have four-year degree; paralegal certificate a plus. Training is not a problem, but you must have an interest in developing computer skills. Demonstrate your commitment and receive respect and recognition from this prestigious firm.

A Few Words About Small to Medium-Size Firms

Litigation paralegal Gayle Lund says, "Smaller law firms, maybe five- or ten-partner firms or sole practitioners, tend not to use paralegals at all. They don't want to spend the money, and they also rely a lot on their legal secretaries to perform what are really paralegal duties." On the other hand, Penny, a placement counselor at the Affiliates, a nationwide legal placement service in Houston, says, "It's not at all mostly larger firms that are hiring paralegals; it runs the gamut. I'm working with a firm right now that has three attorneys. Large firms have the majority of paralegals because they have the overhead to pay the people to have assistants. When you get to the smaller firms, a lot of times you'll see secretary/paralegal jobs. It can be advantageous to go to a small firm because you get a lot of paralegal skills; even though your title is legal secretary, you're really doing paralegal work. A lot of the larger firms have pools of paralegals, whereas maybe a moderate firm has one or two to handle multiple attorneys."

---

everyone should be willing to pitch in, but make sure that your duties are clearly defined when you are hired. Not all attorneys are really aware of the differences between paralegals and legal secretaries. Many of them can't afford to have all the clerical staff they would like. In addition, as computers become more and more a part of our daily life, many of us are doing more clerical work than before. Working in a small firm can be a great experience; just make sure that you and your employer have an understanding about your job duties.

If, as you finish your training and begin job hunting, you are still unsure whether or in what you want to specialize, working in a small to medium-size firm will give you the opportunity to dabble in many different areas of the law. Many paralegals and attorneys prefer to remain generalists throughout their careers; exposure to a variety of legal areas will help you decide if you want to specialize and in what.

Corporations

When you work in the in-house legal department of a corporation, you will probably deal with some of the corporate law topics I talked about earlier and also with the law of the specific industry you are in. On the corporate side, you may assist the corporate attorneys with employee contracts and benefit plans, shareholder agreements, and stock option plans. You may send notices of meetings and take minutes at those meetings.

In addition, you will work in the area of the law that relates to your corporation. It is the responsibility of the legal department to stay on top of all the government regulations that relate to your business, such as antitrust, environmental, and equal employment opportunity, as well as any rules that relate more directly to your industry, such as banking or insurance regulations. Most in-house legal departments are too small to handle all of the legal issues that arise, so you'll be working with outside counsel in some cases.

When you work as a paralegal for a corporation, the company is your client. That's your only client, so you don't have to worry about billable hours. (Which doesn't mean you don't have to account for your working time!) And although unusual things can always happen if there is a lawsuit under way, most of the time you'll work regular, nine-to-five hours. This can be a very important perk if you have a family.

Of course, because you only have one client, you will have less variety than if you had several clients in a law firm. Some people find that it becomes boring after

---

Sample Job Advertisements

In-House Paralegal

Life insurance company, a dynamic, diversified financial services organization. Due to our growth, we are seeking a paralegal for our legal and executive departments. You will be responsible for a variety of legal research and writing activities and will provide an equal amount of support to our legal and executive departments. Specific responsibilities include preparing insurance/regulatory findings, monitoring market compliance, litigation support, and supporting complaint investigations. You have a B.A. or B.S. and a minimum of five years of paralegal experience, with excellent legal research and writing skills. Also, you possess interpersonal skills and experience with spreadsheets, personal computers, and word processing software. You also have a strong interest in continuous learning and self-development. We offer a friendly, professional environment with competitive compensation and benefits. Send your resume and a writing sample.

Computer/Litigation Paralegal

Corporation has an immediate opening for a computer wiz/litigation paralegal with the following software skills: LawTrac, Quest, Lotus, Concordance, Westlaw, LEXIS, Access, Excel. Candidate must be systems oriented. Duties: Tracking/reporting expenses, inputting invoices, legal research, discovery, organization and maintenance of litigation/arbitration files. Exceptional communication skills and flexibility needed; must be a team player. Excellent salary and benefits.

Commercial Loan Closer

Freedom from the office! Travel to three networked banks to do commercial loan closings. Employer needs detail-oriented professional to report directly to bank president. This position requires you to have a car for travel. Employer pays mileage and parking. Terrific position for team-oriented person interested in banking! Good benefits plus FREE checking and other bank perks.

a while. On the other hand, it allows you to become an expert in a particular area of the law, such as banking or insurance or manufacturing. If you feel after a few years that you are ready to move on, you will be in a position to present yourself as an expert, and that can only enhance your job possibilities.

A rather new trend in small corporations is to have a legal department that consists only of a paralegal, although it's rarely called the legal department. Most often the legal assistant will work in human resources or as an assistant to one of the higher-ranking officers. One of the main reasons companies do this is that much of what legal departments do doesn't require an attorney. Taking the minutes at a board meeting, for example, does not involve the practice of law. And when a lawyer is needed, it may be cheaper for the company to hire outside counsel to do the final version of the work. So the paralegal can, for example, draft an employment agreement that fits the needs of the business, and an outside attorney can verify the legal points. Paralegals in these kinds of positions are also responsible for recognizing when outside counsel is needed.

The title of such jobs may not always be paralegal or legal assistant. It may be something like "special assistant to the president" or "human resources specialist." You need to look closely at the job description to realize that the job requires someone with paralegal training.

Government

If you go to work for the government, the kinds of duties and responsibilities you have will depend on what department or agency you work for. Some possibilities include the Department of Justice, the Department of the Interior, the Environmental Protection Agency, the Internal Revenue Service, and the Immigration Service. Many of these agencies have state corollaries, although the names may be different. In addition to all of the departments and agencies, there are the court systems, both federal and state. There, you could work in the offices of the district attorney or public defender. In the courts themselves, there are positions such as court administrator, which involves managing the court's docket and personnel and perhaps conducting research for the judge. Other government positions that may not use the term paralegal or legal assistant in the title include export compliance specialist, a person who investigates commodities and data being exported outside the U.S., and patent examiner, a person who assists in determining if certain inventions are eligible for patent.

Working for the government provides great job security and other benefits. In the legal field, the pay usually starts out higher than in the private sector but

Sample Job Advertisements

Paralegal Specialist, GS-950-7

Salary range: $25,897 to $49,831. Tax division, Department of Justice, various sections (civil, appellate, and criminal), Washington, D.C. Duties: The incumbent will aid attorneys in litigating civil and criminal cases, including conducting investigations, preparing cases for trial, and providing legal advice and assistance. The incumbent is responsible for conducting factual and legal research; collecting, analyzing, and evaluating information; drafting reports, memoranda, pleadings, and correspondence; interviewing persons and preparing interview reports; analyzing documents, organizing material, and preparing synopses; summarizing transcripts; preparing charts and exhibits; and verifying citations and legal references. Qualifications: For GS-7: Applicants must have one full academic year of graduate-level education or law school or superior academic achievement or one year of specialized experience equivalent to the GS-5 level. Nonstatus candidates at the GS-7 level may be appointed using the Outstanding Scholar provision if they possess at least a 3.5 GPA or have graduated in the upper ten percent of the class. Evaluation methods: Applicants will be evaluated on experience, education and training, awards, and supervisory appraisal. How to apply: Applicants may submit a resume, the Optional Form for Federal Employment (OF-612), or any other written format, including the SF-171. In addition, nonstatus applicants must submit a college transcript (the transcript must include grades through the summer 1997 semester). Status (federal) applicants must also submit a copy of their latest Notification of Personnel Action (SF-50) and copy of performance appraisal issued within the last 12 months to U.S. Department of Justice.

Federal government jobs are rated using a General Schedule, which establishes salary rates throughout the government. The ratings range from GS-1 through GS-16. In addition, jobs are classified by occupational group; legal and related jobs are GS-0900. So in GS-950-7, for example, 950 relates to paralegal, and GS-7 is the salary ranking of this paralegal position.

State University Paralegal

Job Summary: Assists attorneys with trial and pretrial matters. Job duties: Organizes, enters, and cross-references documents in a computerized database. Obtains, assembles, and organizes documents pertinent to litigation. Prepares discovery requests and responses. Assists in the preparation of statements and declarations of witnesses. Assists general counsel in organizing and carrying out special projects as assigned. Performs other related duties as assigned or requested. Job qualifications: Must have specialized paralegal training and one year of experience. May combine experience and education as substitute for minimum education or experience. Prefer a bachelor's degree, certificate from an ABA-approved program, and two years of experience. Skills: Must have the ability to assemble and coordinate manuscripts, compose letters, gather data, input data, communicate with others to gather information, maintain filing systems, prioritize different projects, research information, schedule appointments, write memorandums for own signature, coordinate work of others. Must operate personal computer, photocopier, word processor.

> **City Attorney's Office/Internal Litigation Unit Paralegals**
>
> This is paraprofessional legal work of moderate difficulty assisting attorneys in case preparation and processing. An employee of this class is responsible for performing paraprofessional legal tasks routinely handled by attorneys and assisting in the coordination of case activities. Some positions may require working part time or evenings (until 9 p.m.) or require the ability to communicate in Spanish. Minimum qualifications: More than one year of experience in a private or governmental law firm performing primarily litigation related case management and legal research under the direction of an attorney; an associate degree or a certificate of completion from an accredited college or technical school as a legal assistant or paralegal; or an equivalent combination of education, experience and training that provides the desired knowledge, skills and abilities.

caps at a lower level. Getting a government job involves a lot of red tape; whether federal, state, or local, government jobs usually have strict evaluation and hiring guidelines. You have to follow the procedures exactly; there's usually no way for an employer to "give you a break" if you don't.

Nonprofit Organizations

Nonprofit organizations that hire paralegals may be advocacy groups, such as poverty law organizations that provide legal services to disadvantaged persons, or activist groups, such as environmental, women's, or civil rights groups. Often the same group will participate in both activities. For the most part, people who work for these organizations do so because they believe in the cause; the pay usually isn't all that good. The non-monetary rewards of these jobs are significant, however. Nonprofits, although they are serious about the work they do, can rarely be described as stuffy. Usually the office environment is quite casual, and the staff is open to new ideas.

Advocacy nonprofit organizations include groups such as Legal Services Corporation (LSC), a private corporation that was established by Congress in 1974 to provide equal access to the law for impoverished Americans. It seems that Congress threatens to eliminate funding for LSC every year, but so far it's still around. LSC offices are usually strapped for money, as is true of most nonprofits. They occasionally hire paralegals, but they are perhaps better sources for volunteer internships. If you do decide to work for a nonprofit, you may find the work stressful at times, but when you are working for a cause you believe in, it's very rewarding.

As with corporate jobs, sometimes nonprofits won't be looking for a paralegal, but your training will nonetheless qualify you for the position they are trying to fill. If you are committed to working for a nonprofit group, keep your eyes open for all sorts of job titles.

Sample Job Advertisements

Immigration Paralegal

A national public interest law firm dedicated to protecting and promoting the rights of low-income immigrants through impact litigation, policy analysis, training, technical assistance, and the publication of training materials is looking for a paralegal to add to our staff of 11.

Qualifications: Prefer four-year college degree or paralegal training. At least two years of responsible paralegal experience in which independent judgment was utilized and client interaction was emphasized. Thorough knowledge of legal procedures. Familiarity with immigration law and a second language are a plus. Salary: $31,704.47 to $40,515.59.

Community Organizer

A community organization whose goals are to empower parents with the necessary skills to help their children succeed in school, to bring the community and delinquent youth together, and to help citizens take action to improve their neighborhoods needs a community organizer. Job duties include conducting constituent interviews, research, recruiting volunteers, developing volunteer leaders, implementing issue campaigns, writing, media relations, and fundraising. Hours: 45 to 50 hours per week (most evenings; occasional weekends); flextime.

Qualifications: Four-year college degree, excellent written and oral communications skills, commitment to grassroots organizing and citizen empowerment; bilingual (Spanish) and computer skills are helpful. Salary: $21,000 to $24,000 (depending on experience); health insurance and two weeks vacation.

Planned Giving / Major Gifts Paralegal

International non-governmental human rights organization is seeking an assistant to the Advisor for Planned Giving. Responsibilities: Management of terminated estates, bequests, and trusts and administrative assistance to a multimillion-dollar fundraising program that seeks estate-related gifts throughout the U.S. Qualifications: The selected candidate must have three years of paralegal or banking experience specifically related to estates/bequests/trusts. Successful candidates will have management experience in a legal estates department, or as a paralegal handling estates, or as a banker trained in managed trusts. Administration duties include word processing.

Other Workplaces

Contract Paralegals

Contract, or freelance, paralegals are hired by attorneys or companies to work on a case-by-case basis. It is quite rare for a newly graduated paralegal to attempt such a career, but it may be something you'll want to consider after you have several years of experience. The benefits of self-employment include the freedom to structure your own time and to choose the projects you want to work on. The disadvantages include uncertainty about your income and the necessity of paying your own business expenses. In addition, you must be able to market yourself.

Temporary Paralegals

Some paralegals prefer to work through temporary agencies. Some are placed by companies such as Kelly and Manpower that place a variety of workers in a variety of jobs. In a few larger cities, legal temporary agencies are sprouting up. These agencies place attorneys, paralegals, and legal secretaries in temporary positions. Many people enjoy temporary work; it gives you more control over your own time than full-time employment, with a bit more security than freelancing. If, as you finish your paralegal training, you're still unsure about the kind of paralegal work you'd like to specialize in, temporary placements give you an opportunity to try out a variety of positions. But it is less secure than full-time employment. You may have periods in which the agency has no assignment for you, and at times you may have to take positions that you aren't interested in.

Independent Paralegals

Independent paralegals work directly with clients; their work is not directly supervised by an attorney. Independent paralegals help consumers, for example, fill out forms for bankruptcy, estate planning, and taxes. However, they still cannot give legal advice. So your clients need to know before they come to you which bankruptcy chapter they should file under, for example, or whether they should set up a trust. Once these matters have been determined by the client in conjunction with a lawyer, however, the client can save money by hiring a paralegal rather than a lawyer to fill out the forms.

I don't think you should consider being an independent paralegal until you have several years of experience. You will find, even as you attend your paralegal training, that all your friends suddenly have legal questions they want to ask you. Sometimes it can be difficult to distinguish between giving friendly advice and practicing law. You'll find your stock answer to certain questions becomes "You should check with an attorney practicing in that area." In every state in the U.S., it's illegal to practice law without a license, and you must be completely certain about what you can and cannot do.

ENTERING THE FIELD

How Do I Find My First Job?

As you can glean from the above job descriptions, most employers prefer to hire paralegals with some formal training. On the other hand, many employers, particularly large employers, want to train their own paralegals. Most often, this in-house training is in addition to your paralegal education; occasionally, these employers want to hire someone with a bachelor's degree (but no paralegal training), or they promote a legal secretary from within the organization. Sometimes people with a background that is particularly desirable to a law firm or company, such as nursing or tax preparation, will be hired and trained in-house as legal assistants. But most people enter the profession after receiving formal paralegal training.

Many paralegal training programs offer or require an internship for their students. This is an excellent entree into the profession. Many lawyers were hired by their firm after interning there, and the same is true for paralegals. After all, firms don't take on an intern unless they have some work that needs to be done, and the internship period allows them to see if they like you and you like them before either of you contemplate making the arrangement permanent. And even if your internship doesn't result in a job offer, or you decide to decline the offer, an internship provides valuable experience that will help get you your first job.

Most paralegals who don't get their first job through an internship will hear about openings through their paralegal school's placement program. It's very important to find out as much as you can about a placement office before you decide whether to attend a particular school.

Will There Be Jobs When I Start Looking?

In the early 1980s, the Department of Labor said that paralegalism was the fastest growing profession in the country and that by the year 2000 there would be 100,000 paralegals. Their estimates were off a bit. Six years short of 2000, there were already 111,000 paralegals in the U.S. According to the U.S. Bureau of Labor Statistics, employment of paralegals should continue to grow much faster than average through the year 2005. Most of these jobs will be newly created positions as companies and law firms continue to learn about the benefits of adding paralegals to their staffs. Of course, as more and more paralegal jobs open up, more people will enter the job market as paralegals, and the competition for available jobs will continue. This is one reason the training discussed in the next chapter is vital; if you want to become a paralegal, you will want the best possible training to be competitive.

The paralegal profession is affected by economic factors such as recessions, just as other occupations are. But paralegals can usually ride out any economic impact by being creative. In a recession, for example, people might put off spending money on estate planning, but more people will be filing bankruptcy. Also, I can see no sign that Congress or anybody else is considering the possibility of making fewer laws in the future; as long as they keep churning out laws, we will all need legal professionals to help us deal with them.

Where Will Paralegals Be Working?

Most paralegals will work in private law firms in the future, just as they currently do. Private companies, such as banks, real estate firms, insurance companies, and other corporate legal departments, will hire more paralegals in the future as well.

Government agencies and departments on the federal, state, and local levels will also hire more paralegals in the future. Nonprofit organizations will probably continue to hire more paralegals as well, especially if the tide continues to move entitlement programs away from the government into the private sector. And as long as Legal Services Corporation manages to be refunded every year, it will continue to hire more paralegals in an effort to help keep costs down.

What Makes a Good Paralegal?

In the next chapter on training, I discuss some of the traits of a successful paralegal in the context of looking at different kinds of training. Note that, in addition to having good training, paralegals need to be able to communicate well, both orally and in writing. They are expected to attack problems in a logical and methodical way. They must be organized and flexible in their approach to their work assignments. Paralegals have to be able to work well as part of a team and also on their own.

As a paralegal you will often have to deal with the public. Even in large firms, it is often the paralegal who does the initial interview with a potential client. Working with the public takes courtesy and patience, but in a legal setting, it can sometimes take even more. For many of your clients, seeking out a lawyer is not a happy experience. Perhaps they have been arrested or sued; maybe they are getting divorced, or have been injured, or must file bankruptcy. As a paralegal, you may be

National Association of Legal Assistants Code of Ethics and Professional Responsibility

Canon 1.   A legal assistant must not perform any of the duties that attorneys only may perform nor take any actions that attorneys may not take.

Canon 2.   A legal assistant may perform any task which is properly delegated and supervised by an attorney, as long as the attorney is ultimately responsible to the client, maintains a direct relationship with the client, and assumes professional responsibility for the work product.

Canon 3.   A legal assistant must not: (a) engage in, encourage, or contribute to any act which could constitute the unauthorized practice of law; and (b) establish attorney-client relationships, set fees, give legal opinions or advice or represent a client before a court or agency unless so authorized by that court or agency; and (c) engage in conduct or take any action which would assist or involve the attorney in a violation of professional ethics or give the appearance of professional impropriety.

Canon 4.   A legal assistant must use discretion and professional judgment commensurate with knowledge and experience but must not render independent legal judgment in place of an attorney. The services of an attorney are essential in the public interest whenever such legal judgment is required.

Canon 5.   A legal assistant must disclose his or her status as a legal assistant at the outset of any professional relationship with a client, attorney, a court or administrative agency or personnel thereof, or a member of the general public. A legal assistant must act prudently in determining the extent to which a client may be assisted without the presence of an attorney.

Canon 6.   A legal assistant must strive to maintain integrity and a high degree of competency through education and training with respect to professional responsibility, local rules and practice, and through continuing education in substantive areas of law to better assist the legal profession in fulfilling its duty to provide legal service.

Canon 7.   A legal assistant must protect the confidences of a client and must not violate any rule or statute now in effect or hereafter enacted controlling.

Canon 8.   A legal assistant must do all other things incidental, necessary, or expedient for the attainment of the ethics and responsibilities as defined by statute or rule of court.

Canon 9.   A legal assistant's conduct is guided by bar associations' codes of professional responsibility and rules of professional conduct.

The Unlicensed or Unauthorized Practice of Law

What constitutes the practice of law, or the unauthorized practice of law, is determined by each state's judicial branch. Therefore, the definition varies from state to state. It is vital that as a paralegal you are constantly aware of the practice of law in your state and take care that you don't practice law.

The definition of practice of law is continually evolving. The practice of law is often defined in the negative. Someone (a paralegal, a real estate broker, a banker, a notary public, etc.) may undertake an activity that someone else perceives as the practice of law and, therefore, something that should be done by lawyers only. Then a complaint is made against that person, and eventually a court determines whether the activity is or is not the practice of law. And, one more activity is added to one side of the list or the other.

By way of example, here is the definition of Unlicensed Practice of Law according to the Florida Statutes: "The unlicensed practice of law shall mean the practice of law, as prohibited by statute, court rule, and case law of the State of Florida. For purposes of this chapter, it shall not constitute the unlicensed practice of law for a nonlawyer to engage in limited oral communications to assist a person in the completion of blanks on a legal form approved by the Supreme Court of Florida. Oral communications by nonlawyers are restricted to those communications reasonably necessary to elicit factual information to complete the blanks on the form and inform the person how to file the form." (Florida Statutes, chapter 10-2.1(a).) In other words, in any given situation, you must research the statutes, court rules, and case law of Florida to determine if a particular activity constitutes the practice of law.

If you are not an attorney and you want to engage in an activity that you think may constitute the practice of law, and there is no reference to it in the statutes, court rules, or case law, the rules regulating the Florida Bar allow you to request that the Standing Committee on Unlicensed Practice of Law give you an advisory opinion, indicating whether they believe the activity is the practice of law. The Supreme Court of Florida has the final word, however. This procedure is similar in other states. This issue is very important to the future of the paralegal profession and will continue to be high on the agenda of paralegal associations, bar associations, and paralegal educators.

---

the first person clients talk to when they decide to seek help. Like a bartender or cab driver, you must not only perform your professional duties but also be a little bit of a therapist.

Finally, it is imperative that a paralegal always behaves in an ethical manner. There are a variety of sources of ethical standard for paralegals. First of all, every state defines the unauthorized practice of law, which is exactly what you don't want to do. In addition, many state legislatures or state bar associations have addressed the role of paralegals in the legal profession, and professional organizations such as the National Association of Legal Assistants address ethical issues. It is up to every working paralegal to keep abreast of all the ethical concerns of the profession.

Who:	Gayle Lund
What:	Paralegal with a litigation information consultant
Where:	Los Angeles, California
How long:	Three years
Degree:	Associate degree; paralegal certificate

Insider's Advice

I got my first paralegal job through a temp agency. Starting about 1994 up through mid-1996, the law firms in LA were hit very hard by the recession. They were downsizing tremendously, and so there ceased to be an abundance of paralegal jobs. So everyone started going to temp agencies; you get your foot in the door and if they like you and they need you, they'll hire you. My current job was the first temp job I had. They sent me there, and it was supposed to be a three-week job, and I'm still there. But I think I could have had a variety of jobs. There was a big need for document coders at that time and a lot of people were getting those types of jobs. But they didn't pay as well—around eight to nine dollars an hour—so I was lucky I got one with more computer responsibilities, because of my background.

It's tremendously exciting to be involved in a major litigation and to be helping the law firm to have at its disposal all of the evidence and to be able to locate it when they need it, to bring it into court to prove their case. They put everything on the data base in this law firm that's our main customer. For instance, I get the text from the depositions on a floppy and we import that right into the data base so it's immediately searchable. They also have scanned the deposition that was filed, the actual copy that was filed, just to have the signature, and the dates, and everything on it. And the documents that they collect are organized by different sources, so each has its own data base. Other parties in the litigation pay to use portions of the data base—the parts that aren't privileged.

I love the legal field, it's very interesting, very challenging. I originally wanted to be the type of paralegal who did the research and drafted the motions and things like that. And I think I would have been very good at it. But those jobs are hard to get, at least out here. I think in New York, it's a lot easier. But out here you have to work for four or five years, paying your dues, before they'll let you touch that kind of thing.

Insider's Take on the Future

The paralegal field is one that a lot of young people go into, because you can come out of a paralegal certificate class, maybe have an associate degree, and you can start making, minimum, twenty-five thousand a year. For young people that's not bad. And they get bonuses and they get a lot of overtime and that's how they bring their income up to thirty-five, forty-five thousand dollars.

I think the industry has a great future. There really is a wide variety of opportunities in the paralegal field. Especially for young people, who can put in the time to network, and to work a little bit of overtime to get on the exciting projects, and do some volunteer work. I think it's a great field and it has a big future. I'd highly recommend it to anyone.

CHAPTER | 2

Thirty years ago, there was really only one way to receive paralegal training: on the job. Some paralegals began as legal secretaries and gradually took on more and more responsibility; others had bachelor's degrees and actually were hired as paralegal trainees. Now, if you want to become a paralegal, you need to undertake specialized paralegal training, which is discussed in this chapter.

ALL ABOUT TRAINING PROGRAMS

As discussed in the first chapter, the paralegal profession was born in the 1960s, during the "War on Poverty," so it's not surprising that the first paralegal school didn't appear until the late 1960s; by 1971, there were still less than a dozen paralegal training schools. Today there are close to 1,000 paralegal training programs; every state in the U.S. has at least one school, and in most cases, residents have a variety of schools to choose from. With the explosive growth of the paralegal profession since 1960, the choices for training have also grown. If you're interested in becoming a paralegal, the first thing you need to decide is whether you need training and what kind you should get.

Should You Enroll in a Training Program?

Most people interested in becoming paralegals will need some kind of formal training. If you have a bachelor's degree, it is possible for you to get a job as a paralegal without any further training; this will depend a great deal on the market in your area. If most of your job rivals have some kind of specialized training, you will find it difficult to compete with, for example, only a liberal arts degree. Certainly, your situation—because of classes you took or assistantships you held while in college, or even work outside of college—may make you very competitive; see chapter five for resume tips for someone like you.

The National Federation of Paralegal Associations (NFPA) estimates that 85 percent of legal assistants receive some type of specialized paralegal training. In addition, even if you find an opportunity for on-the-job training, that can be a lonely and limiting way to receive your training. As Audrey Casey, a former paralegal, noted, "I wish I'd had that opportunity [specialized training] because it's much more isolated and difficult, doing it on your own." So in most cases, your first step toward becoming a paralegal should be choosing the institution you want to attend to receive your training.

TYPES OF TRAINING PROGRAMS

There is such a variety of training programs available in the paralegal field that it is tempting to lay down some hard-and-fast rules you can use to help you make your choice. Unfortunately, that method ignores the fact that there are many kinds of training programs partly because the market for paralegals varies greatly from place to place. For example, it would be easy for me to tell you that you should only consider training programs that are accredited by the American Bar Association (ABA). But that ignores an important consideration: competition within the market. In the city where I live, there are two paralegal training programs, both at proprietary two-year colleges and both seemingly committed to training competent legal assistants. Neither of these programs is accredited by the ABA, and in this market, at least, I don't think a potential student should be

---

According to the 1995 Compensation and Benefits Survey conducted by the NFPA:

6 percent of paralegals have completed less than 30 semester hours of college

14 percent have at least 30 semester hours of college credits

20 percent have an associate degree

54 percent have a bachelor's degree

6 percent have a graduate degree, Ph.D., or J.D.

unduly concerned about that. The key is finding out the norm in the market in which you plan to work.

So, just how *do* you go about deciding which program is right for you? First, let's talk about the kinds of programs you will likely have to choose from.

Certificate Programs

Among all the choices of programs, there is the greatest variety within certificate programs. Many times, these programs are offered by proprietary colleges—that is, they are private, for-profit institutions. Some of these schools are called, or, used to be called, business schools. In most cases, the length of these certificate programs range from 3 to 24 months. These programs may only require a high school diploma for admission; however, many certificate programs are intended for students who already have an associate or bachelor's degree. In some cases, students who have significant exposure to the law, such as working as a clerk or secretary in a law office, may attend a certificate program even without a degree.

Another type of certificate program is the post-bachelor's certificate, offered at a four-year college or university. These certificates are offered by the continuing education or extension divisions. The courses may or may not bestow college credits and are intended for someone who has completed a bachelor's degree and needs only paralegal-specific training. Many of these programs can be completed in a year or less.

Here is an example of the curriculum of a certificate program. This one is from Northeastern University in Boston and is intended for students who have completed a bachelor's degree or who have significant work experience in a legal setting. This is a twelve-week, full-time program. This list contains "content areas" that all students must complete; the order in which the information is presented may change from session to session.

12-Week Paralegal Certificate Program Curriculum

Probate

Intestacy, Wills, and Trusts

Estate Administration

Federal and State Estate Tax Preparation

Closing the Estate

Real Estate

How Property is Held

Acquisition of Real Property

Leases of Property

Deeds, Mortgages, and Easements

Condominium Practice

Real Estate Closing

Corporations

Partnerships, Corporations, Limited Liability Companies, Trusts, and Joint Ventures

Organization of Corporations

Articles of Organization, Minutes, By-laws, and Stocks

Securities Regulation

Intellectual Property

Termination of Corporate Existence

Litigation

The Court System

Litigation Procedure: Summons and Com-plaints, Service of Process

Answers, Motions to Dismiss, and Counter claims

Motions for Summary Judgment

Interrogatories

Depositions and Other Discovery Pleadings

Legal Research

Fact-Finding and Data Retrieval

Local, State, and Federal Agencies

Registries and Courthouses

Municipal Records

Legal Ethics

Situational Analysis of Ethical Dilemmas

Confidentiality, Conflict of Interest, Moral vs. Legal Obligation

Insider Information

Associate Degree Programs

The associate degree is received after a student completes a two-year program at a community college, proprietary college, or a few four-year colleges and universities. One-quarter to one-half of the classes are law courses, and the remainder are general education classes in, among others, English, math, science, and the humanities. Most students will have the opportunity to choose as many as two classes per semester; most of the curriculum is predetermined, however. The City College of San Francisco offers a two-year program in paralegal studies; upon completion, graduates receive the associate in arts degree, with an Award of Achievement in Legal Assistant/Paralegal. Here is the curriculum.

First semester

Introduction to Legal Assisting

Introduction to Legal Writing

Commercial Law

Legal Resources

Human Relations

Second semester

Civil Litigation

Commercial Law

Legal Research and Writing

Third semester

Tort Law and Claims Investigation

Wills, Trust, and Probate Administration

Law-Office Management

Fourth semester

Family Law

Legal Aspects of Evidence

Investigation, Discovery, and Trial Preparation

Advice on Applying to a Paralegal Program

Kevin Huntington is the admissions officer at the Minnesota Paralegal Institute in Minnetonka, Minnesota. He offers these words on applying to paralegal programs: "Basically, the advice we give to people who are interested in applying to our program is to research the field and make sure it's something that they definitely want to do. We have a really low attrition rate, and one of the reasons is that we really screen people before we allow them into the program, to make sure not only that they are going to be good for our program, but also that our program is going to be good for them. We don't look for any specific background or any particular experience, provided they have a good GPA and a bachelor's degree and they pass the entrance exam. If they pass those screening devices, our main concern is that after they graduate and get their certificate, it will provide them with employment that's going to be satisfactory to them—that they will enjoy. So make sure they research the field and know exactly what they're getting into; and as long as it's something they want to do, we're happy to let them into our school. And help them get to where they want to be."

Bachelor's Degree Programs

Bachelor's degrees are conferred by four-year colleges and universities. A student is expected to complete about 120 semester hours of work; from 18 to 45 of those hours will be in paralegal studies, depending on whether the program is a major or a minor in paralegal studies. A bachelor's program usually combines general education, business, and legal courses. If you are just finishing high school, a four-year liberal arts program allows you time to mature and provides skills that are necessary for the workplace. However, for some people, four years is simply too great an investment in time and money. If that describes you, it might still benefit you to get some information on any four-year programs in your area. In the long run, the more education you acquire, the greater your chance for career advancement will be. Even if you start out with an associate degree, you may some day decide to go on for your bachelor's. Often the credits you received during your associate program may be transferred to a bachelor's. Here is an example of a bachelor's curriculum, from the legal studies program at Illinois State University, which offers a minor in legal studies. Some students at ISU "major" in legal studies by declaring a general studies major and using legal studies courses as a second major. In addition to completing all of the core requirements of the university, legal studies students take:

Required courses (15 credit hours)
Introduction to Law for Paralegals
Legal Research I and II
Litigation I and II

Other paralegal specialty courses (9 hours for a minor or 18 for a major)
Introduction to Torts
Law Office Administration
Investigative Techniques
Probate Law
Domestic Relations Law
Employment Law
Professional Practice Paralegal Internship

Law-related electives
Federal Income Taxation
Advanced Tax

Fundamentals of Criminal Investigation
Juvenile Justice
Criminal Law
Rules of Evidence for the Administration of Justice
Legal Environment of Business
Business Law I
Business Law II
Real Estate Principles
Government Regulation of Business
American Judicial Process
Administrative Law
Constitutional Law: Functions and Powers
Constitutional Law: Due Process Rights
Constitutional Law: Equality and Free Expression

Master's Degree Programs

Master's degree programs are not the same as post-bachelor's certificate programs. Both, of course, require a bachelor's degree for admission. A master's program, however, may also require completion of a graduate school admissions test, such as the GRE (Graduate Record Examination) or even the LSAT (Law School Admission Test). Upon completion of the program, you will be granted a master of arts or science degree (different universities use different designations). Master's programs usually take a minimum of two years to complete and frequently require completion of a thesis or similar project for graduation. If you can afford the time and money to obtain your master's degree, it may enhance your employability. Because the phenomenal growth of the legal assistant field translates into more training programs that are graduating more paralegals, setting yourself apart from other paralegals may help you in your future employment. On the other hand, in some markets you may be considered "overeducated" when employers have the option of hiring paralegals with an associate degree.

One caveat about master's degree programs: Some of these programs are intended to provide top-notch training to paralegals. On the other hand, they may be intended to give legal training to people who are already successful in another profession—in other words, people who are not intending to seek a career as a paralegal but feel their current position would be enhanced with legal training. Programs are usually quite clear about which type of student they were created for. The curriculum of a master's program is similar to an undergraduate curriculum, except that the core courses (in English, science, math, and the humanities) are not included, just the legal courses. Here is the curriculum from Montclair State University in Upper Montclair, New Jersey, where students may obtain a master of arts in legal studies, specializing in general legal studies, dispute resolution, or law office management and technology. Students must complete 36 credit hours of graduate-level courses. They also are required to complete a master's thesis on an approved topic.

Required courses for all students

Ethical and Professional Issues in the Legal Environment

Advanced Legal Research and Writing

Thesis Seminar in Legal Studies

Electives chosen based on specialty

Advanced Civil Litigation

Administrative Law

Criminal Trial Preparation

Cross-Cultural Conflict Resolution

Torts and Contracts

Statutory Analysis

Trademark Law

Negotiation

Mediation

Arbitration

Peer Mediation

Family Mediation

Dispute Resolution: Workplace

Litigation Management

Law Office Management and Technology

Advanced Computer Applications

Private Sector/Public Regulations

Human Resource Management

Distance Education

Distance education—which used to be called correspondence school—is also an option for paralegal training. There is a certain amount of variety among these programs. Some rely very heavily on the computer, providing interactive lessons. Others allow you to read texts and take exams at your own pace; these may also be supplemented with videotapes. You need to be very organized and dedicated to succeed in distance education, and some people shy away from it for those same reasons. I must admit that knowing I was required to attend classes and complete assignments at a certain time was more effective for me. On the other hand, as the National Institute for Paralegal Arts and Sciences notes,

> The skills you learn to be successful as a distance education student are the exact skills you need to be an effective paralegal. Organization, self-reliance, motivation, the desire to learn, the will to succeed, and the ability to solve problems and make decisions are all a part of the distance education and paralegal processes. Success as a self-directed student demonstrates to your employer that you are goal-oriented and have the ability to work independently. Employer surveys taken over the last ten years have indicated overwhelming satisfaction with graduates of accredited paralegal distance education training programs.

By its very nature, distance learning provides a greater possibility for fraud than a school that is established in a particular place, but that is no reason to avoid distance learning; many schools are quite well respected. If home study seems like the best option for you, just be careful in choosing a program. Find out as much as you can about the faculty and how available they will be to answer your questions. Ask for the names of former students whom you can contact for information about their experiences with the school. Get complete information on the course of study, and compare it with the curricula of schools you know to be reputable. Make sure that the distance education school you choose is accredited by an organization such as the National Home Study Council or the Distance Education and Training Council. The U.S. Department of Education can tell you about other accrediting agencies. Its address is 1601 18th St. NW, Washington, DC 20009; phone: 202-234-5100. Finally, check with the Chamber of Commerce, the Better Business Bureau, or the attorney general's office in the state where the school is headquartered to see if the school has had complaints lodged against it.

Here is the curriculum from the Constitutional Educational Research Foundation (CERF), a correspondence school established in California in 1986. CERF provides a two-year course that results in a certificate. It is possible to finish the program in less time.

Introduction to Paralegal Studies

Legal Writing

Contracts

Torts

Civil Procedure and Litigation (elective course)

Criminal Law and Procedure

Business Law

Wills, Trusts, Estates, and the Constitution

Real Property Law (elective course)

Legal Ethics and Professional Responsibility

Family Law (elective course)

A Well-Rounded Curriculum

The National Federation of Paralegal Associations, Inc. (NFPA) states that legal assistant students "need to have exposure to the following theory/practice areas":

Litigation and Civil Procedure

Real Property Transactions

Wills and Trust and Estate Planning

Torts

Legal Research and Writing

Business and Corporate Law

Family Law

Contracts

The NFPA also notes that other courses may be desirable depending on the market. For example, a program may consider offering:

Advanced Legal Research and Writing

Bankruptcy and Debtor / Creditor Rights

Pension and Profit Sharing

Tax Law

Intellectual Property

Immigration Law

Constitutional Law

Elder Law

Advanced Litigation and Civil Procedure

Administrative Law

Law Office Economics and Management

Labor Relations and Employment Law

Criminal Law

Social Security Law

Environmental Law

(*NFPA Suggested Curriculum for Paralegal Studies*)

Ethics Courses

In addition to legal courses, it is very important that a program offer courses in paralegal ethics. Each state has rules that govern the unlicensed practice of law; essentially, only trained attorneys who have been admitted to the Bar of a particular state can give legal advice. This means that if you are not a member of the Bar, you may not counsel clients as to the law. This is not always as clear as it may seem. As a paralegal, you may, for example, help someone fill out a bankruptcy form. You may not, however, help them decide which kind of bankruptcy to file; that constitutes giving legal advice. And, trust me, people are always trying to get free legal advice. So it is imperative that your legal assistant program teaches ethics; it is best if it offers a separate paralegal ethics course. Some schools, however, may choose to teach ethics throughout the curriculum, in conjunction with the other law classes.

A PERSONAL ASSESSMENT

As you can see, many variables come into play when comparing paralegal training programs; in addition to the type and length of the program, cost, location, and reputation of the school must also be taken into account. So how do you begin to determine which program is right for you? Start by taking stock of yourself. You have to figure out what you need to get out of a paralegal training program in order to find the one that's right for you. Use this worksheet to determine the kind of program that is right for you. This assessment looks at four areas:

- **Education.** How much education will you have completed prior to entering paralegal training? Are there areas of your education that are particularly strong or weak?
- **Choosing a specialty.** Do you have work or educational experience that will make you particularly attractive to a certain kind of employer?
- **Where to get your training.** Are you willing to move to a new city to receive paralegal training? Maybe you want to move; maybe you'll have to move.
- **Your schedule; your demands.** How much are you willing /able to pay for your paralegal training? Do you need other special services, such as help with transportation or child care?

Let's look at these areas more closely.

Education

What level of education have you completed?

_____High school or GED

_____Associate degree

_____Bachelor's degree

	Degree you have:		
	High School	Associate	Bachelor's
Programs you	Certificate	Certificate	Certificate
can attend:	Associate	Bachelor's	Master's
	Bachelor's		

Usual Length of Program:

Certificate	Associate	Bachelor's*	Master's
Varies	two-year	four-year	Two-year

*Bachelor's degrees in paralegal studies are relatively unusual, but that doesn't mean that you should discount the idea of getting a bachelor's degree. If the college you want to attend doesn't have a program, you may be able to design a bachelor's degree that will fit your needs. Many Business and Political Science departments offer law courses; if the college is affiliated with a law school, undergraduates may be able to take some law courses. Talk to a counselor at the college or university you are interested in for more information.

Analysis of Your Skills

Successful paralegals possess certain skills. You may have some of these skills now; if you don't, you'll need to seek out a paralegal training program that will teach you the skills you are lacking. For each skill, consider whether, at this time, it is one you already have, one that needs some work, or one that you need to learn. It will help you get the most out of your paralegal training if you are honest with yourself now.

All of these are skills that a good paralegal program will address and give you the opportunity to brush up on. Organization, prioritizing, independent thinking, and the ability to concentrate on several projects at the same time are vital to a successful paralegal. Legal research skills will be taught in paralegal programs, but

	highly skilled	needs work	need to learn
a. Communication skills	_____	_____	_____
b. Research skills	_____	_____	_____
c. Organization skills	_____	_____	_____
d. Prioritizing skills	_____	_____	_____
e. Independent thinking	_____	_____	_____
f. Analytical skills	_____	_____	_____
g. Investigative skills	_____	_____	_____
h. Concentration skills	_____	_____	_____
i. Computer skills	_____	_____	_____

if you feel that your general research skills are lacking, you will want to make sure your program affords you the opportunity to improve them. Analytical and investigative tasks that paralegals undertake are specialized to the law—and you'll learn them in a good program. It will be easier for you, however, if you already have abilities in these areas. The point of this list is for you to look at the work you need to do in order to succeed as a paralegal and make sure that the program you choose gives you the opportunities to do that work.

The two single most important components of an excellent paralegal program, in my opinion, are training in communications and in computers. It is absolutely vital that you are able to communicate effectively, both orally and in writing. And in even the smallest, most rural law offices, computers are becoming more and more common, and dependence on computer research is growing every day.

Communication

When I took the bar exam in 1993, it consisted of two and a half days of writing essays. I passed the first time I took it, but some of my classmates had to take it again, and even again and again, before they passed. In most cases, I believe they may have been as prepared *legally* as I was—but I was able to write well. They may have even known more law than I did, but I knew how to tell what I knew. There are really two points to this story: 1) you need to be able to communicate effectively to be successful in the law and 2) as a paralegal, you may find yourself working for a lawyer who doesn't know how to write or speak well. There's not much you can do about your boss's speaking ability, but whether it's fair or not, your boss may depend on you to make sure that the documents that leave your office are well written. Not only may it fall to you to edit your boss's work, but also as a paralegal you will write many of the documents, and some of them will go out in your name.

It is difficult to be honest with yourself about your communication skills. Most of us think that we manage to speak and write just fine, thank you very much. But the truth is, communication skills are not stressed a great deal, especially in high school and in certain college programs. In the professional world of the law, you must be able to do more than make yourself understood. You must be able to express yourself accurately, succinctly, and correctly. Look back over the grades you received in English and any other classes in which you had to write or speak. Think back over comments you received about your work. If you need to, ask a teacher or school counselor for an assessment of your communication skills. If you feel they are lacking, it is imperative that you choose a program that will help you in this area. And if you feel that your communication skills are pretty good, well, we can all use a little more practice, right?

Computer Skills

If you've never touched a computer in your life, don't panic. Most paralegal programs require, or at least make available, computer training. Keep in mind that there are two skills you need to master. One is the ability to use a computer—keyboarding, really—and common business software; the other is the ability to perform legal research on a computer. Both of these are vitally important. If you run across a paralegal program that *doesn't* teach computer assisted legal research, don't attend. It won't adequately prepare you for a career as a legal assistant.

The ideal paralegal training course will

1. offer you the opportunity to learn/improve your basic keyboarding skills;
2. introduce you to commonly used computer software (legal-specific programs include: Abacus Law, Summation Blaze, and TimeSlips); and
3. offer you training in WestLaw and LEXIS, computer legal research programs.

WestLaw and LEXIS are subscription services; there are other research services on the Web, such as V. Law. A good computer research class will introduce you to several of these services and allow you the opportunity to practice using them.

Much of the drama in television and movie depictions of lawyers occurs in the courtroom. In reality, most attorneys spend little time in the courtroom. One important rule of questioning a witness is to never ask a question that you don't already know the answer to. One way an attorney knows an answer is through questioning a witness before the trial, in a deposition. If the witness should say something different in court from what she or he says in a deposition, it can cast doubt on the witness's entire testimony. But you have to be able to find that discrepancy in the deposition.

Gayle Lund, a litigation paralegal in Los Angeles does a great deal of computer work. On occasion, Gayle's work provides dramatic courtroom moments.

> One of the really interesting things that we do is take videos of depo-sitions, and we match them with the stenographer's transcript, and we put them on CD-ROM. As the person is talking on the video, as the questions are being asked and they're answering, you see that in one-third of the screen. And then in another third of the screen you see the reporter's text, with the actual words typed. A highlighting bar highlights the words on the text as the person is talking....The lawyers take their laptops into the courtroom, and if they want to challenge somebody, they can, within a couple of seconds, do a search and find the portion of the text they're interested in and high-light it...and play it back. What the jury sees is the [video] clip on the screen of the person saying, 'Oh, no, I never did that.'

Most weaknesses in your educational background can be overcome in a good paralegal training program. Be sure you check not only the classes offered in the paralegal program, but also the ones from which you can choose your electives. In addition, ask about the availability of tutoring in your weak areas.

So now you're all depressed from spending all this energy on analyzing your weaknesses. Cheer up. It's time to talk about your strengths.

CHOOSING A SPECIALTY

The question I posed above was *Do you have work or educational experience that will make you particularly attractive to a certain kind of employer?* It may seem a little premature to be talking about employment when you're just worried about where to go to school. But what you want to do as a paralegal has a great deal to do with where you decide to receive your training. And what you want to do as a para-legal depends a lot on your background. This doesn't mean that you shouldn't try to get a good general legal education. Indeed, a general legal education is what most paralegal training programs offer. And I think it is important to be introduced to areas of the law that you are not familiar with. You might find them more interesting than you thought.

Nonetheless, your background may influence your career choices. Do you have any medical training or experience? You might be perfect for a law office that does a lot of medical malpractice. You could take a course in tort law to prepare. Penny, a career counselor with the Affiliates (a nationwide legal placement service) in Houston, Texas, says, "That's a market that doesn't seem to have a lot of competition in it. Registered nurses who have litigation experience—not necessarily practicing nurses, but people who do litigation and have an R.N. degree—we have a lot of those positions open that we can't fill." Do you have experience or training in social work or education? Perhaps you will be drawn to family law, and you will want to be sure that such a course is available. When I started law school, I planned to do something completely different from what I ended up doing. I also have friends who are practicing exactly the kind of law they were interested in on the first day of law school. It is to your benefit to find a paralegal program that offers you as many options as possible for a well-rounded education, while at the same time offering training in the area(s) you are most interested in.

Don't despair if the school or schools you are most interested in lack a particular course you are interested in, such as employment law or administrative law. It may be possible to receive training in your particular area in another way. One of the best alternatives is an internship. In this case, you want to make sure not only that your program will help you get an internship, but also it offers contacts in several different areas of the law. If you were interested in employment or administrative law, for example, you could intern in a human resources office or with a government administrative agency. If an internship simply can't be worked out, you may still be able to receive your specialized training. Perhaps you can take a relevant course at another college, and maybe your program will agree to transfer the credit. As I noted earlier, sometimes law schools let undergraduates take certain law courses; if not, you might be able to audit.

If all of your attempts to find training in a particular specialty seem to fail, go have a chat with the placement counselors in the programs you are interested in. Ask them if they have ever placed someone in your field, what contacts they have, and how much work they are willing to do on your behalf. If their answers satisfy you, consider attending the school, even if it lacks the course you want. Remember,

If you are interested in or have a background in:	Look for courses such as:
The Arts	Contracts Copyrights Entertainment Law Sports Law
Civil Rights	Administrative Law Civil Rights Law Constitutional Law Elder Law Employment Discrimination Law
Corporations	Antitrust Law Business Law or Corporate Law Contracts Employment Law Intellectual Property Labor Law
Criminology	Criminal Law Criminal Procedure Evidence and Trial Practice
Environmental Issues	Administrative Law Environmental Law Property
Financial Matters	Bankruptcy Taxation Trusts and Estates Wills and Probate
Litigation	Civil Procedure Contracts Evidence and Trial Practice Torts
Medicine	Administrative Law Insurance Law Torts
Real Estate	Contracts Landlord / Tenant Law Property Real Estate Law
Social Issues	Administrative Law Family Law Poverty Law

your personal background already gives you an advantage in the field. And it is always possible you will discover you like another area of the law better.

WHERE TO GET YOUR TRAINING

A great many people leave their hometowns when they go off to college or graduate school; people are more apt to attend a two-year college close to home. This doesn't mean you can't move across the country to attend a community college. It is worth your while to consider this issue seriously. It is highly desirable to attend a program that is located in the geographical area in which you want to work. For example, as I mentioned, in the city where I live, neither of the paralegal programs is accredited by the ABA. So that's not a very important consideration for employers here. If you wanted to work here, it would be unnecessary for you to go out of your way to attend an ABA-accredited school. On the other hand, if you want to work in a market where most of the legal assistants graduated from ABA-accredited schools, it would be worth your while to attend one yourself.

Another advantage to attending school in the market in which you want to work is that you learn the laws of that area. I attended law school and joined the Bar in Iowa; that doesn't help me much if I want to know California or Georgia law. Laws can vary a great deal from state to state, and it is to your benefit to learn the local law. Finally, attending paralegal school in the state in which you want to work allows you to make contacts for future job hunting. I will discuss this kind of networking more in chapter five, but having friends from school when you're out in the job market can be a big help. Not to mention that the placement office is best at placing in its own area.

If you can't attend a program in the place where you want to work, you're not out of luck. If you know where you are going to end up, research that area to find out what kind of training most paralegals receive, and duplicate it as best you can. If you're not sure where you are going to end up, it's up to you to make the most of the education you do receive. Are you unable to attend an ABA-accredited school? Try to attend one that at least meets ABA standards. Also, rely on your internships and the faculty of the school you attend. Most of these people will be lawyers who just may have attended law school with, or in some other way, know an attorney in the town where you end up. Well-trained paralegals, with good references from their internships and professors, are always in demand.

YOUR SCHEDULE, YOUR DEMANDS

The final point on your personal inventory is resources. The question of how to pay for your training is addressed in chapter four. Here I'm talking about more than simply the cost of a program, although you should factor in the cost when comparing schools and making a decision. But other resources are important too. Let's say you could attend a paralegal program in your hometown or one in a town 30 miles away. In addition to all the other comparisons, transportation now becomes an issue. No matter which school you attend, child care may be an issue for you. You not only need to get information about any help the schools can give you in these areas; you need to have serious talks with your family and friends about any help they're willing to give. Although I have referred to the programs I've talked about the most as two-year or four-year programs, that is not entirely accurate. Those periods apply to students who are able to attend full time.

Another possibility you might want to consider is attending school part time. Indeed, your resources might dictate that you consider this option.

Part-Time Attendance

By attending classes part time, you can spread the cost of the program over a greater period of time. Schools often charge students based on the credit hours they are taking in a given period. If full-time students take twelve hours and you are taking six, it will cost you half as much for that period. Of course, it will take you longer, and ultimately you will both pay the same amount; you can just take longer doing it. As a part-time student, you will also have more flexibility in your scheduling. This can be a great help, for example, with child care. Finally, a part-time schedule allows you to work, even full time, while you go to school.

Make a list of any special time concerns you have and how you will deal with them. For example, if your spouse or partner can take care of the children, but only if you take classes in the evening, you will have to find a program that offers evening classes. On the other hand, maybe you will need to take classes only while your children are in school; night school won't work for you. If you've decided that you need to keep working while you attend class, you'll need to find a program that will allow you to attend part time and that offers flexible scheduling of classes. Every time you think of one of these "obstacles," jot it down. Then consider how you can solve the problem. If you need to, brainstorm with a friend or relative, or simply call a school in the area (it doesn't even have to be a paralegal school) and ask an admissions counselor what other students in your situation have done.

Here are some things to think about in considering your schedule and your demands:

- **Children.** Are you solely responsible for child care? Who can help you with child care? Family? Friends? Professionals? Who can help you with emergency child care? Is child care available through your paralegal school? Because of the age of your children, are you restricted to attending classes only at certain times of the day (such as when they are in school)?
- **Transportation.** Can you walk to school? Can you take public transportation? Can you join or form a car pool? Is your car reliable? What will you do in an emergency?
- **Finances.** Have you considered nontuition expenses? Textbooks and supplies? New clothes for your internship? Food expenses?
- **Employment.** Will you be working while you attend paralegal training? Full time? Part time? What constraints does your job put on your schooling? Scheduling classes? Scheduling study time? Are your work hours flexible? How will an internship affect your current employment? Will you be forced to quit your job? Can you schedule your job around your internship?
- **Support.** Is your family supportive of your decision to become a paralegal? Will family members help you when you need it? Are your friends supportive of your decision to become a paralegal? Can you count on them for material and spiritual support?

MAKING THE FINAL DECISION

By now, with the help of your personal inventories and the list of schools in the next chapter, you should have narrowed down the number of schools that you are considering. You may be lucky enough to find the final decision quite easy; if not, here are some things to keep in mind while evaluating the programs on your finalist list. You can get most of this information from the program catalog, which the school will be happy to send you. You may have to call an admissions counselor to get answers to some of your questions. Don't be shy about asking for information. Remember, you are the consumer; the schools are interested in selling their program to you.

Is the School Accredited?

As I noted earlier, it may not be necessary to attend an ABA accredited program. ABA accreditation is voluntary, and the process can be quite expensive. For these reasons, many fine programs choose not to seek ABA accreditation. There are more than 1,000 paralegal programs in the U.S.; 217 of these are currently accredited by the ABA. However, many schools model their programs on the ABA guidelines. These guidelines are useful in distinguishing one school from another. The best schools will follow the ABA guidelines fairly closely. In order to be considered for ABA accreditation, a legal assistant program must be a post-secondary school program that

- is part of an accredited educational institution
- offers at least 60 semester hours (or the equivalent) of classroom work These courses must include general education classes and at least 18 semester hours of law courses
- is advised by a committee comprised of attorneys and legal assistants from the public and private sectors
- has qualified instructors who are committed to paralegal education
- has student services available, including counseling and placement
- has an adequate legal library available
- has appropriate facilities and equipment

These ideals are expressed in very general language (get used to it, this is how lawyers talk!). I've already mentioned many of the standards; for example, appropriate facilities *must* include computer terminals. Let me go over a few of the other points on the list.

Make sure that even if the program isn't accredited by the ABA, the school is accredited. There are a variety of accrediting agencies, depending on the kind of school in question. Examples include the Accrediting Council for Independent Colleges and Schools (ACICS), New England Schools and Colleges (NESC), and Distance Education and Training Council (DETC). In addition, in some states the program itself may be accredited or approved by the state bar association.

Are the Faculty Qualified?

The faculty should be comprised of people who are committed to paralegal education and who are up to date on changes in the legal assistant field. This may mean practicing attorneys, but it really isn't necessary for everyone on the faculty to be a practicing attorney. Practicing legal assistants, and former attorneys and paralegals who are dedicated to paralegal education, are perfectly fine instructors.

What Resources Does the School Offer?

Try to get a feel for the student services that are available. These should include, at a minimum, counseling and placement. In a small school, the teaching staff may take most of the responsibility for these tasks. Just make sure that the staff seems as committed to those parts of their job as they are to teaching. A faculty made up of only practicing attorneys and paralegals might be hard to find when you need one-on-one attention. Make sure they are at least expected to have regular office hours. Finally, make sure that the program you are interested in has access to a decent law library, such as one at a law school or courthouse.

Certification

As I mentioned in the previous chapter, there are currently two certifications available to qualified paralegals. They are the Certified Legal Assistant (CLA), administered by the National Association of Legal Assistants (NALA), and the Paralegal Advanced Competency Exam (PACE), administered by the National Federation of Paralegal Associations, Inc. (NFPA). Please note that these are not the same kinds of certificates as those you receive when you complete one of the certificate programs I talked about under Types of Training. Nonetheless, while choosing a program, you may want to keep in mind the requirements you will have to meet if you one day are interested in becoming certified.

The CLA is a credentialing program that was established by the National Association of Legal Assistants in 1976. In order to sit for the CLA, a paralegal must meet *one* of the following requirements:

1. Graduation from a paralegal training program that is accredited by the American Bar Association; or
   a program that is authorized to award an associate degree; or a post-bachelor's certificate program in legal assistant studies; or
   A bachelor's degree program in paralegal studies; or a legal assistant program that consists of a minimum of 60 semester hours (or the equivalent), of which at least 15 semester hours are substantive legal courses

2. A bachelor's degree in any field *and* one year of experience as a legal assistant (successful completion of at least 15 semester hours of substantive

legal courses will be considered equivalent to one year's experience as a legal assistant)

3. A high school diploma or GED *and* seven years experience as a legal assistant under the supervision of a member of the Bar, *plus* a minimum of twenty hours of continuing legal education credit, completed within a two-year period prior to the examination date

Specifics of the examination are discussed in chapter one.

In order to sit for the PACE, a legal assistant must meet *all* of the following requirements:

1. At least two years of paralegal experience
2. A bachelor's degree
3. Completion of a paralegal program at an accredited school (paralegal education need not be separate from the bachelor's degree; until December 31, 2000, paralegals who are lacking a bachelor's degree or completion of a paralegal program may substitute four years of paralegal experience)
4. No felony convictions or revoked license, registration, or certification

Details of this examination are discussed in chapter one.

Although it is possible to take the CLA test as soon as you graduate from a paralegal program, most legal assistants wait until they have a few years of experience before obtaining a certification. It's not a bad idea to keep the standards in mind, though.

Note: When you are job hunting, keep in mind the difference between having a certificate (because you graduated from a paralegal program) and having certification (either CLA or PACE). Employers may be confused about this, and when they advertise for a "certified" paralegal, they may actually mean a legal assistant with a certificate.

MAKING THE MOST OF YOUR TRAINING PROGRAM
Internships

An internship is a temporary job, arranged through your paralegal program, for which you receive either academic credit or pay or both. Claire Andrews notes, "It's really important to me that the students do get out there, whether it's through a part-time job or through the internship, to get the practical experience. Otherwise, waving that certificate means nothing."

Internships can provide you with the single most valuable part of your legal assistant education. They allow you to leave the rarified halls of an educational institution to see what the real world is like. If you are interested in specializing in a particular area of the law, an internship provides an invaluable education. One thing you should be prepared for, however, is the possibility that you won't like an area of the law as much as you thought you might. In my opinion, this doesn't make an internship any less valuable; indeed, it's better to "waste" a semester at a job you don't like than spend several years at it.

Before you choose an internship, however, you will take many classes and exams. Keep yourself open, as you take your substantive law classes, to the possibility of being surprised. You may never dream that criminal law or real estate law will interest you. Once you study them, however, you may find them fascinating.

Getting the Most Out of Your Classes

The law is a discipline in which concepts build on one another. For this reason, the law lends itself well to an outline style of notetaking. For example, your notes from an evidence or trial practice course lecture on admitting evidence at trial might look like this:

I. Admitting Evidence
  A. Only if Relevant—if it tends to make a fact more or less likely than without it
    1. FRE 401—all rel. ev. admitted
    2. All rel. ev. must be:
      a. Probative—relationship between ev. and fact
      b. Material—link between fact and sub. law
    3. May be excluded if prob. value is outweighed by danger of:
      a. unfair prejudice—HOW DECIDE??
      b. confusion of issues
      c. misleading jury
      d. delay, waste of time or needless (because cumulative)
  B. Direct v. circumstantial ev.

If you haven't had much experience with outline formats, the table of contents of your textbook can be an effective starting point. Notice that this student has made use of abbreviations to make notetaking go faster. Students in this course have already been introduced to the Federal Rules of Evidence, which is abbreviated FRE (line I.A.1.). Also, this student has developed a habit of abbreviating repeated concepts rather than writing them out each time. So the word relevant becomes "rel." and the word evidence becomes "ev." "Sub. Law" (line I.A.2.b.) is substantive law, a concept that repeats in several classes. Some of these abbreviations you will come up with on your own; some have become standard in the law.

K = contract

Δ = defendant

Π = plaintiff

v. = versus, as in Brown v. Board of Education. Also, lawyers usually say "v" rather than "versus."

e.g. = for example

i.e. = that is

∴ = therefore

Most compilations of laws and cases are referred to in some abbreviated fashion, such as:

FRE = Federal Rules of Evidence

CFR = Code of Federal Regulations

Notice that this student also made a note to find out more about I.A.3.a., unfair prejudice. This concept was not entirely clear to the student, and this note serves as a reminder to investigate further. I was a great fan of colored highlighters in law school. I had different colors for the plaintiff, the defendant, and the judge, state law versus federal law, and the new rules versus the old. Remember, the reason you are taking notes is to give yourself a concise and clear summary of each class session. Whatever method makes it most clear for you is a good method.

Because learning the law involves building concepts one on another, it is important to attend class regularly. It is also vital to be prepared, but if for some reason you are unable to prepare, don't use that as an excuse not to attend class. You need to do both, but one is better than neither. Each instructor conducts class differently, but to the extent that it is appropriate, I urge you to participate in class. It is also helpful to briefly read over your notes as soon after class as possible, so you can make sure you understand everything you've written.

Preparing for Exams

Begin preparing for an exam by reading over your notes. Look for any areas that you indicated you didn't understand at the time, and make sure you understand them now. If you don't, talk to your instructor or do some extra reading until the concept is clear. Then try making an outline of the class. If you are an outlining expert, you've essentially done this—all you have to do is put each day's notes in order. But if, like most of us, your notes are a little sloppier, you might want to start fresh in creating an outline. (This can provide some extra computer practice!) Sometime when you're in a bookstore, take a look at *Emanuel Law Outlines* or *Smith's Review* or the *Black Letter Law Series.* These are commercial study aids for law students—don't be alarmed to discover they're several hundred pages long— but they will give you an idea of what an outline for an entire course looks like. (Law students' textbooks are quite different from most paralegal texts; it probably would be a waste of money for you to purchase any of these books.)

Most important, the evening before the exam, relax, eat a good dinner, and get a good night's sleep. In the morning, eat a good breakfast (and lunch, if it's an afternoon test). Try to take a walk or get some other light exercise, if you have time before the exam. Most of all, stay calm and have faith in yourself and your abilities.

Networking with Students and Instructors

Part of making the most of your training is taking advantage of the interesting people who are sitting next to you in class and who are teaching your classes. These people all have experiences and knowledge that can be a benefit to you. You can help each other by studying together and sharing informal information (some-times called gossip) that is part of every educational experience. You can also share all the latest lawyer jokes. And after graduation, these are the people who will help you get your first job and keep you sane in the workplace.

If the program you're in offers social events, take advantage of them as often as you can. If the events offered don't appeal to you, suggest others. Or arrange something on your own. When I was in law school, the big social event every week was "law night" at a local bar. As I was in my mid-thirties, this wasn't very inter-esting to me. So a friend and I founded a nontraditional-age students' organiza-tion. We had a potluck once a month, which was held at an hour we were more comfortable with and allowed us to include our families. Some of the students who participated are still my closest friends.

Finally, make it a point early in your academic career to get to know the folks in your counseling and placement offices. These people know the answers to almost all your questions, and they are an invaluable resource.

Your paralegal education is the first, essential step on the road to becoming a paralegal. But don't view it simply as something to get through, as an ordeal you must overcome before you can begin work and start your real life. School is the time to learn as much about the profession and yourself as you possibly can. Along the way, you will make friends and contacts—sometimes they'll be the same person—who will be equally valuable to you as you finish school and embark on your career.

THE INSIDE TRACK

Who:	Audrey M. Casey, PLS, CLA
What:	Paralegal Chair; Creator of the Paralegal Program at Andover College
Where:	Portland, Maine
How long:	Fifteen years
Degree:	Bachelor's degree in business education

Insider's Advice

I tell students who say, "Oh, I hate real estate law, I'd never want to do it," that learning it and doing it are a lot different. So I try to have them keep an open mind about that. A lot of their frustration comes from having to learn the theory. As a paralegal you won't spend a lot of time analyzing contracts, you'll basically be helping to draft them and helping to format them and doing some research on a particular contract issue. So, if the whole theory of contracts is boring, I think it's boring to everybody, basically. But when you're actually dabbling in your theory but also dabbling in your technology skills, then it's a lot different.

We have one legal research and writing class, and some students just love it and want more of it, and other students really struggle with it and feel it's very difficult. Then we have the issue of should it be offered first, like it is in law school, or should it not be. I know some students could handle it and could really benefit from it. But a lot of our students are high school graduates, entry level, and they would have a really difficult time. They could learn the procedure, but could they apply, without some background, some of these legal theories? So I continue to contend that it's a better course for them at the end.

Insider's Take on the Future

Right now, everybody here takes the same law courses, and are, you could say, "specializing" in the business skills they want to use on the job. Somebody who is just starting out in a career, who's coming from high school or a home environment, would probably take the Paralegal-Office Management course, because they're going to get a position more easily with those office skills. The other two are Paralegal-Accounting, so you have accounting and taxation skills as the specialty, or Paralegal-Business Management, which is paralegal plus management.

I think legal specialization is something that we want to look at. Because we have open admissions, we have a wide variety of people, and some of them are definitely capable at this point in their lives of specializing. They've worked in a law firm, or they have a lot of business experience, so they have the experience to get into a specialized position, and could do quite nicely there. So, I think the trend for paralegal education is going to be specializing.

CHAPTER | 3

This chapter contains the most comprehensive listing of paralegal programs you'll find in any one place. The list contains over 900 paralegal programs, catalogued by state. All programs provide school name and address so you can contact each school directly to get more information and application forms for the programs that interest you. Phone numbers, fax numbers, and/or e-mail addresses have been provided where available.

DIRECTORY OF PARALEGAL TRAINING PROGRAMS

In the last chapter, you discovered what you should look for in a paralegal program; now it's time to look into *where* you'll find paralegal programs. Whether you are looking for a program near where you live or you want to move, this list will probably contain a program that is right for you. Because the paralegal field is growing all the time, more and more schools are offering paralegal programs. If you don't find the right school for you, check with your state bar association, which usually will have information on paralegal programs. Most counties and cities have bar associations as well. Or check with one of the local paralegal organizations that are affiliated with one of the national associations. For a complete listing of national organizations, state bar associations, and affiliated organizations of the National Federation of Paralegal Associations, see Appendix A.

Keep in mind that most paralegal programs are found at two-year colleges—community, junior, technical, or business. If there is one near you that isn't included on the list, call and ask if it has such a program.

Even if not, the school may point you in the direction of a program elsewhere. Also check with any four-year college or university near you; if it has a program, it may or may not be four years long. While the specific schools included in this chapter are not endorsed or recommended by LearningExpress; they are intended to help you begin your search for an appropriate school by offering a representative listing of schools in each state.

ALABAMA
Alabama Christian Academy
5345 Atlanta Hwy.
Montgomery 36109-3323
334-277-1985

Auburn University at Montgomery
Legal Assistant Education Program
209 Goodwyn Hall, 7300 University Dr.
Montgomery 36117-3596
334-244-3697; FAX: 334-244-3826
bailey@strudel.aum.edu

Community College of the Air Force
Maxwell Air Force Base 36112
334-953-6436

Draughons Junior College
Paralegal Program
122 Commerce St.
Montgomery 36104-2538
334-263-1013

Faulkner University
5345 Atlanta Hwy.
Montgomery 36109-3398
334-260-6200

Gadsden State Community College
Legal Assistant Education Program
P.O. Box 227, 231 Allen Hall
Gadsden 35902-0227
205-549-8368; FAX: 205-549-8444

Huntingdon College
Continuing Education
1500 E. Fairview Ave.
Montgomery 36106-2148
334-834-3300

John C. Calhoun Community College
Paralegal Program
P.O. Box 2216
Decatur 35602-2216
205-233-3300

Miles College
Paralegal Studies
P.O. Box 3800
Birmingham 35208
205-923-2771

National Academy of Paralegal Studies
1572 Montgomery Hwy., Suite 100
Birmingham 35216-4512
800-922-0771

Northeast Alabama State Community
College
P.O. Box 159
Rainsville 35986-0159
205-638-4418

Phillips Junior College
Paralegal Program
115 Office Park Dr
Birmingham 35223
205-879-5100

Samford University
Division of Paralegal Studies
800 Lakeshore Dr. , SU Box 2200
Birmingham 35229-0001
205-870-2783; FAX: 205-870-2783

Spring Hill College
Legal Studies Program
4000 Dauphin St.
Mobile 36608-1791
205-460-2077

University of Alabama
Special Studies
917 Eleventh St.
Birmingham 35294-0001
205-934-8221

University of South Alabama
Special Courses
2001 Old Bay Front Rd.
Mobile 36615-1427
205-431-6411

Virginia College
Paralegal Program
1900 28th Ave. S.
Birmingham 35209
205-802-1200

Wallace State Community College
Paralegal Program
P.O. Box 2000
Hanceville 35077-2000
205-352-8000; FAX: 205-352-8228

ALASKA
Alaska Junior College
800 E. Dimond Blvd. , Suite 3-350
Anchorage 99515-2043
907-394-1905

Charter College
Paralegal Studies Program
1221 E. Northern Lights Blvd., Suite 120
Anchorage 99508-9990
907-277-1000; FAX: 907-274-3342

University of Alaska Anchorage
Paralegal Certificate Program
3211 Providence Dr. , Justice Center
Anchorage 99508
907-786-1810; FAX: 907-786-7777

University of Alaska Southeast
Paralegal Studies
11120 Glacier Hwy.
Juneau 99801
907-465-6347; FAX: 907-465-6383
jfrch@acad1.alaska.edu

ARIZONA
Northland Pioneer College
Legal Assistant Program
P.O. Box 610
Holbrook 86025
520-536-7871; FAX: 520-524-2313

Academy of Business College
Legal Assistant Program
3320 W. Cheryl Dr. , Suite 115
Phoenix 85051-9576
602-942-4141; FAX: 602-942-9082
aob@netzone.com

American Institute of Paralegal Studies
3443 N. Central Ave., #1800
Phoenix 85012-2213
602-252-4986; FAX: 602-274-1440

Arizona Paralegal Training Program
General Practice Paralegal Program
111 W. Monroe, Suite 800
Phoenix 85003
602-252-2171; 800-990-2380;
FAX: 602-252-1891

Chaparral College
Paralegal Program
4585 E. Speedway Blvd. , Suite 204
Tucson 85712
520-327-6866

Interstate Career College
Paralegal Program
6367 E. Tanque Verde Rd., Suite 100
Tucson 85715
520-327-6851

Lamson Junior College
Legal Assistant Dept.
1980 W. Main St., Suite 250
Mesa 85201-6933
602-898-7000

Lamson Junior College
Legal Assistant Program
1126 N. Scottsdale Rd.
Tempe 85281
602-898-7000; FAX: 602-967-6645

Paralegal Institute Inc.
2933 W. Indian School Rd.
Phoenix 85017
602 212 0501

Phoenix College
Legal Assisting Program
1202 West Thomas Rd.
Phoenix 85013-4234
602-285-7568; FAX: 602-285-7591

Pima Community College
Legal Assistant Studies
1255 N. Stone Ave.
Tucson 85709-3030
520-884-6788; 520-884-6369;
FAX: 520-884-6201

Scottsdale Community College
9000 E. Chaparral Rd.
Scottsdale 85250-2614
602-243-8120

Yavapai College
Paralegal Studies
1100 E. Sheldon St.
Prescott 86301-3297
520-776-2343; FAX: 520-776-0438
susan@yavapai.cc.az.us

ARKANSAS
Ouachita Technical College
Malvern 72104
501-332-3658

Remington College
Paralegal Program
3448 N. College Ave.
Fayetteville 72703-3815
501-442-2364

Remington College
Paralegal Program
7601 Scott Hamilton Dr.
Little Rock 72209
501-565-7000

Shorter College
604 Locust St.
North Little Rock 72114
501-374-6305

Westark Community College
Division of Business
Legal Assistance/Paralegal
5210 Grand Ave., P.O. Box 3649
Fort Smith 72913-3649
501-788-7805; FAX: 501-788-7816
mlowe@systema.westark.edu

CALIFORNIA
American River College
4700 College Oak Dr.
Sacramento 95841-4286
916-484-8282

Barclay College
Paralegal Program
3151 Airway Ave., Suite A1
Costa Mesa 92626-4620
916-448-8758

California Paralegal College
461 Grass Valley Hwy.
Auburn 95603-3701
916-272-576

California State University–Chico
Paralegal Certificate Program
Chico 95929-0455
916-895-6478

California State University–Dominquez
Hills
Paralegal Program
1000 E. Victoria St.
Carson 90747-0001
310-516-3696

California State University–Hayward
Paralegal Studies Program, Extended
Education
25800 Carlos Bee Blvd.
Hayward 94542-3012
510-885-3605 x312; 510-881-2312;
FAX: 510-885-4817

California State University
Paralegal Program
1250 N. Bellflower Blvd.
Long Beach 90840-0001
562-985-4111

California State University–Los Angeles
Certificate Program in Paralegal Studies
5151 State University Dr.
Los Angeles 90032-8000
213-343-2022; FAX: 213-343-4954

California State University
Paralegal Studies Dept.
5500 University Pkwy.
San Bernardino 92407-2393
714-887-7268

Canada College
Paralegal Program
4200 Farm Hill Blvd.
Redwood City 94061-1099
415-364-1212

Cerritos Community College
Paralegal Program
11110 E. Alondra Blvd.
Norwalk 90650-6203
310-860-2451 x2710; FAX: 310-
467-5005

City College of San Francisco
Legal Assistant/Paralegal Program
50 Phelan Ave., C106
San Francisco 94112-1821
415-239-3508; FAX: 415-239-3919 (call
ahead)
mvota@ccsf.cc.ca.us

Coastline Community College
Legal Assistant Program
11460 Warner Ave.
Fountain Valley 92708
714-960-7671; 714-241-6213 x17319;
FAX: 714-751-3806
chet@cccd.edu

College of the Redwoods
Business Division
7351 Tompkins Hill Rd.
Eureka 95501-9300

College of the Sequoias
Paralegal Program
915 S Mooney Blvd.
Visalia 93277-2234
209-733-2050

Compton Community College
1111 East Artesia Blvd.
Compton 90221
310-637-2660

CSB Plus
Attorney Assistant Certificate Program
9001 Stockdale Hwy.
Bakersfield 93311-1022

De Anza College
Paralegal Studies
21250 Stevens Creek Blvd.
Cupertino 95014-5797
408-864-8563; FAX: 408-864-5309

Edison Tech College
8520 Balboa Blvd.
Northridge 91325-3561

El Camino College
Legal Assistant Program
16007 Crenshaw Blvd.
Torrance 90506
310-660-3773; FAX: 310-660-3774
ohadley@admin.elcamino.cc.ca.us

Evergreen Valley College
1236 Sierra Ave.
San Jose 95126-2642
408-287-1010

Ewing University
Paralegal Program
2007 E. Compton Blvd.
Compton 90221-3548

Fresno City College
Paralegal Studies
1101 E. University Ave.
Fresno 93741
209-442-4600 x8485;
FAX: 209-265-5719

Fullerton College
Legal Assistant Program
321 E. Chapman Ave.
Fullerton 92632-2095
714-992-7077

Gavilan College
15713 Kings Creek Rd.
Boulder Creek 95006-9648
408-338-3295

Humphreys College
Paralegal Program
Suite 605, 11344 Colomia Rd.
Gold River 95670-4463
916-635-3996

Humphreys College
Paralegal Program
Suite 3a, 3600 Sisk Rd.
Modesto 95356-0539
209-543-9411

Humphreys College
Paralegal Program
6650 Inglewood Ave.
Stockton 95207-3896
209-478-0800

Imperial Valley College
P.O. Box 158
Imperial 92251-0158
760-352-8320

Kelsey-Jenney College
Paralegal Studies
201 A St.
San Diego 92101
619-525-1799; FAX: 619-544-9610

Lake Tahoe Community College
One College Dr.
South Lake Tahoe 96150-4524
916-541-4660

Los Angeles City College
855 N. Vermont Ave.
Los Angeles 90029-3500
213-953-4381

Los Angeles SW College
Legal Assistant Program
1600 W. Imperial Hwy.
Los Angeles 90047-4810
213-241-5320

Merritt College
12500 Campus Dr.
Oakland   94619-3196
510-466-7369

Mission Valley College
Paralegal Studies
1212 San Fernando Rd.
San Fernando   91340-3212

Mt. San Antonio College
Paralegal Studies Program
1100 N. Grand Ave.
Walnut   91789
909-594-5611 x4906;
FAX: 909-468-3936

MTI Western Business College
Legal Assistant Studies
5221 Madison Ave.
Sacramento   95841-3003
916-339-1500; FAX: 916-339-0305

Napa Valley College
Napa   94558
707-253-3000

National University School of Law
Paralegal Studies
8380 Miramar Rd., # 240
San Diego   92126-4331
619-492-5201

Orange Coast College
2701 Fairview Rd
Costa Mesa   92626-5561
714-432-0202

Oxnard College
4000 S. Rose Ave.
Oxnard   93033-6699
805-986-5843

Pacific Coast College
Legal Assistant Program
P.O. Box 1540
La Canada   92701-4634

Palomar College
San Marcos   92069
619-744-1150

Pasadena City College
Legal Assistant Program
1570 E. Colorado Blvd.
Pasadena   91106-2041
818-578-7397; FAX: 818-585-7915

Phillips College
Inland Empire Campus
4300 Central Ave.
Riverside   92506-2918
909-787-9300

Rancho Santiago College
Legal Assistant Program
17th at Bristol
Santa Ana   92706
714-564-6813; FAX: 714-564-6755
deboerc@msn.com

Rio Hondo College
Paralegal Education Program
3600 Workman Mill Rd.
Whittier   90601
562-692-0921; FAX: 562-699-2699

Riverside Community College
4800 Magnolia Ave.
Riverside   92506-1299
909-222-8615

Saddleback College
Legal Assistant Program
28000 Marguerite Pkwy.
Mission Viejo   92692-3699
714-582-4773; FAX: 714-347-2431
BOEN_P@sccd.cc.ca.us

Saint Mary's College
Paralegal Program
P.O. Box 3052
Moraga 94575
510-631-4509; 510-273-8350;
FAX: 510-631-9869; 510-835-1451
http://simon.stmarys-ca.edu:70/0/study
/law/legal.html
cmoscrip@stmarys-ca.edu

San Bernadino Valley College
Legal Administration Program
701 S. Mount Vernon Ave.
San Bernardino 92410-2748

San Diego City College
1313 Twelfth Ave.
San Diego 92101
619-230-4787

San Diego Miramar College
San Diego 92126
619-536-7854

San Diego State University
Legal Assistant Specialist Certificate
Program
5250 Campanile Dr.
College of Extended Studies
San Diego 92182-1924
619-594-7078; 619-594-4800;
FAX: 619-594-8566
http://www.sdsu.edu/
ngeiser@mail.sdsu.edu

San Francisco State University
Paralegal Studies Certificate Program
425 Market St.
Downtown Center, 2nd Fl.
San Francisco 94105-2406
415-904-7770; FAX: 415-904-7760
http://www.cel.sfsu.edu
leeg@sfsu.edu

San Joaquin College of Law
Paralegal Program
3385 East Shields Ave.
Fresno 93726
209-225-4953; FAX: 209-225-4322

San Joaquin College of Law
Paralegal Program
901 5th St.
Clovis 93612-1312
209-323-2100; FAX: 209-323-5566

San Rafael Dominican College
50 Acacia Ave.
San Rafael 94901-2298
415-485-3228

Santa Ana College
Seventeenth at Bristol
Santa Ana 92706

The Santa Barbara and Ventura
Colleges of Law
911 Tremonto Rd.
Santa Barbara 93103
805-569-1567; FAX: 805-682-1135

Santa Clara University
Institute for Paralegal Education
500 El Camino Real
Santa Clara 95053-0440
408-554-4535; FAX: 408-554-5188

Santa Monica College
Legal Assistant Program
1900 Pico Blvd.
Santa Monica 90405-1644
310-450-5150

Sawyer College
Paralegal Program
8475 Jackson Rd.
Sacramento 95826
916-383-1909

Sawyer College
Paralegal Program
441 W. Trimble Rd.
San Jose 95131
408-954-8200

Shasta College
Redding   96049
916-225-4841

Sierra College
5000 Rocklin Rd.
Rocklin 95677-3397
916-624-3333

Skyline College
Paralegal Program
3300 College Dr.
San Bruno 94066-1698
415-355-7000

Sonoma State University
Attorney Assistant Certificate Program
1801 East Cotati Ave.
Rohnert Park 94928
707-664-2394; FAX: 707-664-2613
diane.petropulos@sonoma.edu

Southern California College of Business
and Law
Paralegal Program
595 W. Lambert Rd.
Brea 92621
714-256-8830; FAX: 714-256-8858

Southern California College of Court
Reporting
Paralegal Program
1360 S. Anaheim Blvd.
Anaheim 92805
714-758-1500

State Center Community College
1525 E. Weldon Ave.
Fresno 93704-6340

University of California–Davis
Legal Assisting Certificate Program
University Extension
Davis 95616
916-757-8895; FAX: 916-754-5105
mchaix@unexmail.ucdavis.edu

University of California–Irvine
Certificate Program in Legal
Assistantship
P.O. Box 6050
Irvine 92716-6050
714-824-3437; 714-824-1228;
FAX: 714-824-3651; 714-824-1547
http://www.unex.uci.edu.~unex

University of California–Los Angeles
Attorney Assistant Training Program
10995 Le Conte Ave., Rm. 517
Los Angeles 90024-2883
310-825-0741; FAX: 310-825-9242

University of California–Riverside
Legal Assistantship Certificate Program
1200 University Ave., Extension Center
Riverside 92507-4596
909-787-4111 x1614;
FAX: 909-787-2456
http://www.unex.ucr.edu/legal.htm

University of California–San Diego
Legal Assistant Program
UCSD Ext. 0176, 9500 Gilman Dr.
La Jolla 92093-0176
619-534-3434; 619-534-0706; FAX:
619-534-7385
http://www-esps.ucsd.edu
cboyl@ucsd.edu

University of California–Santa Barbara
Legal Assistant Program
6550 Hollister Ave.
Goleta 93117
805-893-4200; FAX: 805-893-4943

University of California–Santa Cruz
UCSC Extension Program
Legal Assistant
740 Front St., #155
Santa Cruz 95060-4536

University of La Verne
Paralegal Studies Program
1950 3rd St.
La Verne 91750-4401
909-596-1848; FAX: 909-392-2707
sanjuanv@ulvacs.ulaverne.edu

University of Laverne
College of Law
21300 Oxnard St.
Woodland Hills 91367-5016A
818-981-4529

University of Northern California
Paralegal School
7623 Southbreeze Dr.
Sacramento 95828-5107

University of San Diego
Paralegal Program
5998 Alcala Park, Serra Hall 316
San Diego 92110
619-260-4579; FAX: 619-260-2252

University of Southern California
Paralegal Program
200 University Park
Los Angeles 90089-0071
213-743-2008

University of West Los Angeles
School of Paralegal Studies
1155 West Arbor Vitae St.
Inglewood 90301-2902
310-215-3339; 310-342-5203;
FAX: 310-342-5295

Watterson College
2030 University Dr.
Vista 92083-7736

West Los Angeles College
Paralegal Studies
4800 Freshman Dr.
Culver City 90230-3500
310-287-4200; 310-412-0319;
FAX: 310-841-0396

West Valley College
Paralegal Program
14000 Fruitvale Ave.
Saratoga 95070-5640
408-741-2415; FAX: 408-741-2145
bobdiane@ix.netcom.com

COLORADO
Aims Community College
5401 20th St.
Greeley 80634-3002
303-330-8008

Arapahoe Community College
Legal Assistant Program
2500 W. College Dr.
P.O. Box 9002
Littleton 80160-9002
303-797-5900; FAX: 303-797-5935

Blair College
Paralegal Program
828 Wooten Rd.
Colorado Springs 80915
719-574-1082

Center for Legal Studies
22316 Sunset Dr.
Golden 80401-9537
303-526-9777; 800-522-7737

Colorado Community College
1391 N. Speer Blvd., Suite 600
Denver 80204-2554
303-620-4000

Colorado Mountain College
P.O. Box 10001
Glenwood Springs 81602
800-621-8559

Colorado Northwestern Community
College
Rangely 81648-3598
970-675-3217
http://www.cncc.cc.co.us/

Community College of Aurora
Paralegal/Legal Assistant Program
16000 E. Centre Tech Pkwy., C208
Aurora 80011-9036
303-361-7407; FAX: 303-361-7374

Community College of Denver
1111 W. Colfax Ave., Rm. Ca-313
Denver 80204-2026
303-556-2600

Denver Business College
Paralegal Program
7350 N. Broadway
Denver 80221
303-426-1000

Denver Community College
P.O. Box 173363
Denver 80217-3363

Denver Paralegal Institute
105 E. Vermijo Ave., #415
Colorado Springs 80903-2005
719-444-0107

Denver Paralegal Institute
General Practice Program
1401 19th St.
Denver 80202-1213
303-295-0550; 800-848-0550;
FAX: 303-295-0102
covingtonb@aol.com

Metropolitan State College
Legal Assistant Program
1006 11th St.
Denver 80204-2025

North Eastern Junior College
100 College Dr.
Sterling 80751-2344

Parks College
Paralegal Program
9065 Grant St.
Denver 80229-4339
303-457-2757

Pikes Peak Community College
Legal Assistant Program
5675 South Academy Blvd.
Colorado Springs 80906
719-540-7261; 800-456-6847;
FAX: 719-540-7254

Pueblo Community College
900 West Orman Ave.
Pueblo 81004-1499
719-549-3013
http://www.pcc.cccoes.edu/

Red Rocks Community College
13300 West Sixth Ave.
Lakewood 80401-5398
303-988-6160

Trinidad State Junior College
600 Prospect St.
Trinidad 81082-2356
719-846-5011

CONNECTICUT
Branford Hall Career Institute
1 Summit Place
Branford 06405
203-488-2525; 800-959-7599

Branford Hall Career Institute
Paralegal Program
995 Day Hill Rd.
Windsor 06095
860-683-4900

Briarwood College
Legal Assistant/Paralegal Program
2279 Mount Vernon Rd.
Southington 06489-1057
203-628-4751

Fairfield University
School of Continuing Education
Fairfield 06430
203-254-4220

Hartford College for Women
Legal Studies Dept
1265 Asylum Ave.
Hartford 06105
860-768-5600; FAX: 860-768-5693

Katharine Gibbs School
142 East Ave.
Norwalk 06851-5714
203-838-4173

Manchester Community-Technical
College
Legal Assistant Program
P.O. Box 1046
60 Bidwell Ave., Mail Station 8
Manchester 06045-1046
860-647-6108; FAX: 860-647-6238

Mattatuck Community College
Legal Assistant Program
750 Chase Pkwy.
Waterbury 06708-3000
203-575-8002

Morse School of Business
Paralegal Program
275 Asylum St.
Hartford 06103-2002
203-522-2261

Naugatuck Valley Community/Technical
College
Legal Assistant Program
750 Chase Pkwy.
Waterbury 06708-3000
203-596-8744; 203-575-8040

National Academy of Paralegal Studies
P.O. Box 4102
Wallingford 06492-1452
800-922-0771

Northwestern Connecticut Community
College
Park Place East
Winstead 06098
203-738-6390

Norwalk Community College
Legal Assistant Program
188 Richards Ave.
Norwalk 06854-1655
203-866-3504
Norwalk Community-Technical College
188 Richards Ave.
Norwalk 06854-1655
203-857-7060

Paralegal Studies Institute–London
306 26th St.
Stamford 06905-4605
203-325-2181

Post College
Legal Assistant Program
800 Country Club Rd.
Waterbury 06708-3200

Quinnipiac College
Legal Studies Department
Mt. Carmel Ave.
Hamden 06518
203-281-8712; FAX: 203-281-8709
martin@quinnipiac.edu

Sacred Heart University
Legal Assistant Program
5151 Park Ave.
Fairfield 06432-1023
203-371-7960; FAX: 203-365-7538
sdonohue@shy.sacred.heart.edu

Teikyo Post University
Paralegal Program
P.O. Box 2540
Waterbury 06723-2540
203-596-4648

University of Bridgeport
Legal Assistant Studies
169 University Ave., Rm. 130
Bridgeport 06604-5795
203-576-4641

University of Hartford
Legal Studies Program
200 Bloomfield Ave.
W. Hartford 06117-1599
203-243-4980

University of New Haven
300 Orange Ave.
West Haven 06516-1999
203-932-7088

DELAWARE
Career Institute
711 Market St. Mall
Wilmington 19801

Delaware Technical Community College
Southern Campus
Legal Assistant Technology
Georgetown 19947
302-856-5400

University of Delaware
Legal Assistant Education Program
Clayton Hall
Newark 19716
302-831-3474

Wesley College
Paralegal Studies Program
Dover 19901
302-736-2429; 302-736-2309

Widener University Law Center
Legal Education Institute
4601 Concord Pike
Wilmington 19803
302-477-2012; FAX: 302-477-2054

DISTRICT OF COLUMBIA
George Washington University
Legal Assistant Program
2029 K St. NW, Suite 600
Washington 20006
202-496-2274; FAX: 202-973-1165
parr@gwis2.circ.gwu.edu

Georgetown University
Legal Assistant Program
37th and O St. NW, 306 ICC-SSCE
Washington 20057-0001
202-687-6245; FAX: 202-687-8954
silversg@guner.georgetown.edu

NRI Paralegal School
McGraw Hill Continuing Education
Center
4401 Connecticut Ave. NW
Washington 20008-2322
202-244-1600

U.S. Dept of Agriculture
Graduate School
Rm. 1, 14th St. & Independence Ave.
Washington 20250-0001
202-447-5885

FLORIDA
Atlantic Coast Institute
Paralegal Program
5225 W. Broward Blvd.
Ft. Lauderdale 33317
954-581-2223

Barry University
Paralegal Studies Program
11300 NE 2nd Ave.
Miami Shores 33161-6695
305-899-3300; FAX: 305-899-3346

Broward Community College
Legal Assisting Program
7200 Hollywood Pines Blvd.
Pembroke Pines 33024
305-986-8011; FAX: 954-963-8990

Career Training Institute
Paralegal Studies Program
3326 Edgewater Dr.
Orlando 32804-3742

Central Florida Community College
Legal Assistant Program
P.O. Box 1388
Ocala 34478-1388
904-237-2111

City College
Paralegal Program
1401 W. Cypress Creek Rd.
Ft. Lauderdale 33309
954-492-5353

Cooper Career Institute
Paralegal Program
2247 Palm Beach Lakes Blvd., Suite 110
West Palm Beach 33409
407-640-6999

Daytona Beach Community College
Daytona Beach 32120
904-254-4426

Edison Community College
P.O. Box 06210
Fort Myers 33906-6210
813-489-9318

Florida Atlantic University
Institute for Legal Assistants
P.O. Box 3091
Boca Raton 33431-0991
407-367-3179

Florida Community College
Legal Assisting Program
3939 Roosevelt Blvd.
Kent Campus, C-205
Jacksonville 32205-8999
904-381-3589 x3476;
FAX: 904-381-3462

Florida Metropolitan University
Paralegal Program
Ft. Lauderdale College
1040 Bayview Dr.
Ft. Lauderdale 33304-2522
954-568-1600

Florida Metropolitan University
Paralegal Program
Orlando College, N.
5421 Diplomat Circle
Orlando 32810
407-628-5870

Florida Metropolitan University
Paralegal Program
Tampa College
3319 W. Hillsborough Ave.
Tampa 33614
813-879-6000

Florida National College
4206 West 12th Ave.
Hialeah 33012
305-821-3333

Gulf Coast Community College
Panama City 32401-1058
904-769-1551

Hillsborough Community College
P.O. Box 30030
Tampa 33620
813-253-7004

Indian River Community College
Ft. Pierce 34981-5599
407-462-4740

International College
Paralegal Program
2654 E. Tamiami Trail
Naples 33962-5790
941-774-4700

Jones College
Paralegal Program
5353 Arlington Expwy.
Jacksonville 32211-5588
904-743-1122

Keiser College of Technology
Melbourne 32901-1461
407-255-2255

Keiser College of Technology
Sarasota 34236
941-954-0954
http://www.keisercollege.cc.fl.us/

Keiser College of Technology
Tallahassee 32308
904-906-9494

Manatee Community College
Legal Assisting
P.O. Box 1849, A.S. 134
Bradenton 34206
941-755-1511 x4656;
FAX: 941-755-1511 x4330

Manatee Community College
Paralegal Student Association
4231 Berkshire Dr.
Sarasota 34241-5916
813-755-1511

Miami-Dade Community College
Legal Assistant Program
300 NE 2nd Ave.
Miami 33132-2204
305-237-3151; FAX: 305-237-7541

National Center for Paralegal Training
Lawyer's Assistant Program
1799 SE 17th St.
Fort Lauderdale 33316-3013

National School of Technology
Paralegal Program
9020 SW 137th Ave.
Miami 33186
305-386-9900

Nova Southeastern University
Paralegal Studies Program
3301 College Ave.
Ft. Lauderdale 33314
305-465-7340

Okaloosa-Walton Community College
Niceville 32578-1295
904-729-5223

Palm Beach Community College
4200 Congress Ave.
Lake Worth 33461-4705
407-439-8106

Palm Beach Junior College
3160 PGA Blvd.
Palm Beach Gardens 33410
407-622-2440

Paralegal Support Service
338 N. Magnolia Ave.
Orlando 32801-1653

Pensacola Junior College
Legal Assistant Program
10000 College Blvd.
Pensacola 32504
904-484-2509

Prospect Hall School of Business
Paralegal Program
2620 Hollywood Blvd.
Hollywood 33020
954-923-8100

Rollins College
Suite G-20, 2203 N. Lois Ave.
Tampa 33607-2370

Rollins College
1000 Holt Ave.
Winter Park 32789-4499
800-688-2450

St. Petersburg Junior College
Legal Assistant Program
2465 Drew St.
Clearwater 34625-2898
813-791-2530; FAX: 813-791-2736

St. Petersburg Junior College
Legal Assistant Program
P.O. Box 13489
St. Petersburg 33733-3489
813-791-2501

Santa Fe Community College
Legal Assistant Program
3000 NW 83rd St.
Gainesville 32606
352-395-5139; FAX: 352-395-4127

Sarasota Vocational/Technical School
Legal Assistant Program
4748 Beneva Rd.
Sarasota 34233-1798

Schiller International University
Paralegal Program
453 Edgewater Dr.
Dunedin 34698
813-736-5082

Seminole Community College
Sanford 32773-6199
407-328-2041

South College
Paralegal Studies Program
1760 N. Congress Ave.
West Palm Beach 33409-5178
407-697-9200; FAX: 407-697-9944

Southern College
Paralegal Program
5600 Lake Underhill Rd.
Orlando 32807-1699
407-273-1000; FAX: 407-273-0492

Southwest Florida College of Business
Paralegal Program
1685 Medical Ln., Suite 200
Fort Myers 33907
941-939-4766

Tallahassee Community College
444 Appleyard Dr.
Tallahassee 32304-2895
904-921-2265
http://www.tallahassee.cc.fl.us

Tampa College
Paralegal Program
15064 U.S. Hwy. 19N
Clearwater 34624-7188
813-530-9495

Tampa College
Paralegal Program
1200 U.S. Hwy. 98 S
Lakeland 33801-5939
813-686-1444

Tampa College
Paralegal Program
3924 Coconut Palm Dr.
Tampa 33619-1354
813-621-1141

University of Central Florida
Legal Studies Program
P.O. Box 161600
Orlando 32816-1600
407-823-5364; FAX: 407-823-5360

University of Miami
400 SE 2nd Ave., Fl. 4
Miami 33131-2140
305-372-0120

University of North Florida
Division of Continuing Education
4567 St. Johns Bluff Rd. S.
Jacksonville 32224-2645
904-620-2690

University of West Florida
Legal Administration
11000 University Pkwy., Bldg. 50
Pensacola 32514-5751
904-474-2336; FAX: 904-474-2373

Valencia Community College
Legal Assisting Program
P.O. Box 3028, MC3-25
Orlando 32802-3028
407-299-5000 x2514;
FAX: 407-299-5000 x2552

Ward Stone College
Dadeland Campus
9020 SW 137th Ave., Fl. 2
Miami 33186-1410
305-670-2082

GEORGIA
Academy of Paralegal Studies
8493 Campbellton St.
Douglasville 30134-1820

Academy of Paralegal Studies, Inc.
691 Cherry St.
Macon 31201-2666

American Institute for Paralegal Studies
1 Dunwoody Park, #114
Atlanta 30338-6708
800-343-9776

American Institute for Paralegal Studies,
Inc.
Paralegal Program
(sites in Lawrenceville and Marietta)
800-624-3933

Athens Area Technical Institute
Paralegal Studies Program
800 U.S. Highway 29
North Athens 30601-1500
706-355-5041; 706-355-5000;
FAX: 706-369-5753
http://admin1.athens.tec.ga.us
dacahill@admin1.athens.tec.ga.us

Clayton State College
Legal Assistant Program
P.O. Box 285
Morrow 30260-0285
770-961-3500

Floyd College
Rome 30162-1864
706-295-6339
http://www.fc.peachnet.edu

Gainesville College
Legal Assistant Program
P.O. Box 1358
Gainesville 30503
770-718-3760; FAX: 770-718-3761
jmarler@hermes.gc.peachnet.edu

Kennesaw State College
P.O. Box 444
Marietta 30061-0444

Middle Georgia College
Cochran 31014-1599
912-934-3036
http://www.mgc.peachnet.edu

Morris Brown College
Legal Assistant Program
643 Martin Luther King Jr. Dr. NW
Atlanta 30314-4195
814-886-4131

National Center for Paralegal Training
Paralegal Studies Program
3414 Peachtree Rd. NE, Suite 528
Atlanta 30326
404-266-1060; FAX: 404-233-4891

School of Paralegal Studies
6065 Roswell Rd. NE
Atlanta 30328-4011

South College
Paralegal Program
709 Mall Blvd.
Savannah 31406-4881

Valdosta State University
Paralegal Program
Valdosta 31698-0001

HAWAII
Kapiolani Community College
Legal Assistant Program
4303 Diamond Head Rd.
Honolulu 96816
808-734-9100; FAX: 808-734-9147

IDAHO
Boise State University
Paralegal Education Program
1910 University Drive
Boise 83725-0399
208-385-3306

Lewis-Clark State College
Paralegal Program
500 8th Ave.
Lewiston 83501-2466
208-799-2466; FAX: 208-799-2856
bbowen@lcsc.edu

North Idaho College
Coeur d'Alene 83814-2199
208-769-3311
http://www.ni.edu

ILLINOIS
American Institute for Paralegal Studies
Paralegal Program
17 W. 705 Butterfield Rd., Suite A
Oakbrook Terrace 60181
630-916-6880

Belleville Area College
Belleville 62221-5899
618-235-2700

Elgin Community College
Paralegal Program
1700 Spartan Dr.
Elgin 60123
847-697-1000 x7466;
FAX: 847-888-7995

Gem City College
Paralegal Program
700 State St.
Quincy 62301
217-222-0391

Illinois Central College
Paralegal Studies Program
One College Dr.
East Peoria 61635-0001
309-694-5386; FAX: 309-673-9501

Illinois State University
Legal Studies Program
Campus Box 4600
Normal 61790-4600
309-438-8638; FAX: 309-438-5310
http://www.ilstu.edu/depts/polisci/legs.
htm
teeimer@ilstu.edu

John Marshall Law School
315 S. Plymouth St.
Chicago 60604-3968
312-427-2737

Lincoln College
Lincoln 62656-1699
217-732-3155

Loyola University Chicago
Institute for Paralegal Studies
820 N. Michigan Ave., Rm. 307
Chicago 60611
312-915-6820; FAX: 312-915-6448

MacCormac Junior College
506 S. Wabash Ave./Congress Pkwy.
Chicago 60605-1667
708-941-1200

MacCormac Junior College
615 N. West Ave.
Elmhurst 60126-1887
708-941-1200

Midstate College
Paralegal Services
P.O. Box 148
Peoria 61650-0148
309-673-6365

NorthEastern Business College
8020 W. 87th St.
Hickory Hills 60457-1189
708-430-0990

NorthWestern Business College
Paralegal Program
4829 North Lipps
Chicago 60630-2298
773-777-4220

Roosevelt University
Lawyer's Assistant Program
430 S. Michigan Ave., Rm. 462
Chicago 60605
312-341-3882; FAX: 312-341-6356
http://www.hc.net/~/ap
sreardon@acfsysv.roosevelt.edu

Sangamon State University
Paralegal Studies
PAC 429
Springfield 62794
217-786-6535

South Suburban College
8568 Cedar St.
Orland Park 60462-1620

South Suburban College
Paralegal/Legal Assistant Program
15800 South State St.
South Holland 60473
708-596-2000; FAX: 708-210-5758

Southern Illinois University
Paralegal Studies for Legal Assistants
c/o History Department
Carbondale 62901
618-536-2162; FAX: 618-453-5440

University of Illinois at Springfield
Legal Studies Program
PAC 340
Springfield 62708
217-786-6535

William Rainey Harper College
Legal Technology Program
1200 W. Algonquin Rd.
Palatine 60067-7398
847-925-6407; FAX: 847-925-6043
http://www.harper.cc.il.us
pguymon@harper.cc.il.us

INDIANA
American Institute for Paralegal
Studies, Inc.
Paralegal Program
(sites in Indianapolis and Ft. Wayne)
800-624-3933

American Institute for Paralegal Studies
1777 Market Tower, 10 W. Market St.
Indianapolis 46204-2954
800-624-3933

Ball State University
Legal Assistance Studies
NW 240, Dept. of Political Science
Muncie 47306
317-285-8780; FAX: 317-285-8980
rg.hollands@bsu.edu

Butler University
Legal Assistant Program
4600 Sunset Ave.
Indianapolis 46208-3485
317-283-9230

Commonwealth Business College
Paralegal Program
4200 W. 81st Ave.
Merrillville 46410
219-769-1076

Indiana University
P.O. Box 9003
Kokomo 46904-9003
317-455-9405

Indiana University
1700 Mishawaka Ave.
South Bend 46615-1408
219-237-4261

Indiana University–Purdue
Division of Continuing Studies
626 Union Dr., Suite 318
Indianapolis 46202-5130
317-274-5047

Indiana Vocational Technical College
3800 N. Anthony Blvd.
Ft. Wayne 46805-1430

Indiana Voctech College
P.O. Box 1763
Indianapolis 46206-1763
317-921-4443

International Business College
Paralegal Program
3811 Old Illinois Rd.
Ft. Wayne 46804
219-432-8702

International Business College
7205 Shadeland St.
Indianapolis 46256-3997
317-841-6400

Ivy Tech State College–Central Indiana
1 W. 26th St.
P.O. Box 1763
Indianapolis 46206-1763
317-921-4612
http://www.ivy.tec.in.us

Ivy Tech State College–Northeast
3800 North Anthony Blvd.
Fort Wayne 46805-1430
219-480-4211
http://www.ivy.tec.in.us

Saint Mary-of-the-Woods College
Paralegal Studies Program
Guerin Hall
Saint Mary-of-the-Woods 47876
812-535-5235; FAX: 812-535-4613

Sawyer College
Paralegal Program
3803 E. Lincoln Hwy.
Merrillville 46410
219-947-4555

University of Evansville
Legal Studies Program
1800 Lincoln Ave., School of Business
Evansville 47722
812-479-2851; FAX: 812-479-2872
http://cedar.evansville.edu/~dh4/index.
html
dh4@evansville.edu

University of Indianapolis
1400 E. Hanna Ave.
Indianapolis 46227-3697

Vincennes University
Legal Assistant/Paralegal Program
Davis Hall #64
Vincennes 47591
812-885-5764; FAX: 812-882-2237
lstearns@vunet.vinu.edu

IOWA
American Institute for Paralegal
Studies, Inc.
Paralegal Program
Sioux City 51101
800-624-3933

American Institute of Commerce
Legal Assistant Program
2302 West First St.
Cedar Falls 50613

American Institute of Commerce
Paralegal Program
1801 E. Kimberly Rd.
Davenport 52807
319-355-3500

Des Moines Area Community College
Legal Assistant Program
1100 7th St.
Des Moines 50314
515-248-7208; FAX: 515-248-7253

Iowa Lakes Community College
Legal Assistant Program
300 S. 18th St.
Estherville 51360
712-362-2604; FAX: 712-362-7649

Iowa Western Community College
Council Bluffs 51502
712-325-3288

Kirkwood Community College
Legal Assistant/Paralegal Program
P.O. Box 2068
Cedar Rapids 52214
319-398-5576; FAX: 319-398-1021
http://www.kirkwood.cc.ia.us:80/catalo
g/career_option/social/paralegal.html
wgeertz@kirkwood.cc.ia.us

Marycrest College
1607 W. 12th St.
Davenport 52804-4096
319-332-9190

National Academy of Paralegal Studies
627 Frances Bldg.
Sioux City 51101
800-922-0771

University of Northern Iowa
Cedar Falls 50613

University Teikyo Marycrest
Paralegal Program
Davenport 52070

KANSAS
American Institute for Paralegal
Studies, Inc.
Paralegal Program
800-624-3933

Barton County Community College
Legal Assisting
Great Bend 67530

Brown Mackie College
Legal Assistant Program
8000 W. 110th St.
Overland Park 66210-2315

Brown Mackie College
Salina 67401-2810
913-825-5422; 800-365-0433

Brown Mackie College–Olathe Campus
100 E. Santa Fe, Suite 300
Olathe 66061
913-768-1900

Hutchinson Community College
Legal Assistant Programs
1300 N. Plum St.
Hutchinson 67501-5894
316-665-3476

Hutchison Community College
P.O. Box 12951
Kansas City 66112-9978
316-665-3536

Johnson County Community College
Paralegal Program
12345 College Blvd.
Overland Park 66210-1299
913-469-8500 x3184;
FAX: 913-469-2380
atebbe@johnco.cc.ks.us

Kansas City Kansas Community College
Kansas City 66112-3003

National Academy of Paralegal Studies
105 S. Kansas Ave.
Olathe 66061-4434

Washburn University
Legal Assistant Program
17th & College
Topeka 66621
913-295-6619

Wichita State University
Legal Assistant Program
P.O. Box 48
Wichita 67201-0048
316-689-3200

KENTUCKY
Career Commercial Junior College
1102 S. Virginia St.
Hopkinsville 42240-3579

Draughons Junior College
Paralegal Program
2424 Airway Dr. & Lovers Ln.
Bowling Green 42103
502-843-6750

Eastern Kentucky University
Paralegal Programs
McCreary 113
Richmond 40475
606-622-1025; FAX: 606-622-4378
govmccor@acs.eku.edu

Midway College
Paralegal Studies Program
512 East Stephens St.
Midway 40347-9731
606-846-4421 x5331;
FAX: 606-846-5349

Morehead State University
Paralegal Studies Program
350 Rader Hall
Morehead 40351
606-783-2655; FAX: 606-783-2678
k.schafe@morehead-stedu

Owensboro Junior College of Business
Paralegal Program
1515 E. 18th St.
Owensboro 42303
502-926-4040

Sullivan College
Institute for Paralegal Studies
3101 Bardstown Rd.
Louisville 40205-3000
502-456-6504; FAX: 502-458-7467

Sullivan College
Institute for Paralegal Studies
2659 Regency Rd.
Lexington 40503
606-276-4357; FAX: 606-276-1153

University of Louisville
Paralegal Studies Program
406 Ford Hall, Belknap Campus
Louisville 40292
502-852-3249; FAX: 502-852-7923

LOUISIANA
Elaine P. Nunez Community College
Chalmette 70043-1249
504-278-7350

Herzing College of Business and
Technology
Paralegal Program
201 Evans Rd., Suite 400
New Orleans 70123
504-733-0074

Louisiana State University
Paralegal Studies Program
271 Pleasant Hall
Baton Rouge 70803-1530
504-388-6760; FAX: 504-388-6761
amccror@lsuvm.sncc.lsu.edu

Louisiana State University
8515 Youree Dr.
Shreveport 71115-2301
800-256-1530

Louisiana State University at Eunice
Eunice 70535-1129
318-457-7311

Nicholls State University
Legal Assistant Studies
Box 2089, Dept. of Government
Thibodaux 70310
504-448-4610

Phillips Junior College
Paralegal Studies Program
822 S. Clearview Pkwy.
New Orleans 70123-3449

Remington College
Paralegal Program
303 Rue Louis XIV
Lafayette 70508
318-981-4010

Southern University at
Shreveport–Bossier City Campus
3050 Martin Luther King Jr. Dr.
Shreveport 71107
318-674-3345

Southwest Paralegal College
P.O. Box 92247
Lafayette 70509-2247
318-233-4959

Tulane University
Paralegal Studies Program
Rm. 125, Gibson Hall
New Orleans 70115
504-865-5555; FAX: 504-865-5562

University of New Orleans
Paralegal Studies Program
226 Carondelet St., Suite 310
New Orleans 70130-2933
504-568-8585; FAX: 504-568-8596
klwpa@uno.edu

MAINE
Andover College
Paralegal Program
901 Washington Ave.
Portland 04103-2791
207-774-6126

Beal College
Paralegal Program
629 Main St.
Bangor 04401-6896
207-947-4591

Casco Bay College
Paralegal Certificate Program
477 Congress St.
Portland 04101
207-772-0196; FAX: 207-772-0636

Husson College
1 College Circle
Bangor 04401-2999

University College of Bangor
Legal Technology, Paralegal Studies
Program
210 Texas Ave., Katahdin Hall
Bangor 04401
207-581-6212; FAX: 207-581-6069

University of Maine
Admission and Student Services
Acadia Hall
216 Texas Ave.
Bangor 04401
207-581-6161

MARYLAND
Abbie Business Institute
Paralegal Program
5310 Spectrum Dr.
Frederick 21701
301-694-0211

Anne Arundel Community College
Paralegal Studies Program
101 College Pkwy.
Arnold 21012
410-315-7390; FAX: 410-315-7099

Baltimore City Community College
600 E. Lombard St.
Baltimore 21202-4031
410-333-8329

Catonsville Community College
Legal Assistant/Paralegal Program
800 S. Rolling Rd.
Catonsville 21228-5384
410-455-6912

Charles County Community College
P.O. Box 910
La Plata 20646-0910
301-934-2251
http://www.charles.cc.md.us

Chesapeake College
P.O. Box 8
Wye Mills 21679-0008
410-822-5400

Community College of Baltimore
Paralegal Program
Lombard St. at Market Place
Baltimore 21202
301-396-5870

Dundalk Community College
Paralegal Studies Program
7200 Sollers Point Rd.
Dundalk 21222
410-285-9794; FAX: 410-285-9665

Frederick Community College
7932 Opossumtown Pike
Frederick 21702-2097
301-846-2571

Hagerstown Business College
Legal Assistant Program
1050 Crestwood Dr.
Hagerstown 21742-2797
301-739-2670

Hagerstown Junior College
Hagerstown 21742-6590
301-790-2800
http://www.western-md.com/hjc

Harford Community College
Paralegal Studies
401 Thomas Run Rd.
Bel Air 21015-1698
410-836-4434; FAX: 410-836-4198
dsmith@smtpgate.harford.cc.md.us

Montgomery College
Legal Assistant Program
7600 Takoma Ave.
Takoma Park 20912-4197
301-650-1343

National Academy for Paralegal Studies
P.O. Box 20148
Baltimore 21284-0148
800-922-0771

Prince George's Community College
Paralegal Program
301 Largo Rd. #B208
Upper Marlboro 20772-2199
301-322-0703

University of Maryland
University College
Paralegal Studies Program
University Blvd. at Adelphi Rd.
College Park 20742
301-985-7733; FAX: 301-985-4615
hkaufman@nova.umuc.edu

Villa Julie College
Paralegal Program
1525 Greenspring Valley Rd.
Stevenson 21153
410-602-7423; FAX: 410-486-3552
dea-joyc@wpmsgsvr.vjc.edu

MASSACHUSETTS
Anna Maria College
Paralegal Studies Dept.
Sunset Lane
Paxton 01612
508-849-3380; FAX: 508-849-3362

Aquinas College
303 Adams St.
Milton 02186-4296
617-696-3100

Assumption College
Paralegal Studies
500 Salisbury St.
Worcester 01609-1294
508-752-5616

Atlantic Union College
P.O. Box 1000
South Lancaster 01561-1000
508-368-2235

Bay Path College
Legal Studies
588 Longmeadow St.
Longmeadow 01106
413-567-0621; FAX: 413-567-9324
jspadoni@baypath.edu

Becker Junior College
61 Sever St.
Worcester 01609-2165
508-791-9241

Bentley College
Institute of Paralegal Studies
175 Forest St.
Waltham 02154-4705
617-891-2800; FAX: 617-891-3449
fsalimbene@bentley.edu

Boston University, Metropolitan College
Paralegal Studies
755 Commonwealth Ave., Rm. 205
Boston 02215
617-353-2061; FAX: 617-353-5532
swidoff@bu.edu

Bridgewater State College
100 State St.
Bridgewater 02325-0001
508-697-1237

Cape Cod Community College
West Barnstable 02668-1599
508-362-2131

Dean College
Franklin 02038-1994
508-541-1508; 800-852-7702
http://www.dean.edu

Elms College
30 Chestnut St.
Amherst 01002

Elms College
Paralegal Institute
291 Springfield St.
Chicopee 01013-2839
413-594-7787; FAX: 413-594-8173
currierk@elms.edu

Endicott College
376 Hale St.
Beverly 01915-2098
508-921-1000

Fisher College
118 Beacon St.
Boston 02116-1500
617-236-8800; 800-821-3050 (in-state); 800-446-1226 (out-of-state)

Hampshire College
893 West St.
Amherst 01002-3359

Katharine Gibbs School
Paralegal Program
126 Newbury St.
Boston 02116-2904

Kinyon-Campbell Business School
Paralegal Program
1041 Pearl St.
Brockton 02401
508-584-6869

Massachusetts Bay Community College
50 Oakland St.
Wellesley Hills 02181-5359
617-239-2500

Masssachusetts Bay Community College
19 Flagg Dr.
Framingham 01702
508-270-4000
http://www.mbcc.mass.edu

Massachusetts Continuing Legal Education, Inc.
10 Winter Place
Boston 02108-4751
617-350-7006

Mildred Elley
Paralegal Program
St. Luke Square, 7 Whipple St.
Pittsfield 01201
413-499-8618

Middlesex Community College
P.O. Box 1
Bedford 01730-0001
617-275-8910

Mount Ida College
Paralegal Studies Program
777 Dedham St.
Newton 02159-3310

National Academy for Paralegal Studies
53 Winter St.
Weymouth 02188-3367
800-922-0771

Newbury College
Legal Studies
129 Fisher Ave.
Brookline 02146
617-738-2407; FAX: 617-730-7095

North Shore Community College
Paralegal Program
1 Ferncroft Rd.
Danvers 01923
508-762-4000

Northeastern University
Paralegal Professional Program
370 Common St.
Dedham 02026-4097
617-320-8023

Northern Essex Community College
Paralegal Program
Elliott Way
Haverhill 01830
508-374-3969; FAX: 508-374-3729

Quincy College
34 Coddington St.
Quincy 02169-4522
617-984-1700

Regis College
235 Wellesley St.
Weston 02193-1571
617-893-1820

Stonehill College
320 Washington St.
North Easton 02357-0001
508-238-1081

Suffolk University
Paralegal Studies
41 Temple St.
Boston 02114
617-573-8228; FAX: 617-722-9440
dahlborg@aol.com

University of Massachusetts
Paralegal Training Program
Harbor Campus
Boston 02125
617-287-7290

University of Massachusetts
Division of Continuing Education
1 University Ave.
Lowell 01854-2887
508-934-2495

MICHIGAN
Academy of Court Reporting
Paralegal Program
26111 Evergreen Rd.
Southfield 48076
248-353-4880

American Institute for Paralegal Studies
615 Griswold, Suite 320
Detroit 48226
313-964-1452

Charles Stewart Mott Community
College
Paralegal Technology
1401 E. Court St.
Flint 48503-6208
313-232-7901

Davenport College
Paralegal Studies
415 E. Fulton
Grand Rapids 49503
616-451-3511; FAX: 616-732-1142
http://www.davenport.edu
rstevens@davenport.edu

Davenport College
Paralegal Studies Program
4123 W. Main St.
Kalamazoo 49006-2791
616-382-2835

Delta College
Legal Assistant Studies
Office F-45
University Center 48710
517-686-9093; FAX: 517-686-9144

Eastern Michigan University
Legal Assistant Program
14 Sill Hall
Ypsilanti 48197
313-487-4330; FAX: 313-487-8755

Ferris State University
Legal Assistant Program
Bus. 124E, 119 South St.
Big Rapids 49307
616-592-2416; FAX: 616-592-3548

Gogebic Community College
Paralegal Program
Greenbush & Jackson
Ironwood 49938

Grand Rapids Community College
143 Bostwick Ave. NE
Grand Rapids 49503-3201
616-771-3850

Grand Valley State University
Legal Studies Program
237 Mackinac
Allendale 49401
616-895-2910; FAX: 616-895-2915

Grand Valley State University
Legal Studies Program
25 Commerce St.
Grand Rapids 49503
616-771-6577

Great Lakes Junior College of Business
320 South Washington Ave.
Saginaw 48607-1158
517-755-3457

Henry Ford Community College
Legal Assistant Program
22586 Ann Arbor Trail
Dearborn Heights 48127-2508
313-271-2750

Kellogg Community College
Legal Assistant Program
450 North Ave.
Battle Creek 49017
616-965-3931 x2520;
FAX: 616-965-4133

Lake Superior State University
Legal Assistant Studies
1000 College Dr.
Sault Sainte Marie 49783-1637
906-632-1755

Lansing Community College
Legal Assistant Program
P.O. Box 40010
Business Careers Dept.
Lansing 48901-7210
517-483-1503; FAX: 517-483-9740

Macomb Community College
Legal Assistant Technology Program
14500 Twelve Mile Rd.
Warren 48093
810-445-7350; FAX: 810-445-7014

Madonna University
Legal Assistant Program
36600 Schoolcraft
Livonia 48150
313-432-5549; FAX: 313-432-5393
cote@smtp.munet.edu

Mercy University of Detroit
Legal Assistant/Legal Administrator
8200 W. Outer Dr.
Detroit 48219-3580

Michigan Christian College
800 W. Avon Rd.
Rochester 48307-2764

Montcalm Community College
Sidney 48885-0300
517-328-1250
http://www.montcalm.cc.mi.us

Muskegon Business College
Paralegal Program
141 Hartford Ave.
Muskegon 49442-3453

Northwestern Michigan College
Traverse City 49686-3061
616-922-1022; 800-748-0566
http://www.nmc.edu

Oakland Community College
Legal Assistant Program
27055 Orchard Lake Rd.
Farmington Hills 48334
810-471-7643; FAX: 810-471-7544

Oakland University
Legal Assistant Diploma Program
265 S. Foundation Hall
Rochester 48309-4401
810-370-3120; FAX: 810-370-3137
gjboddy@oakland.edu

St. Clair Community College
323 Erie St.
Port Huron 48060-3812
810-984-3881

LearningExpress

20 Academy Street, P.O. Box 7100, Norwalk, CT 06852-9879

FREE! TEN TIPS TO PASSING ANY TEST

To provide you with the test prep and career information you need, we would appreciate your help. Please answer the following questions and return this postage paid survey. As our Thank You, we will send you our "Ten Tips To Passing Any Test" – surefire ways to score your best on classroom and/or job-related exams.

Name : _____

Address : _____

_____

Age : _____   Sex : ☐ Male   ☐ Female

Highest Level of School Completed : ☐ High School ☐ College

1) I am currently :

    A student — Year/level: _____

    Employed — Job title: _____

    Other — Please explain: _____

2) Jobs/careers of interest to me are :

    1. _____

    2. _____

    3. _____

3) If you are a student, did your guidance/career counselor provide you with job information/materials? _____

    Name & Location of School: _____

_____

_____

_____

4) What newspapers and/or magazines do you subscribe to or read regularly? _____

_____

5) Do you own a computer? _____

    Do you have Internet access? _____

    How often do you go on-line? _____

6) Have you purchased career-related materials from bookstores?

_____

    If yes, list recent examples: _____

_____

7) Which radio stations do you listen to regularly (please give call letters and city name)?

_____

_____

8) How did you hear about this LearningExpress book?

    An ad? _____

    If so, where? _____

    An order form in the back of another book? _____

    A recommendation? _____

    A bookstore? _____

    Other? _____

9) Title of the book this card came from:

_____

LearningExpress books are also available in the test prep/study guide section of your local bookstore.

LEARNINGEXPRESS

The new leader in test preparation and career guidance!

LearningExpress is an affiliate of Random House, Inc.

Southwestern Michigan College
Dowagiac 49047-9793
616-782-5113; 800-456-8675

Washtenaw Community College
4800 E. Huron River Dr.
Ann Arbor 48105-9572
313-973-3300

MINNESOTA

Hamline University
Paralegal (Legal Assistant) Program
1536 Hewitt Ave.
Saint Paul 55104
612-641-2207; FAX: 612-641-2956
http://www.hamline.edu/depts/legal/index.html
foreilly@piper.hamline.edu

Inver Hills Community College
Legal Assistant Program
2500 80 St. E.
Inver Grove Heights 55076-3224
612-450-8567; FAX: 612-450-8679

Itasca Community College
1851 E. Hwy. 169
Grand Rapids 55574
218-327-4205

Mankato State University
Political Science Department
Box 7
South Rd. & Ellis Ave.
Mankato 56002
507-389-2572; 507-389-2721

Mesabi Community College
1001 Chestnut St. W.
Virginia 55792
218-749-7752

Minnesota Paralegal Institute
12450 Wayzata Blvd., Suite 318
Minnetonka 55305
612-542-8417; FAX: 612-545-1524

Minnesota School of Business
Globe College of Business
1401 W. 76th St.
Richfield 55423
612-861-2000

Moorhead State University
Legal Assistant Program
1104 7th Ave.
South Moorhead 56563
218-236-2862; FAX: 218-236-2238
nordick@mhb.moorhead.msus.edu

North Hennepin Community College
Legal Assistant Program
7411 85th Ave.
North Brooklyn Park 55445
612-424-0915; FAX: 612-424-0889

Northland Community College
Hwy. 1 E.
Thief River Falls 56701
800-628-9918; 218-681-0701

Rasmussen College Mankato
Paralegal Program
501 Holly Ln.
Mankato 56001-9938
507-625-6556

Winona State University
Paralegal Program
212 Minne Hall, P.O. Box 5838
Winona 55987
507-457-5400; FAX: 507-457-5086
histdept@vax2.winona.msus.edu

MISSISSIPPI

Hinds Community College
103 Gibbes Hall
Raymond 39154
601-857-3488

Mississippi College
Paralegal Studies Program
P.O. Box 4092
Clinton 39058
601-925-3812; FAX: 601-925-3932

Mississippi Gulf Coast Community
College
8468 Louise St.
Biloxi 39532-8274

Mississippi Gulf Coast Junior College
Paralegal Program
2226 Switzer Rd.
Gulfport 39507-3824

Mississippi University for Women
Paralegal Studies
Box W-1634
Columbus 39701
601-329-7154

Northeast Mississippi Community
College
Booneville 38829
601-728-7751

Northwest Mississippi Community
College
Legal Assistant Program
300 N. Panola St.
Senatobia 38668-2009
601-562-3345

Phillips Junior College
Legal Assistant Program
1 Hancock Plaza
Gulfport 39501
509-535-7771

University of Mississippi
Paralegal Studies Program
655 Eason Blvd.
Tupelo 38801-5955

University of Southern Mississippi
Paralegal Studies
Box 5108, Southern Station
Hattiesburg 39406
601-266-4310; FAX: 601-266-5800

MISSOURI
American Institute for Paralegal Studies,
Inc.
Paralegal Program
13550 Conway Rd.
St. Louis 63141-7232
314-576-9400; 800-624-3933

Avila College
Legal Assistant Program
11901 Wornall
Kansas City 64145
816-942-8400 x2244; FAX: 816-
942-3362
gibbsja@avila.edu

Columbia College
Legal Assistant Program
Columbia 64201

Concorde Career Institute
Legal Assistant Program
P.O. Box 26610
Kansas City 64196-6610

Drury Evening College
Continuing Education Division
Legal Assistant Studies
900 N. Benton Ave.
Springfield 65802-3712

Hickey School
Paralegal Program
940 West Port Plaza
St. Louis 63146
314-434-2212

Mineral Area College
R.R. 1, Box 133
Caledonia 63631-9702
314-779-3881

Missouri Western State College
Legal Studies
4525 Downs Dr., Rm. PS204
St. Joseph 64507
816-271-5837; FAX: 816-271-5849
katz@griffon.mwsc.edu

Patricia Stevens College
Paralegal Program
1415 Olive St.
St. Louis 63103
314-421-0949

Penn Valley Community College
Legal Technology Program
3201 Southwest Trfy.
Kansas City 64111-2764
816-759-4000

Rockhurst College
Paralegal Program
5225 Troost Ave.
Kansas City 64110-2599
816-926-4200

Sanford-Brown College
Des Peres 63131-4499
314-822-7100

Sanford-Brown College
Hazelwood 63042
314-731-1101

Sanford-Brown College
Paralegal Program
520 E. 19th Ave.
No. Kansas City 64116
816-472-7400

Sanford-Brown College
Paralegal Program
3555 Franks Dr.
St. Charles 63301
314-724-7100

Southern Missouri State University
900 Normal Ave.
Cape Girardeau 63701-4710
314-651-2094

Southwest Missouri State University
West Plains Campus
128 Garfield Ave.
West Plains 65775-2715
417-256-5761

Southwestern Missouri State University
Dept. of Political Science
901 S. National Ave.
Springfield 65804-0027
471-836-5630

Springfield College
Paralegal Program
1010 W. Sunshine
Springfield 65807
717-864-7220

St. Louis Community College–Florissant
Valley
Legal Assistant Program
3400 Pershall Rd.
St. Louis 63135
314-595-4568; FAX: 314-595-4544

St. Louis Community College–Meramec
Legal Assistant Program
11333 Big Bend Blvd.
St. Louis 63122
314-984-7376; 314-984-7575;
FAX: 314-984-7117

Stephens College
Columbia 65215-0001

Vatterott Education Center
3925 Industrial Dr.
St. Ann 63074-1807

Webster University
Legal Studies
470 East Lockwood Ave.
St. Louis 63119
314-968-7496; FAX: 314-968-7403
harpoogd@webster2.websteruniv.edu

William Jewell College
Paralegal Program
Liberty 64068

William Woods University
Paralegal Studies Program
200 W. 12th St.
Fulton 65251
314-592-4293; FAX: 314-592-4574
sstratto@iris.wmwoods.edu

MONTANA
College of Great Falls
Paralegal Studies Program
1301 20th St. S.
Great Falls 59405
406-791-5339; FAX: 406-791-5394

May Technical College
Paralegal Program
1306 Central
Billings 59103
800-8-MAYTEC

May Technical College
Paralegal Program
1807 3rd St. NW
Great Falls 59404
800-7-MAYTEC

Missoula Voctech Center
Legal Assistant Certificate Program
909 South Ave. W.
Missoula 59801-7910

Rocky Mountain College
Legal Assistant Program
1511 Poly Dr.
Billings 59102-1796
406-657-1047

NEBRASKA
Central Community College
Paralegal Studies
3134 W. Hwy. 34
Grand Island 68802-4903
308-384-5220; FAX: 308-389-6398

College of Saint Mary
Paralegal Program
1901 S. 72nd St.
Omaha 68124
402-399-2418; FAX: 402-399-2686

Lincoln School of Commerce
Paralegal Studies
1821 K St.
Lincoln 68508
402-474-5315; FAX: 402-474-5302

McCook Community College
McCook 69001-2631
308-345-6303; 800-658-4348
http://www.mcc.mccook.cc.ne.us

Metropolitan Community College
Legal Assistant Program
P.O. Box 3777
Omaha 68103
402-449-8559; FAX: 402-449-8532
vkorslmn@metro.mccneb.edu

Nebraska College of Business
Paralegal Program
3350 N. 90th St.
Omaha 68134
402-572-8500

Nebraska Wesleyan College
Legal Assistant Program
50th & St. Paul
Lincoln 68504

Northeast Community College
Norfolk 68702-0469
402-644-0459; 800-348-9033 (in-state)

NEVADA

Clark County Community College
Legal Assistant Program
3200 E. Cheyenne Ave.
North Las Vegas 89030-4228

Community College of Southern
Nevada
North Las Vegas 89030-4296
702-651-4060

Las Vegas College
Paralegal Program
3320 E. Flamingo Rd., Suite 30
Las Vegas 89121-4306
702-434-0486

Morrison College
Paralegal Program
140 Washington St.
Reno 89503
702-323-4145

Reno Business College
Paralegal Program
140 Washington St.
Reno 89503-5620

NEW HAMPSHIRE

Castle College
Windham 03087-1297
603-893-6111

Hesser College
3 Sundial Ave.
Manchester 03103-7245
603-338-6660; 800-526-9231

McIntosh College
Legal Assistant Program
23 Cataract Ave.
Dover 03820-3990
603-742-1234

New Hampshire Community Technical
College, Nashua / Claremont
505 Amherst St.
Nashua 03061-2052
603-882-6923

New Hampshire Technical College
Paralegal Studies Program
11 Institute Dr.
Concord 03301-7400
603-225-1874

Rivier College
Paralegal Studies Program
420 South Main St.
Nashua 03060-5086
603-888-1311 x8266;
FAX: 603-888-6447
repost@mighty.riv.edu

University of New Hampshire
Continuing Education Center
220 Hackett Hill Rd.
Manchester 03102-8503
603-862-1360

University of New Hampshire
Paralegal Studies Program
Brook House, 24 Rosemary Ln.
Durham 03824-3528
603-862-1088

NEW JERSEY

American Institute for Paralegal Studies
5 Fox Haven Lane
Mullica Hill 08062-9609
800-533-2420

Atlantic Community College
Legal Assistant Program
5100 Blackhorse Pike
Mays Landing 08330-2699
609-343-4941; FAX: 609-343-5122

Bergen Community College
Legal Assistant Program
400 Paramus Rd.
Paramus 07652
201-447-7191; FAX: 201-447-0934

Berkeley College of Business
44 Rifle Camp Rd.
West Paterson 07424-3353
201-278-5400

Brookdale Community College
765 Newman Springs Rd.
Lincroft 07738-1543
201-842-1900

Burlington Community College
Legal Assistant Program
County Rte. 530
Pemberton 08068-1599
609-894-9311

Cumberland County College
Legal Assistant Program
P.O. Box 517
College Dr. & Orchard Rd.
Vineland 08360-0517
609-691-8600 x290;
FAX: 609-478-0671

Essex County College
Paralegal Program
503 University Ave.
Newark 07102-1798
201-877-1906

Fairleigh Dickinson University
Paralegal Studies Program
285 Madison Ave.
Madison 07940
201-593-8990; FAX: 201-593-8178

Harris School of Business
Paralegal Program
654 Longwood Ave.
Cherry Hill 08002
609-662-5300

Horizon Institute for Paralegal Studies
453 N. Wood Ave.
Linden 07036-4144
908-486-0404

Hudson County Community College
168 Sip Ave.
Jersey City 07306
201-714-2115
http://www.hudson.cc.nj.us

Katharine Gibbs School
Paralegal Program
33 Plymouth St.
Montclair 07042-2699
201-744-6967

Katharine Gibbs School
80 Kingsbridge Rd.
Piscataway 08854-3948
908-885-1580

Mercer County Community College
Legal Assistant Program
P.O. Box B
Trenton 08690
609-586-4800 x479;
FAX: 609-890-6338

Middlesex County College
Legal Assistant Program
155 Mill Rd., North Hall
Edison 08818-3050
908-906-2576; FAX: 908-906-4194

Montclair State University
Paralegal Studies Program
Normal Ave. & Valley Rd.
Upper Montclair 07043
201-655-4152; FAX: 201-655-7951
http://www.shss.montclair.edu/leclair/
msu2.html
tayler@saturn.montclair.edu

National Academy of Paralegal Studies
P.O. Box 621
Ridgewood 07451-0621
800-922-0771

Ocean County College
College Dr.
Toms River 08753-2102
908-255-0400

Omega Institute
7050 Rte. 38 E.
Pennsauken 08109-4417
609-663-4299

Raritan Valley Community College
Legal Assistant Program
P.O. Box 3300, Lamington Rd.
Somerville 08876-1265
908-526-1200 x8236;
FAX: 908-429-0268

Somerset Community Technical
Institute
P.O. Box 6350
Bridgewater 08807-0350
201-526-8900

Stockton State College
Pomona 08240-9988
609-652-1776

Stuart School of Business
Administration
2400 Belmar Blvd.
Belmar 07719-3970

Sussex Community College
1 College Hill Rd.
Newton 07860-1149
201-579-5400

Technical Institute of Camden County
Paralegal Studies Program
343 Berlin Cross Keys Rd.
Sicklerville 08081
609-767-7002

Warren County Community College
475 Rte. 57
Washington 07882-9605
908-689-1090

NEW MEXICO

Albuquerque Career Institute
11300 Lomos Blvd. NE
Albuquerque 87112
505-268-2000

Albuquerque Technical Vocational
Institute
Legal Assistant Studies
525 Buena Vista SE, Business
Occupations Dept.
Albuquerque 87106
505-224-3845; FAX: 505-224-3850

Dona Ana Branch Community College
Legal Assistant Program
P.O. Box 300001, Dept. 3da
Las Cruces 88003-0001
505-527-7500

Eastern New Mexico University at
Roswell
Paralegal Program
P.O. Box 6000
Roswell 88202-6000
505-624-7213

New Mexico State University–Grants
Grants 80702-2025
505-287-7981

San Juan College
Paralegal Program
4601 College Blvd.
Farmington 87402-4699
505-326-3311

Santa Fe Community College
Paralegal Program
P.O. Box 4187
Santa Fe 87502-4187
505-438-1306

University at Carlsbad
Paralegal Program
1500 University Dr.
Carlsbad 88220-3509
505-885-8831

University of New Mexico Law School
1117 Stanford NE
Albuquerque 87131-0001
505-277-2446

University of New Mexico
Paralegal Program
1634 University Blvd. NE
Albuquerque 87131-0001
800-522-7737

NEW YORK
Berkeley College
Paralegal Program
40 West Red Oak Ln.
White Plains 10604
914-694-1122; FAX: 914-694-5832

Berkeley College
Paralegal Studies Program
3 E. 43rd St.
New York 10017-4604
212-986-4343

Betty Owen
Secretarial Systems
130 William St.
New York 10038
212-267-2627

Briarcliffe College
Bethpage 11714
516-470-6000
http://www.bcl.org

Bronx Community College
Paralegal Studies Program
University Ave. & West 181 St.
Bronx 10451
718-289-5635; FAX: 718-289-6303

Brooklyn College
Paralegal Program
1212 Boylan Hall
Brooklyn 11210
718-951-5013; FAX: 718-951-4873

Broome Community College
Paralegal Assistant Program
P.O. Box 1017
Binghamton 13902-1017
607-778-5000

Bryant & Stratton Business Institute
Paralegal Program
1028 Main St.
Buffalo 14202
716-884-9120
http://www.bryantstratton.com

Bryant & Stratton Business Institute
Paralegal Program
Liverpool 13090-1315
315-652-6500
http://www.bryantstratton.com

Bryant & Stratton Business Institute
Paralegal Program
Rochester 14623-3136
716-292-5627
http://www.bryantstratton.com

Bryant & Stratton Business Institute,
Eastern Hills Campus
Paralegal Program
Williamsville 14231
716-631-0260
http://www.bryantstratton.com

City University of New York, St. George
Campus
130 Stuyvesant Pl.
Staten Island 10301-1907

Corning Community College
Paralegal Studies
One Academic Dr.
Corning 14830-3297
607-962-9424; FAX: 607-962-9287

Erie Community College
Paralegal Unit
121 Ellicott St.
Buffalo 14203-2698
716-851-1588

Eugenio Maria de Hostos Community
College
City University of New York
500 Grand Concourse
Bronx 10451
718-518-6633
http://www.cuny.hostos.edu

Finger Lakes Community College
Canandaigua 14424-8395
716-394-3500
http://www.fingerlakes.edu

Fiorello H. LaGuardia Community
College of the City University of New
York
31-10 Thomson Ave.
Long Island City 11101-3071
718-482-5105
http://www.lagcc.cuny.edu

Genesee Community College
Paralegal Program
One College Rd.
Batavia 14020-9704
716-343-0055

Herkimer County Community College
Paralegal Program
Reservoir Rd.
Herkimer 13350
315-866-0300; 800-947-4432

Hilbert College
Legal Assistant Program
5200 South Park Ave.
Hamburg 14075
716-649-7900; FAX: 716-649-0702

Hofstra University
Paralegal Studies Program
375 Hofstra University, Republic Hall
Hempstead 11550
516-463-6599; FAX: 516-463-4814
engb@hofstra.edu (Admissions)

Interboro Institute
Lawyer's Assistant (Paralegal Studies)
Program
450 West 56th St.
New York 10019
212-399-0091; FAX: 212-765-5772

Jefferson Community College
Watertown 13601
315-786-2408
http://www.sunyjefferson.edu

Kingsborough Community
College–CUNY
Paralegal Studies Program
2001 Oriental Blvd.
Brooklyn 11235
718-368-5052; FAX: 718-368-4781

Lehman College
Paralegal Studies Program
250 Bedford Park Blvd.
Bronx 10468
718-960-8512; FAX: 718-733-3254

Long Island University
Paralegal Studies Program
1 University Plaza, Rm. LLC 302
Brooklyn 11201
718-488-1066; FAX: 718-488-1367
ssobel@aurora.liunet.edu

Long Island University
C. W. Post Legal Studies Institute
Paralegal Program
720 Northern Blvd.
Brookville 11548-1300
516-299-2238; FAX: 516-299-2066

The Madison School
Paralegal Program
500 Eighth Ave., 2nd Fl.
New York 10018
212-695-2759

Marist College
Paralegal Program
Division of Humanities
Fontaine Building, 290 North Rd.
Poughkeepsie 12601-1381
914-575-3000 x2167;
FAX: 914-471-6213

Marymount Manhattan College
Paralegal Studies Program
221 E. 71st St.
New York 10021-4501
212-517-0564; FAX: 212-628-4208

Mercy College
Paralegal Studies Major
555 Broadway
Dobbs Ferry 10522
914-674-7320; FAX: 914-693-9455

Mercy College
Paralegal Studies Program
277 Martine Ave.
White Plains 10601
914-948-3666; FAX: 914-948-6732

Mildred Elley
Paralegal Program
Two Computer Dr. S.
Albany 12205
518-446-0595

Monroe Community College
Paralegal Studies
1000 E. Henrietta Rd.
Rochester 14623-5701
716-292-3324

Nassau Community College
Paralegal Program
Garden City 11530
516-572-7774; FAX: 516-572-7750
birdofj@sunynassau.edu

New York City Technical College (CUNY)
Legal Assistant Studies Program
300 Jay St., N622
Brooklyn 11201
718-260-5124; FAX: 718-260-5387
msdny@cunyum.edu

New York Institute of Technology
Paralegal Studies Program
Bldg. 66, Rm. 224
Carlton Ave.
Central Islip 11722
516-348-3013; FAX: 516-348-3399

New York Paralegal School
Paralegal Program
299 Broadway, Suite 200
New York 10007-1901
212-349-8800; FAX: 212-349-8968

New York University
Diploma Program in Paralegal Studies
11 W. 42nd St., Rm. 429
New York 10036
212-790-1320; FAX: 212-790-1366

Niagara County Community College
Legal Assistant Program
3111 Saunders Settlement Rd.
Sanborn 14132-9460

Olean Business Institute
Paralegal Program
301 N. Union St.
Olean 14760
716-372-7978

Queens College
Paralegal Studies Program/CEP
65-30 Kissena Blvd.
Flushing 11367
718-997-5709; FAX: 718-997-5723

Rockland Community College
Legal Assistant Program
145 College Rd.
Suffern 10901-3699
914-353-4300

Sage Junior College of Albany
140 New Scotland Ave.
Albany 12208-3491
http://www.sage.edu
518-445-1730

St. John's University
Paralegal Studies Program
8000 Utopia Pkwy.
Jamaica 11439
718-990-6161 x7417;
FAX: 718-990-1882
http://www.stjohns.edu
ylbhssc@st.johns.edu

Schenectady County Community
College
78 Washington Ave.
Schenectady 12305-2215
518-346-6211

Skidmore College
Paralegal Program
Saratoga Springs 12866
518-854-5000

The Sobelsohn School
Paralegal Program
370 Seventh Ave.
New York 10011
212-244-3900; FAX: 212-244-0500

Spencer Business & Technical Institute
Paralegal Program
200 State St.
Schenectady 12305
518-374-7619

Stenotopia Business School
Paralegal Program
45 South Service Rd.
Plainview 11803
516-777-1117

Suffolk County Community College
Paralegal Program
533 College Rd.
Selden 11784-2851
516-451-4663; FAX: 516-451-4887

Sullivan County Community College
Paralegal Program
P.O. Box 4002
Loch Sheldrake 12759
914-434-5750 x338;
FAX: 914-434-4806

Syracuse University
Legal Assistant Program
610 E. Fayette St.
Syracuse 13244-6020
315-443-2894; FAX: 315-443-1928
dhking@syr.edu

Tompkins Cortland Community College
Paralegal Program
170 North St.
Dryden 13053
607-844-8211

Westchester Community College
Valhalla 10595-1698
914-785-6735

NORTH CAROLINA
American Institute for Paralegal Studies,
Inc.
Paralegal Program
(sites in Charlotte, Raleigh, and
Greensboro)
800-624-3933

Appalachian State University
Department of Criminal Justice and
Political Science
Boone 28606
704-262-2120

Caldwell Community College and
Technical Institute
Hudson 28638-2397
704-726-2245

Cape Fear Community College
411 North Front St.
Wilmington 28401-3993
910-251-5180

Carteret Community College
Paralegal Technology
3500 Arendell St.
Morehead City 28557
919-247-6000 x230; FAX: 919-247-1828
http://gofish.carteret.cc.nc.us
mcneillr@sco.ncc.cc.nc.vus

Cecils College
Paralegal Program
1567 Patton Ave.
P.O. Box 6407
Asheville 28806
704-252-2486

Central Carolina Community College
1105 Kelly Dr.
Sanford 27330-9000
919-775-5401

Central Piedmont Community College
Paralegal Technology
P.O. Box 35009
Charlotte 28235
704-342-6873; FAX: 704-342-5930
pam_hendricks@cpcc.cc.nc.us

Coastal Carolina Community College
Paralegal Technology Program
444 Western Blvd.
Jacksonville 28546-6899

CPCC
Paralegal Program
P.O. Box 35009
Charlotte 29235-5009

Davidson Community College
Old Greensboro Rd. & Int. 40
Lexington 27292
704-892-2231

Durham Technical Community College
1637 Lawson St.
Durham 27703-5023
919-686-3629

Edgecombe Community College
Tarboro 27886-9399
919-823-5166

Fayetteville Technical Community
College
Paralegal Technician Program
P.O. Box 5236
Fayetteville 28303
919-323-1961

Forsyth Technical Community College
Winston-Salem 27103-5197
910-723-0371

Gaston College
Dallas 28034-1499
704-922-6214
http://www.gaston.cc.nc.us

Greensboro College
Department of Business Administration
/ Legal Administration
815 W. Market St.
Greensboro 27401-1875
919-272-7102

Guilford Technical Community College
Jamestown 27282-0309
910-334-4822
technet.gtcc.cc.nc.us

Johnston Community College
Paralegal Program
P.O. Box 2350
Smithfield 27577-2350

King's College
Paralegal Program
322 Lamar Ave.
Charlotte 28204
704-372-0266

Meredith College
Legal Assistants Program
3800 Hillsborough St.
Raleigh 27607-5298
919-829-8353; FAX: 919-829-2898
http://www meredith.edu/meredith

Pitt Community College
Paralegal Technology
P.O. Box 7007
Greenville 27835
919-321-4304; FAX: 919-321-4433

Rockingham Community College
Wentworth 27375-0038
910-342-4261

Rowan-Cabarrus Community College
Salisbury 28145-1595
704-637-0760

Sandhills Community College
Paralegal Program
2200 Airport Rd.
Pinehurst 28374

Southwestern Community College
P.O. Box 95
Sylva 28779-0095
704-586-4091
http://www.southwest.cc.nc.us

Surry Community College
P.O. Box 304
Dobson 27017-0304
910-386-8121

Western Piedmont Community College
Paralegal Program
1001 Burkemont Ave.
Monganton 28655-9978

Wilson Technical Community College
Wilson 27893-3310
919-291-1195

NORTH DAKOTA
National Academy of Paralegal Studies
116 N. 4th St.
Bismarck 58501-4001
800-922-0771

University of North Dakota
Legal Assistant Program
Lake Region
Devils Lake 58301
701-662-8683

OHIO
Academy of Court Reporting
Paralegal Program
614 Superior Ave. NW
Cleveland 44113
216-861-3222

American Institute for Paralegal Studies
Paralegal Program
Apt. 5, 1809 Pleasantdale Rd.
Cleveland 44109-5753

American Institute for Paralegal Studies, Inc.
Paralegal Program
(sites in Cincinnati, Dayton, Canton, and Columbus)
800-624-3933

Bohecker's Business College
Paralegal Program
326 E. Main St.
Ravenna 44266
330-297-7319

Bradford School
Paralegal Program
6170 Busch Blvd.
Columbus 43229
614-846-9410

Capital University Law Center
Certified Legal Assistant Program
665 South High St.
Columbus 43215
614-445-8836; FAX: 614-445-7125

Cincinnati Law Library Association
Paralegal Program
601 Court House
Cincinnati 45202

Clark State Community College
P.O. Box 570
Springfield 45501-0570
937-328-6027

College of Mount St. Joseph
Paralegal Studies Program
5701 Delhi Rd.
Cincinnati 45233-1670
513-244-4952; FAX: 513-244-4222
http://www.msj.edu
georgana_taggart@mail.msj.edu

Columbus State Community College
550 E. Spring St.
Columbus 43215-1722
614-227-2487

Cuyahoga Community College
Paralegal Studies Program
11000 Pleasant Valley Rd., C247
Parma 44130
216-987-5112; FAX: 216-987-5050
http://www.tri-c.cc.oh.us/
ellen.erzen@tri-c.cc.oh.us

David N. Myers College
Paralegal Education Program
112 Prospect Ave.
Cleveland 44115-1096
216-696-9000 x691;
FAX: 216-696-6430
apiazza@dnmyers.edu

Edison Community College
Legal Assisting
1973 Edison Dr.
Piqua 45356
513-778-8600; FAX: 513-778-1920
cooper@edison.cc.oh.us

ETI Technical College
2076 Youngstown Warren Rd.
Niles 44446-4398

Lake Erie College
Legal Studies Program
391 W. Washington
Painesville 44077
216-352-3361; FAX: 216-352-3533

Lakeland Community College
Paralegal Studies Program
7700 Clocktower Dr.
Kirkland 44094
216-953-7352; FAX: 216-975-4333

Lima Tech College
4240 Campus Dr.
Lima 45804
419-995-8404

Marion Technical College
1465 Mount Vernon Ave.
Marion 43302-5628

Muskingum Area Technical College
Paralegal Program
1555 Newark Rd.
Zanesville 43701
614-454-2501 x439

North Central Technical College
P.O. Box 698
Mansfield 44901-0698
419-755-4888

Northwestern College
Lima 45805-1498
419-227-3141
http://www.bsd-server.nc.edu

Northwest State Community College
Archbold 43502-9542
419-267-5511

Notre Dame College of Ohio
Paralegal Studies Program
4545 College Rd. S.
Euclid 44121-4293
216-381-1680 x229; FAX: 216-381-3802

RETS Tech Center
Centerville 45459-4815
513-433-3410

Raedel College and Industrial Welding
School
Paralegal Program
137 Sixth St. NE
Canton 44702
330-454-9006

Sawyer College of Business
Paralegal Program
3150 Mayfield Rd.
Cleveland Heights 44118
216-932-0911

Shawnee State University
Legal Assistant Program
940 2nd St.
Portsmouth 45662-4344
614-355-2575

Sinclair Community College
Legal Assisting Program
444 W. Third St.
Dayton 45402-1462
513-226-2923; FAX: 513-449-5192
gmcdonou@sinclair.edu

University College
Legal Assisting (Paralegal) Technology
P.O. Box 210207
Cincinnati 45221-0207
513-556-1731; FAX: 513-556-3007

University of Akron
Paralegal Program
Polsky Bldg. 161
Akron 44325-4304

University of Cincinnati–University
College
Legal Assisting Program
MC 207 University of Cincinnati
Cincinnati 45221-0207
513-556-1731; FAX: 513-556-3007

University of Cincinnati–Clermont
4200 Clermont
Batavia 45103
513-732-5302

University of Toledo
Legal Assistant Technology
Scott Park Campus
Toledo 43606-3390
419-530-3332; FAX: 419-530-3047

University of Toledo, Community and
Technical College
Legal Assisting Program
2801 West Bancroft
Toledo 43606-3390
419-530-3363; FAX: 419-530-3047

OKLAHOMA
American Institute for Paralegal Studies
530 NW 33rd St.
Oklahoma City 73118-7347
800-533-2420

Northeastern State University
Paralegal Program
Criminal Justice Department
Tahlequah 74464
918-456-5511

Oklahoma City University
Legal Assistant Program
2501 N. Blackwelder
Sarkeys Law Center 209
Oklahoma City 73106
405-521-5189; FAX: 405-521-5185

Rogers State College
Will Rogers & College Hill
Claremore 74017-2099
918-343-7546
http://www.rogersu.edu

Rose State College
Legal Assistant Program
6420 S.E. 15th St.
Midwest City 73110
405-733-7460; FAX: 405-733-7447

Tri-County Area Vocational/Technical
School
6101 Nowata Rd.
Bartlesville 74006-6029

Tulsa Community College
6111 Skelly Dr.
Tulsa 74135-6198
918-595-7811

Tulsa Junior College
Legal Assistant Program
909 S. Boston, Rm. 416
Tulsa 74119
918-595-7317; FAX: 918-595-7343

University of Oklahoma College of Law
Department of Legal Assistant
Education
300 Timberdell Rd., Rm. 314
Norman 73019
405-325-1726; FAX: 405-325-7158
rscott@hamilton.law.uoknor.edu

University of Tulsa
Legal Assistant Program
600 South College Ave.
Tulsa 74104-3189
918-621-2937

OREGON
College of Legal Arts
Paralegal Studies
University Center Bldg.
527 SW Hall, No. 308
Portland 97201
503-223-5100; FAX: 503-273-8093

Pioneer Pacific College
Paralegal Program
25195 Southwest Pkwy. Ave.
Wilsonville 97070
503-682-3903

Portland Community College
Legal Assistant Program
12000 SW 49th Ave.
Portland 97219-7199
503-244-6111

Western Business College
Paralegal Program
425 SW Washington
Portland 97204
503-222-3225

PENNSYLVANIA
Academy of Medical Arts and Business
Paralegal Program
279 Boas St.
Harrisburg 17102-2940
717-233-2172; FAX: 717-233-2211

American Institute for Paralegal Studies
609 County Line Rd.
Huntingdon Valley 19006-1105

American Institute for Paralegal Studies,
Inc.
Paralegal Program
(sites in Philadelphia, Bethlehem, York,
and Blue Bell)
800-624-3933

Bradford School
Paralegal Program
707 Grant St., Gulf Tower
Pittsburgh 15219
412-391-6710

Bucks County Community College
Newtown 18940-1525
215-968-8119
http://www.bucks.edu

Cedar Crest College
Paralegal Studies
100 College Dr.
Allentown 18104-6196
610-740-3792 x3412;
FAX: 610-606-4614
gmglasco@cedarcrest.edu

Central Pennsylvania Business School
Legal Assistant Program
College Hill Rd.
Summerdale 17093
717-728-2230; FAX: 717-732-5254

Clarion University of Pennsylvania
Legal Business Studies
1801 West First St.
Oil City 16301
814-676-6571

Community College of Alleghany
County
808 Ridge Ave.
Pittsburgh 15233
412-325-6614
http://www.ccac.edu

Community College of Allegheny
County–Boyce Campus
595 Beatty Rd.
Monroeville, PA, 15146-1348
412-327-1327

Community College of Philadelphia
Paralegal Studies Curriculum
1700 Spring Garden St.
Philadelphia 19130-3991
215-751-8961; FAX: 215-972-6388
markphila@aol.com

DuBois Business College
Paralegal Program
1700 Moore St.
Huntington 16652
814-641-3674

DuBois Business College
Paralegal Program
701 E. Third St.
Oil City 16301
814-677-1322

DuBois Business College
Paralegal Program
One Beaver Dr.
DuBois 15801
814-271-6920

Duff's Business Institute
Paralegal Program
110 Ninth St.
Pittsburgh 15222
412-261-4520

Duquesne University
Paralegal Institute
201 Rockwell Hall
Pittsburgh 15282-0102
412-396-5128; FAX: 412-396-5072
klein@duq2.cc.duq.edu

Erie Business Center
Paralegal Program
246 W Ninth St.
Erie 16501
814-456-7504

Gannon University
Paralegal Program
Box 1027, University Sq.
Erie 16541
814-871-5897; 814-864-1311

Harrisburg Area Community College
Paralegal Studies
One HACC Dr.
Harrisburg 17110-2999
717-780-2515; FAX: 717-236-0709

Indiana University
Finance and Legal Studies Dept
202 McElhaney Hall
Indiana 15705-0001
412-357-2929

Lansdale School of Business
Paralegal Program
201 Church Rd.
North Wales 19454-4137
215-699-5700

Main Line Paralegal Institute
100 E. Lancaster Ave.
Wayne 19087-4177
215-687-4600

Lehigh Carbon Community College
Schnecksville 18078-2598
610-799-1134
http://www.lib3.lccc.edu

Luzerne County Community College
Nanticoke 18634-9804
717-740-7336
800-377-5222 (in-state)

Manor Junior College
Paralegal Studies
700 Fox Chase Rd.
Jenkintown 19046-3399
215-885-2360; FAX: 215-576-6564

Marywood College
Legal Studies/Legal Assistant Program
2300 Adams Ave.
Scranton 18509
717-348-6288; FAX: 717-961-4742

McCann School of Business
47 South Main St.
Mahanoy City 17948
717-773-1820

McCann School of Business
101 N. Centre St.
Pottsville 17901
717-622-7622; FAX: 717-622-7770

Misericordia College
Legal Assistant Program
Department of History and Government
Dallas 18612

Mount Aloysius College
Legal Assistant Studies
7373 Admiral Peary Hwy.
Cresson 16330
814-886-6304

Northampton Community College
Legal Assistant Certification Program
3835 Green Pond Rd.
Bethlehem 18017-7599
215-861-5396

Peirce College
Paralegal Studies
1420 Pine St.
Philadelphia 19102
215-545-6400; FAX: 215-546-5996

Penn Commercial, Inc.
Paralegal Program
82 S. Main St.
Washington 15301
412-222-5330

Pennsylvania Business Institute
81 Robinson St.
Pottstown 19464-6439

Pennsylvania College of Technology
Legal Assistant Program
One College Ave.
Williamsport 17701
717-327-4517; FAX: 717-327-4529

Pennsylvania State University
Rm. 115a, 1600 Woodland Rd.
Abington 19001-3918
215-320-4800

Pennsylvania State University
Allentown Campus
6090 Mohr Ln.
Fogelsville 18051-1629
215-285-4811

Pennsylvania State University
5091 Station Rd.
Erie 16563-1000
412-565-7018

Pennsylvania State University
Continuing Education, Delaware County
Campus
25 Yearsley Mill Rd.
Media 19063-5522
215-320-4800

Pennsylvania State University
Fayette Campus
P.O. Box 519
Uniontown 15401-0519
215-320-4800

Pennsylvania State University
Continuing Education
Highacres
Hazelton 18201
215-320-4800

Pennsylvania State University
Continuing Education
McKeesport Campus
University Dr.
McKeesport 15132
412-675-9044

Pennsylvania State University
Mont Alto Campus
Mont Alto 17237
215-320-4800

Pennsylvania State University
Continuing Education, Shenango Valley
Campus
147 Shenango Ave.
Sharon 16146-1537
215-320-4800

Pennsylvania State University
State College Area
409 Business Administration Bldg.
University Park 18602
814-863-2479

Pennsylvania State University
Wilkes Barre Campus
General Delivery
Lehman 18627-9999
215-320-4800

Pennsylvania State University
Worthington/Scranton Campus
120 Ridgeview Dr.
Dunmore 18512-1699
215-320-4800

Pennsylvania State University
Continuing Education
1031 Edgecombe Ave.
York 17403-3326
215-320-4800

Philadelphia College, Textile and
Science
School House & Henry Lns.
Philadelphia 19144-5497

PJA School
7900 W. Chester Pike
Upper Darby 19082-1917

Robert Morris College
Legal Assistant Certificate Program
600 Fifth Ave.
Pittsburgh 15219
412-227-6478; FAX: 412-281-5539

St. Vincent College
Career Development Center
Latrobe 15650-2690

Tri-State Business Institute
Paralegal Program
5757 W. 26th St.
Erie 16506
814-838-7673

University of Pittsburgh
Legal Studies Program
435 Cathedral of Learning
Pittsburgh 15260

Villanova University
Paralegal Program
102 Vasey Hall, 800 Lancaster Ave.
Villanova 19085
610-519-4304; FAX: 610-519-7910

Western School of Health and Business
Careers
Paralegal Program
Chamber of Commerce
421 7th Ave., 6th Fl.
Pittsburgh 15219-1907
412-281-2600

Westmoreland County Community
College
Youngwood 15697
412-925-4060

Widener University
Main Campus
Chester 19013-5792
610-499-4126 FAX 610-876-9751

RHODE ISLAND
Community College of Rhode Island
Warwick 02886-1807
401-825-2285

Johnson & Wales University
Paralegal Program
Eight Abbott Park Pl.
Providence 02903-2807
401-598-1000

Providence College
School of Continuing Education
River and Eaton Sts.
Providence 02918-0001
401-865-1000

Roger Williams University
Paralegal Department
One Old Ferry Rd.
Bristol 02809
401-254-3172; FAX: 401-254-3431

SOUTH CAROLINA
American Institute for Paralegal Studies,
Inc.
Paralegal Program
(site in Charleston)
800-624-3933

Beaufort Technical College
Paralegal Program
P.O. Box 1288
Beaufort 29901-1288
803-525-8328

Central Carolina Technical College
506 N. Guignard Dr.
Sumter 29150-2468
803-778-7859

Clemson University
Department of Legal Studies
201 Sirrine
Clemson 29634-1330
803-656-2287

Columbia Junior College
Professional Center for Paralegal
Studies
1207 Lincoln St.
Columbia 29201
803-254-6065; FAX: 803-779-5009

Columbia Junior College of Business
Paralegal Program
3810 Main St., P.O. Box 1196
Columbia 29202
803-799-9082

Florence-Darlington Technical College
Legal Assistant/Paralegal Program
P.O. Box 100548
Florence 29501-0548
803-661-8047; FAX: 803-661-8268
fergusonf@flo.tec.sc.us

Greenville Technical College
Paralegal/Legal Assistant Program
P.O. Box 5616, Station B
Greenville 29606-5616
803-250-8255; FAX: 803-250-8455
http://www.gvltec.edu/www/business/
legalasstpara.html
fisherrsf@gvltec.edu

Horry-Georgetown Technical College
Paralegal Program
P.O. Box 1966
Conway 29526-1966
803-347-3186

Midlands Technical College
Legal Assistant/Paralegal Program
Box 2408
Columbia 29202
803-822-3312; FAX: 803-882-3631

Orangeburg-Calhoun Technical College
Orangeburg 29118-8299
803-535-1218; 800-813-6519 (in-state)
http://www.octech.org

Professional Center for Paralegal
Studies
Paralegal Studies
1207 Lincoln St., Suite 201
Columbia 29201
803-254-6065; FAX: 803-779-5009

Technical College of the Lowcountry
Beaufort 29901-1288
803-525-8207

Trident Technical College
Legal Assistant/Paralegal Program
P.O. Box 118067, 66 Columbus St.
Charleston 29403
803-722-5526; FAX: 803-722-5545

University of South Carolina
171 University Pkwy.
Aiken 29801-6309
803-648-6851

SOUTH DAKOTA
National Academy
Cummings Legal Clinic
335 N. Main St., Suite 300
Sioux Falls 57102-0348
800-922-0771

National College
Paralegal Studies
321 Kansas City St.
Rapid City 57701
605-394-4800; FAX: 605-394-4871

Nettleton Career College
Paralegal Program
100 S. Spring Ave.
Sioux Falls 57104
605-336-1837

Western Dakota Vocational/Technical
Institute
Paralegal Program
800 Mickelson Dr.
Rapid City 57701
605-394-4034

TENNESSEE

American Institute for Paralegal Studies,
Inc.
Paralegal Program
(site in Memphis)
800-624-3933

Bristol College
P.O. Box 4366
Bristol 37625-4366

Chattanooga State Technical
Community College
Legal Assistant Technology Program
7158 Lee Hwy.
Chattanooga 37421-1732
615-697-4400
http://www.chattanooga.net/clscc/
index.html

Cleveland State Community College
Legal Assistant Program
P.O. Box 3570, Adkisson Dr.
Cleveland 37320-3570
423-472-7141; 800-604 2722;
FAX: 423-478-6255
amccoin@clscc.cc.tn.us

Draughons Junior College
Paralegal Program
Plus Park Pavillion Blvd., P.O. Box 17386
Nashville 37217
615-361-7555

Jackson State College
Office of Continuing Education
P.O. Box 2467
Jackson 38302-2467
901-425-2677

Jackson State Community College
2046 North Pkwy.
Jackson 38301-3797
901-425-2627
jstephens@jscc.cc.tn.us

Knoxville Business College
Paralegal Program
720 N. Fifth Ave.
Knoxville 37917
423-524-3043; FAX: 423-637-0127

Miller Motte Business College
Paralegal Program
1820 Business Park Dr.
Clarksville 37040-6023
615-553-0071

Milligan College
Legal Assistant Studies
P.O. Box 500
Milligan 37682
423-461-8941; FAX: 423-461-8716
http://www.milligan.milligan-college.tn.
us
cchartier@kegley.milligan.milligan-
college.tn.us

Pellissippi State Technical Community
College
Legal Assistant Technology Program
10915 Hardin Valley Rd., P.O. Box
22990
Knoxville 37933-0990
423-971-5200; FAX: 423-971-5221
aballew@pstcc.cc.tn.us

Southeastern Paralegal Institute
Legal Assistant Program
2416 21st Ave. S., Suite 300
Nashville 37212
615-269-9900; FAX: 615-383-4800

Directory of Paralegal Training Programs

State Technical Institute at Memphis
Legal Assistant Technology
5983 Macon Cove
Memphis 38134-7693
901-383-4130; FAX: 901-383-4377
ghutton@stim.tec.tn.us

University of Memphis
Paralegal Studies
University College, Johnson Hall, G-1
Memphis 38152
901-678-2716; FAX: 901-678-4913
cdewitt@msuvx2.memphis.edu

Volunteer State Community College
Paralegal Studies
1360 Nashville Pike
Gallatin 37066
615-452-8600 x300;
FAX: 615-230-3317

TEXAS
Alvin Community College
Alvin 77511-4898
281-388-4615

Austin Community College
5930 Middle Fiskville Rd.
Austin 78752-4390
512-223-7000
http://www.austin.cc.tx.us

Blackstone School of Law
2801 Carriage Ln.
Carrollton 75006-4831
214-418-5141

Center for Advanced Legal Studies
Paralegal Program
3910 Kirby Dr., Suite 200
Houston 77098
713-529-2778; FAX: 713-523-2715

Central Texas College
P.O. Box 1800
Killeen 76542-4199
817-526-1104; 800-792-3348

Collin County Community College
Legal Assistant Program
2200 W. University Dr.
McKinney 75070
214-548-6823; FAX: 214-548-6801

Del Mar College
Legal Assisting
101 Baldwin Blvd.
Corpus Christi 78404-3897
512-886-1491; FAX: 512-886-1524
http://www.viking.delmar.edu
svanwie@davlin.net

Delta Career Institute
Paralegal Program
1310 Pennsylvania Ave.
Beaumont 77701
409-833-6161

East Texas State University
Department of Political Science
Commerce 75428
214-886-5317

El Centro College
Legal Assistant Program
Main & Lamar Sts., 5th Fl.
Dallas 75202
214-746-2429; FAX: 214-746-2268

El Paso Community College
P.O. Box 20500
El Paso 79998-0500
915-594-2433

Executive Secretarial School
Paralegal Program
4849 Greenville Ave., Suite 200
Dallas 75206-4125
214-369-9009

Grayson County Junior College
Legal Assistant Program
6101 Hwy. 691
Denison 75020-8297
214-465-6030

Houston Community College System
4310 Dunlavy St.
Houston 77006-5221
713-630-7205

International Business College
Paralegal Program
4121 Montana Ave.
El Paso 79903
915-566-8644

Kilgore College
Legal Assisting Program
1100 Broadway Blvd.
Kilgore 75662-3299

Kingwood College
Program Coordinator
2000 Kingwood Dr.
Kingwood 77339
713-359-1697

Kingwood Technical Center
Paralegal Program Director
250 N. Sam Houston Pkwy. E.
Houston 77060-2000

Lamar University
P.O. Box 10008
Beaumont 77710-0008
409-880-8432

Lamar University–Port Arthur
P.O. Box 310
Port Arthur 77641-0310
409-984-6156; 800-477-5872 (in-state)

Lee College
511 S. Whiting St.
Baytown 77520-4796
713-427-5611

McLennan Community College
Legal Assistant Program
1400 College Dr.
Waco 76708
817-756-6551

Midland College
Legal Assistant Program
3600 N. Garfield
Midland 79705
915-685-4666; FAX: 915-685-4761
nlhtex@aol.com

Navarro College
3200 W. 7th Ave.
Corsicana 75110-4899
903-874-6501; 800-628-2776

North Central Texas College
Gainesville 76240-4699
817-668-7731

North Harris Community College
Paralegal Program
2700 W. Thorne Blvd.
Houston 77073-3410
713-443-5737

Odessa College
Legal Assistant Program
201 W. University Blvd.
Odessa 79764-7127
915-335-6400

St. Edwards University
Legal Assistance Program
3001 S. Congress Ave.
Austin 78704-6489
512-448-8500

St. Philip's College
1801 Martin Luther King Dr.
San Antonio 78203-2098
210-531-3290

San Antonio College
Legal Assistant Program
1300 San Pedro Ave.
San Antonio 78284-0001
512-733-2000

San Jacinto College–North Campus
5800 Uvalde
Houston 77049-4599
713-458-4050

South Plains College
Paralegal Program
1302 Main St.
Lubbock 79401-3224
915-264-3700

South Texas Community College
Uvalde 78801-6297
210-278-4401

Southeastern Paralegal Institute
Paralegal Program
5440 Harvest Hill Rd., Suite 200
Dallas 75230
214-385-1446; FAX: 214-385-0641
skstoner@cyberramp.net

Southern Career Institute
5333 Everhart Rd.
Corpus Christi 78411-4835

Southwest Texas State University
Lawyer's Assistant Program
601 University Dr., Political Science
Department
San Marcos 78666
512-245-2233; FAX: 512-245-7815

Southwestern Paralegal Institute
Legal Assistant Studies
4888 Loop Central Dr., Suite 800
Houston 77081
713-666-7600; FAX: 713-666-2030

Stephen F. Austin State University
Legal Assistant Program
Department of Criminal Justice
Box 13064 SFA
Nacogdoches 75962-3064
409-468-4408
http://www.sfasu.edu/aas/criminalj
crimj@sfasu.edu

Tarrant County Junior College
Northeast Campus
828 W. Harwood Rd.
Hurst 76054-3219
817-281-7860

Texas School of Business
Paralegal Program
711 E. Airtex Dr.
Houston 77073
713-876-2888

Texas Technical University
Division of Continuing Education
P.O. Box 42191
Lubbock 79409-2191
806-742-2352

Texas Wesleyan University
University Applied Legal Services
1201 Wesleyan
Forth Worth 76105-1536
817-531-4422

Texas Woman's University
Government Degree with Paralegal
Emphasis
P.O. Box 425889
Denton 76204-5889
817-898-2148; FAX: 817-898-2130
f_robb@twu.edu

University of Houston–Clear Lake City
Legal Studies Program
P.O. Box 20
Houston 77058
713-488-9233

University of Houston
Division of Arts and Sciences
2302 C Red River
Victoria 77901
512-576-3151

University of North Texas
Paralegal Certificate Program
Professional Development Institute
P.O. Box 310769 UNT
Denton 76203-0769
800-433-5676

University of Texas–Arlington
Legal Assistant Program
P.O. Box 19197
Arlington 76019-0197
817-265-2820

University of Texas–Austin
Legal Assistant Program
P.O. Box 7879
Austin 78713-7879
512-471-8921

University of Texas–Pan American
Legal Assistant Program
Edinburg 78539

West Texas University
Department of History and Political
Science
Box 807, W. Station
Canyon 79016-0001
806-656-2424

Woodlands Paralegal Institute
5 Grogans Park Dr., Suite 200
The Woodlands 77380-2190
713-367-6448

UTAH
Lake Community College
1575 S. State St.
Rm. N109C
Salt Lake City 84115-1610
801-461-3205

Mountain West College
Paralegal Program
3098 Highland Dr.
Salt Lake City 84106
801-485-0221

Phillips Junior College
Director, Paralegal Program
Suite 100, 3098 Highland Dr.
Salt Lake City 84016-3047

Salt Lake Community College
P.O. Box 30808
Salt Lake City 84130-0808
801-957-4297

Utah Valley Community College
Legal Assistant Program
800 W. 1200 S.
Orem 84058-5999
801-222-8000; 801-226-5207

Washington Institute of Graduate
Studies
Washington College of Law
2268 Newcastle Dr.
Sandy 84093-1743

Westminster College of Salt Lake City
Legal Assistant Certificate Program
1840 S. 1300 E.
Salt Lake City 84105
801-488-4159; FAX: 801-487-9507
k-dehill@whitewater.wcslc.edu

VERMONT
Champlain College
Legal Assistant Program
163 South Willard St.
Burlington 05402-0670
802-658-0800; FAX: 802-860-2750
stgeorge@champlain.edu

Woodbury College
Paralegal Studies
660 Elm St.
Montpelier 05602
802-229-0516; FAX: 802-229-2141
tbuckles@aol.com

VIRGINIA

American Institute for Paralegal Studies, Inc.
Paralegal Program
(site in Virginia Beach)
800-624-3933

Central Virginia Community College
3506 Wards Rd.
Lynchburg 24502-2448
804-386-4617

Christopher Newport University
Legal Studies
50 Shoe Ln.
Newport News 23606
804-594-7820; FAX: 804-594-7481
hgreenle@powhatan.cc.cnu.edu

Commonwealth College–Hampton
1120 W. Mercury Blvd.
Hampton 23666-3309
757-838-2122

Commonwealth College–Richmond
8141 Hull St. Rd.
Richmond 23235-6411
804-745-2444

Commonwealth College–Virginia Beach
Paralegal Program
301 Centre Pointe Dr.
Virginia Beach 23462
757-499-7900

Dominion Business School
Paralegal Program
4142-1 Melrose Ave. NW, #1
Roanoke 24017
703-362-7738

Ferrum College
Legal Assistant Program
Ferrum 24088
703-365-4290

J. Sargeant Reynolds Community College
Legal Assisting Program
P.O. Box 85622
Richmond 23285-5622
804-371-3265; FAX: 804-371-3588

James Madison University
Paralegal Program
Department of Political Science
Harrisonburg 22807-0001
703-568-3767

Marymount University
Paralegal Studies/MA in Legal Administration
2807 N. Glebe Rd.
Arlington 22207-4299
703-284-5910; FAX: 703-527-3830

Mountain Empire Community College
Legal Assistant Program
P.O. Drawer 700
Big Stone Gap 24219-0700
540-523-2400

National Academy, Paralegal Studies
P.O. Box 1359
Lynchburg 24505-1359
800-922-0771

National Institute of Paralegal Training
1880 Howard Ave., Suite 302
Vienna 22182-2611
703-442-0723

New River Community College
Dublin 24084-1127
540-674-3600

Northern Virginia Community College
Alexandria Campus
3001 N. Beauregard St.
Alexandria 22311-5065

Paralegal Institute
9524 Lee Hwy.
Fairfax 22031-2303
703-734-0430

Thomas Nelson Community College
Legal Assistant Program
P.O. Box 9407
Hampton 23670-0407
804-825-2743

Tidewater Community College
Legal Assistant Program
1700 College Crescent
Virginia Beach 23456-1918
757-822-1000

University of Richmond
Paralegal Studies
University College Evening School
Richmond 22317
804-289-8000

University of Virginia
104 Midmont Ln.
Charlottesville 22903-2449
804-924-0311

Virginia Intermont College
Paralegal Studies Program
1013 Moore St.
Bristol 24201
540-669-6101; FAX: 540-669-5763

Virginia Western Community College
Legal Assisting Program
3095 Colonial Ave. SW
Roanoke 24038
540-857-7272; FAX: 540-857-7544

WASHINGTON
Bellevue Community College
3000 Landerholm Circle SE
Bellevue 98007-6484
206-641-2224

Central Washington Union
Program in Law and Justice
Ellensburg 98926
509-963-1111

Clark College
1800 E. McLoughlin Blvd.
Vancouver 98663-3598
206-694-6521

Columbia Basin College
Legal Assistant Program
2600 N. 20th Ave.
Pasco 99301-3397
509-946-9669

Edmonds Community College
Legal Assistant Program
20000 68th Ave. W.
Lynnwood 98036-5999
206-640-1658; FAX: 206-771-3366
http://www.edmonds.ctc.edu/
mfitch@ec.ctc.edu

Highline Community College
P.O. Box 98000
Des Moines 98198
206-878-3710

Lower Columbia College
Legal Assistant Program
1600 Maple St.
Longview 98632-3995
360-577-2300

Pacific Lutheran University
Legal Studies
S. 121st St. & Park Ave.
Tacoma 98447-0001
253-531-6900

Pierce College
Paralegal Studies
9401 Farwest Dr. SW
Tacoma 98498-1999
206-964-6638; FAX: 206-964-6318

Skagit Valley College
Paralegal Program
2405 E. College Way
Mount Vernon 98273
360-428-1278; FAX: 360-428-1186
http://www-svc.ctc.edu/
tmaloney@ctc.ctc.edu

South Puget Sound Community College
2011 Mottman Rd. SW
Olympia 98512-6218
206-754-7711

Spokane Community College
N. 1810 Greene St.
Spokane 99207
509-536-7398

Whatcom Community College
Paralegal Program
237 W. Kellogg Rd.
Bellingham 98226-8003
206-676-2170

WEST VIRGINIA
College of West Virginia
Legal Studies
P.O. Box AG
Beckley 25802-2830
304-253-7351; 800-766-6067;
FAX: 304-253-0789

Fairmont State College
Legal Assistant Program
Division of Social Science
Fairmont 26554

Marshall University Community &
Technical College
Legal Assistant Program
400 Hal Greer Blvd.
Huntington 25755-2700
304-696-3646; FAX: 304-696-3013

Mountain State College
Paralegal Program
Spring & Sixteenth Sts.
Parkersburg 26101-3993
304-485-5487

University of Charleston
2300 MacCorkle Ave. SE
Charleston 25304-1099
304-357-4812

Webster College
Paralegal Program
144 Willey St.
Morgantown 26505-5521
304-363-8824

West Virginia Business College
Paralegal Program
1052 Main St.
Wheeling 26003
304-232-0631

West Virginia Career College
Paralegal Program
148 Willey St.
Morgantown 26505
304-296-8282

WISCONSIN
American Institute for Paralegal Studies
710 M. Plakington Ave., #500
Milwaukee 53203
800-533-2420

American Institute for Paralegal Studies,
Inc.
Paralegal Program
(sites in Milwaukee, Madison, and
Green Bay)
800-624-3933

Carthage College
Paralegal Program
2001 Alford Dr.
Kenosha 53140-1994

Chippewa Valley Technical College
Paralegal Program
620 W. Clairemont Ave.
Eau Claire 54701-6162
715-833-6355; FAX: 715-833-6470

Concordia University Wisconsin
Paralegal Program
12800 North Lake Shore Dr.
Mequon 53097
414-243-5700; FAX: 414-243-4351
jarratt@bach.cuw.edu

Lakeshore Technical College
Paralegal Program
1290 North Ave.
Cleveland 53015
414-458-4183 x202; FAX: 414-457-6211

MBTI Business Training Institute
Paralegal Program
606 W. Wisconsin Ave.
Milwaukee 53203
414-272-2192

Madison Area Technical College
3550 Anderson St.
Madison 53704-2599

Milwaukee Area Technical College
Paralegal Association
700 West State St.
Milwaukee 53233-1433

Northeast Wisconsin Technical College
Paralegal Program
2740 W. Mason St.
Green Bay 54307
414-498-6277; 414-498-6811

University of Wisconsin
905 University Ave., Rm. 401
Madison 53715-1005
608-262-3961

Western Wisconsin Technical College
Sixth & Vine Sts.
LaCrosse 54601
608-785-9616

WYOMING
Casper College
Legal Assistant Program
125 College Dr.
Casper 82601
307-268-2618; FAX: 307-268-2224

Jets Technical Institute
P.O. Box 1777
Riverton 82501-1777
307-856-7279

Laramie County Community College
Legal Assistant Program
1400 E. College Dr.
Cheyenne 82007-3204
307-778-1178

PUERTO RICO
Liseo de Arte, Diseño y Comercio
Calle Union #50
P.O. Box 1009
Fajardo 00738-1009
787-863-0593

CANADA
Capilano College
2055 Purcell Way
North Vancouver, BC V7J 3H5
604-986-1911

Humber College, North Campus
205 Humber College Blvd.
Etobicoke, Ontario M9W5-7
416-675-3111

Red Deer College
Box 5005
Red Deer, Alberta T4N 5H5
403-342-3266

Distance Learning

American Institute for Paralegal Studies
17 W. 705 Butterfield Rd., Suite A
Oakbrook Terrace, IL 60181
630-916-6880

Constitutional Educational Research
Foundation
11357 Pyrites Way, Suite A3
Gold River, CA 95670-4439
800-830-1333

National Institute for Paralegal Arts and
Sciences
164 W. Royal Palm Rd.
P.O. Box 2158
Boca Raton, FL 33427-2158
800-669-2555

THE INSIDE TRACK

Who:	John Gleeson
What:	Owner of *We The People*, an Independent Paralegal Service
Where:	Nashua, New Hampshire
How long:	Seven years
Degree:	Paralegal certificate (distance learning program)

Insider's Advice

This is a one-man operation; most places like this are. We prepare documents for people who are known as *pro se* filers [people who serve as their own attorneys], or for people who just want to handle their own affairs without going through a lawyer. So for *pro se* filers, people who do it themselves in court, we do divorces, bankruptcies and so on; and then for business people we do incorporations; and then, wills, deeds and so on. So the documents are prepared for people who decide to do it themselves instead of paying lawyers to do the paperwork for them. One thing we don't do, of course, is we don't give legal advice—it's not part of the service.

Since we stay away from legal advice, we basically only prepare forms. The format of the forms is what is important; the content is the responsibility of the customer. We just guarantee that the forms will be okay. And if somebody says that was the wrong form that I used, well, that's their responsibility. We don't advise them which forms to use—we're not allowed to do that.

Insider's Take on the Future

In California, they've been doing this [independent paralegal services] for over twenty years, and down in Florida, after going through a lot of upheaval and people being thrown in jail, they are now well on the way to a lot of people doing independent paralegal work. It's actually active in just about every state. A lot of states are still persecuting people who try it. I still get harassed occasionally by lawyers, though the attorney general in this state has chosen to say if the public isn't complaining and they're happy, then we'll leave you alone. [Some states] really don't want us out there, but it's difficult to stop us. I was the first in New Hampshire in 1991 and I know of three or four now.

CHAPTER | 4

Post-secondary education of any kind can be quite expensive. However, that's no reason not to go to school; if you are determined to get training, there's financial aid available for you. As much as possible, plan ahead to handle your education costs. The federal government offers student loans and grants, and many states offer financial aid as well. This chapter will help you figure out ways to pay for your paralegal training.

FINANCIAL AID FOR THE TRAINING YOU NEED

Your best resource for information on financial aid is the officer at the school you are planning to attend. If you are still in high school, your guidance counselor will be able to help you locate sources of financial aid. If you don't yet know which school you want to attend or are no longer in high school, you can receive information from various lending agencies or educational opportunity centers. It is much easier to undertake this search with a guide. Try your high school counselor—even if you've been out of high school a few years—or the financial aid officer at a school you're considering. This chapter, by necessity, concentrates on federal financial aid. States, schools, and private agencies give out millions of dollars every year. Make sure you find out, from your counselor or financial aid officer, how you apply for that aid.

STATE AID

Your best source for information about aid that does not come from the federal government—that is, state, school, or private aid—is the financial aid office at your paralegal school. If you want more information on aid available from a particular state, you can contact one of the higher education agencies listed in Appendix A.

GATHERING FINANCIAL RECORDS

It's important that you keep good records about all of your finances and your financial aid. Find a place to keep files with all the information you get on various aid programs, and make sure you have a highly visible calendar on which you can note deadlines and other important dates. Keep copies of everything you send to any agency, and include a record of when things were sent.

First, you need to know whose finances are going to determine the aid you receive—yours and your spouse's (if you have one) or yours and your parents. In order to be considered independent of your parents for financial aid purposes, you must meet one of the following requirements:

- be 25 years old or older
- be a veteran of the U.S. military
- be a graduate or professional (that is, post-bachelor's degree) student
- be married
- be an orphan or a ward of a court
- have dependents (other than a spouse)

In some rare cases, a financial aid administrator can adjudge a student independent, even if none of the above categories apply. But this doesn't happen just because your parents won't help you with college costs; it may be the case for students whose parents are, for example, imprisoned or have engaged in documented abuse of the student. If none of these categories apply to you, then you, like most undergraduates, will be considered a dependent of your parents.

Whether you are dependent or independent, the first step toward obtaining your financial aid is filling out the Free Application for Federal Student Aid (FAFSA). **You cannot get financial aid if you do not fill out a FAFSA.** You can get this form from your high school guidance office, paralegal school financial aid office, the public library, or by calling 800-4-FED-AID. If you have applied for aid in the past, you may only need to file the shorter Renewal FAFSA. If you are independent, you will need to fill out the FAFSA about you and, if you're married, your spouse. If you are dependent, you will provide information about yourself, and your parents will supply information about themselves. Your school's financial aid office can also tell you about any other forms you need to fill out to qualify for state aid or assistance that the school itself sponsors.

It's very important that you fill out the FAFSA—and any other forms—completely and accurately. Make sure that all signatures are included. If the form is incorrect, it will be returned to you, which will delay the processing of your application. And unfortunately, there isn't an unlimited supply of aid; what is available is awarded on a first come, first served basis. After you complete your FAFSA, check it over and make a copy of it. Then send it to the appropriate processor as soon as possible after January 1. Note that you must send in the original; photocopies are not accepted. You do not need to have been admitted into an educational program to file a FAFSA. However, you will have to be admitted before you receive any money.

FAFSA Tips

The Financial Aid Office at Metropolitan Community College in Omaha, Nebraska, offers this advice on filling out your FAFSA:

- Avoid waiting until the last minute to complete financial aid application materials. An early start will leave time to collect and correct information, ask questions, and solve problems.
- Use a pen with black or dark ink or a number 2 pencil. Print clearly and neatly. Do not use correction fluid anywhere on the form.
- Do not use a FAFSA that is torn, crumpled, or stained.
- Write only in the response areas and answer boxes on the form. Shade ovals to indicate correct responses.
- Set aside at least one full afternoon or evening to work on the application.
- Assemble the needed materials ahead of time, including:
  - the FAFSA and any additional application materials required by the college
  - Social Security number
  - your U.S. income tax return (Form 1040, 1040A, 1040EZ) if you can complete it by early January (if you have not filed your tax return, estimate income on the FAFSA)
  - W-2 forms and other records of money earned

- current bank statements, mortgage information, and business or farm records; records of medical and dental bills paid in the previous year
- records of veterans benefits or Social Security payments
- documentation of untaxed income (AFDC, military allowances, 401k plans, etc.)

+ Work carefully through the application. Follow all directions.

+ If there are additional circumstances you feel should be considered, bring the additional information directly to the financial aid office along with the FAFSA. Be sure to put your name and Social Security number at the top of each page.

+ Make a list of unanswered questions, and before mailing the application, check to make sure each question has been answered, unless otherwise indicated by the FAFSA instructions.

+ Make a photocopy of the completed application materials and keep the work copies of financial statements.

+ Bring the completed FAFSA and supporting documents to a campus financial aid office for review.

+ Send the original FAFSA (not a photocopy) in the preaddressed envelope in the booklet by first-class mail.

+ Do not send any documents or tax forms with the FAFSA.

+ Do not use a special mailing service such as registered mail; it will delay processing of your form.

Some funds are limited, so apply and complete your file as soon as possible after January 1. Applications are processed on first-received basis. See the Sample FAFSA form at the end of this chapter.

In about a month, you will receive your Student Aid Report (SAR). The SAR tells you the amount your family is expected to pay toward your course of study. This is called your expected family contribution (EFC). Make sure the information on the SAR is correct, and if it isn't, make any necessary changes and send it to the address noted on the SAR.

Once you are accepted at a paralegal school, the financial aid office will determine your eligibility for aid, based on your FAFSA, and send you a financial aid award letter. This will tell you the amount of aid you have been awarded and the types of aid that make up your aid package. These can include grants, loans, and work-study. If you were accepted by more than one paralegal school, the aid package that each offers, coupled with the factors listed in chapter two, will help you make your final selection.

If you get frustrated and confused by your aid applications, view it philosophically as good practice for work in the legal field. Remember, these regulations were written by lawyers, and lawyers just *love* abbreviations. When you're finished, throw yourself a party. Just NIMBY.

FINANCIAL AID DOCUMENTS

Let's look at some financial aid documents in detail.

Free Application for Federal Student Aid

The FAFSA evaluates your income and assets, and your parents', to arrive at your EFC. The FAFSA is based, for the most part, on information on your income tax forms from last year. Remember, you want to send in your FAFSA as soon after January 1 as possible. If you or your parents have not filed your taxes yet, you can estimate and correct inaccuracies later. Make sure you check all appropriate boxes to be considered for loans, work-study, and grants.

If your parents are divorced, things can get confusing. Parenthood is defined differently in different financial aid situations. For example, the FAFSA should be filled out by the parent with whom you have lived the most during the past 12 months, even if that parent doesn't have legal custody. If you didn't live with either parent, the one who supplied the most financial support should complete the FAFSA. If you haven't received support in the last year, use the most recent year. Remember that your parent needs to report any child support on the FAFSA.

However, in determining "household size" on the FAFSA, you should use the household of the parent who has provided, and will continue to provide, more than half of your support, regardless of where you lived. Often, the parent who should fill out the FAFSA and whose household will determine household size is the parent who has legal custody of you and claimed you as a dependent on his or her tax return. That's not a given, though, and these factors (legal custody and tax dependency) are only used when the other ones are unclear. And this doesn't even include the issue of step-parents, whose income and assets may have to be reported. Read the directions carefully and don't be afraid to ask for help.

In order to fill out the FAFSA, gather these records for both you and your parents, for last year:

- income tax returns, that is, IRS Form 1040, 1040A, or 1040EZ (or an income estimate) and W-2 and 1099 forms
- records of any untaxed income, such as Social Security benefits, child support, welfare, pensions, and veterans benefits
- current bank statements
- mortgage information
- medical and dental expenses (if they weren't covered by health insurance)
- farm and/or business records
- records of any investments, for example, stocks, bonds, mutual funds, certificates of deposit and money market accounts
- Social Security numbers

After you have completed and double-checked your FAFSA—and you and your family are on speaking terms again—make a copy and send it in to the appropriate processor, whose address is on the form. Do this as soon after January 1 as possible, but not before!

Recently, the Department of Education began accepting FAFSA information online, with a program called FAFSA Express. If you have a Windows operating system and a modem, you can contact the Department of Education at http://www.ed.gov/offices/OPE/express.html and fill out your FAFSA online. You will want to print out the Releases and Signatures page of the application, sign it, and send it in. If you don't, you will still receive an SAR, but you will need to sign

If you are not an independent student, your parents must provide information on the FAFSA. For various reasons, parents sometimes balk at furnishing this information. They may give you lots of reasons, but often their concern is about keeping the information confidential. Perhaps they don't want an ex-spouse to know about their financial situation; perhaps they don't want *you* to know. There are all kinds of myths out there about who can receive financial aid and what can result from a determination that you qualify for aid. The bottom line is this: You can't get aid if you don't file a FAFSA. The information on financial aid forms is confidential; it will only be seen by the federal processor and the financial aid officers at the schools you've applied to. If a financial aid officer detects fraud in your FAFSA, he or she is required to report it to the Department of Education (which does *not* share the information with the IRS). In any other case, the person who provided information for a FAFSA must give express written permission for that information to be released. And even if your parents refuse to help pay for your education, if you're not otherwise independent, you will be considered a dependent student and will need to have a FAFSA on file. Beg, plead, or bribe your parents, whatever it takes to get them to fill out the FAFSA. If they refuse, ask your financial aid officer for help and any alternatives.

and send in your SAR before the process can continue. If you don't have a home computer or yours is lacking some of the necessary equipment, you may be able to use FAFSA Express on a computer at a library, guidance or financial aid office, or educational opportunity center. Remember, you'll need all the records that you would need for a paper FAFSA.

Student Aid Report (SAR) and Expected Family Contribution (EFC)

About a month after you file your FAFSA, you will receive a SAR that details your EFC—remember, that's expected family contribution, the amount the government feels your family can contribute toward your education. (If you don't receive a SAR, contact Federal Student Aid Programs, P.O. Box 4038, Washington, DC 52243-4038.) The other important number is the COA, cost of attendance at the school you plan to go to. Your financial need is calculated by subtracting your EFC from your COA. This is the amount your financial aid office wants to help you receive from financial aid. The school will tell you what your financial aid package is by sending you a financial aid award letter. (Remember, you've already found out what forms are required for state aid and aid from the school, and you've filed these forms in the appropriate places.)

In addition to the EFC and COA, you'll see some other acronyms on the SAR; these represent interim conclusions reached in the course of analyzing your EFC.

TI	=	total income
ATI	=	allowances against total income
STX	=	state and other tax allowance
EA	=	employment allowance
IPA	=	income protection allowance
AI	=	available income
CAI	=	contribution from available income (independent student)
DNW	=	discretionary net worth
APA	=	education savings and asset protection allowance
PCA	=	parents' contribution from assets
AAI	=	adjusted available income
TPC	=	total parents' contribution
TSC	=	total student's contribution
PC	=	parents'contribution
SIC	=	dependent student's income contribution
SCA	=	dependent student's contribution from assets

This might be a good time to take some of your AI and get some R & R!

In calculating your EFC, the processor considers factors such as family size, how many family members are in college, how much the family has in savings, and the amount of the family's current earnings. For dependent students, the parents' and student's contributions are added together to arrive at the *family* contribution.

Currently, a student who last year earned less than $1,750 and has no assets is not expected to contribute anything. But 35 percent of any assets a student does have

> You can estimate your EFC at the Web site maintained by Sallie Mae, at http://www.salliemae.com

and 50 percent of any income over $1,750 is counted toward the student's portion of the EFC. The parents' share of the EFC is a bit more complicated; it includes assets and income but is affected by the number of undergraduate students in the family, whether one or both parents work, and a number of "unusual circumstances" that can alter the parental contribution.

YOUR FINANCIAL AID PACKAGE

Once it receives your SAR, the financial aid office at the school you will be attending will send you a financial aid award letter that outlines your financial aid package. Assuming you've filled out all proper forms for state and school aid, here are some of the things that might be in your package.

Loans: Federal, State, School, Private

Most students receive at least some of their financial aid in the form of loans that have to be paid back. It would be nice to finance your education completely with grants and scholarships, but you shouldn't count on that. The majority of education loans are available through the Federal Family Education Loan Program (FFELP) and the Federal Direct Student Loan Program (FDSLP). Your school may participate in one or both of these programs. The two programs are essentially the same, but in the FFELP your bank, credit union, or the school provides the loan, and in the FDSLP the U.S. Department of Education is the lender. Your financial aid officer will determine which program applies to you.

Federally sponsored loan programs include Stafford loans (either subsidized or unsubsidized), PLUS loans, and Perkins loans. Subsidized Stafford loans are available to students who have demonstrated need, according to their SAR. The government pays the interest on subsidized Stafford loans while the student is in school, as well as during any grace or forbearance periods. Students who don't qualify for a subsidized loan can obtain an unsubsidized Stafford loan, available regardless of the student's financial need. The student is responsible for all the interest on the loan, even that which accrues while the student is in school, although payments don't begin until after graduation. If you do not qualify for a subsidized Stafford loan for all the money you need, you can combine the two.

Federal Perkins loans are for students who have demonstrated extraordinary financial need. These are low interest loans (currently 5 percent) that are funded by the federal government but administered by individual schools. The amount you can receive depends not only on your financial need, but also on how much the school has available.

Parent Loans for Undergraduate Students (PLUS) are for parents of dependent students. Parents can borrow up to the full educational cost, minus any aid or grants the student has received. PLUS loans are not based on financial need; however, credit histories are checked. With good credit, a parent may borrow for any number of dependent students in the family, as long as the students attend school at least half time. This is usually the "loan of last resort." It is intended to make up any shortfall after all other avenues are explored. Note that parents must begin repaying these loans within 60 days of the date the money is disbursed.

In addition to these federally sponsored loans, most states offer guaranteed student loans, and many educational institutions do as well. Your high school guidance counselor or your financial aid officer is your best source for information on these loans. Private loan sources are most often available to parents, but on occasion they are available to students as well. The requirements and characteristics of these loans vary, depending on the institution offering them.

Grants and Scholarships

Grants and scholarships provide money that doesn't have to be repaid. Two of the largest grant programs are funded by the federal government: the Pell grant program and the Federal Supplemental Educational Opportunity Grant (FSEOG) program. These are need-based grants, reserved for the neediest students. If you qualify for a Pell grant, it will be indicated on your SAR, assuming you checked all the appropriate boxes on the FAFSA.

Pell grants are only available to undergraduate students who have not yet received a bachelor's or professional degree. The amount available to each student depends on the funding for the program; in 1996 the maximum award was less than $2,500. If you receive a Pell grant, your school will either apply the money directly to the cost of your tuition or pay you directly. The school must inform you, in writing, about the amount of your grant and how and when it will be disbursed.

Federal Supplemental Educational Opportunity Grants (FSEOG) are awarded to undergraduate students with exceptional financial need. Students who receive Pell grants are given priority for this program. Even if you are attending school less than half time, you can be considered for this grant.

In addition to these federal programs, there are several state grant programs available. The school you are planning to attend may also provide some educational grants. Many scholarships are administered by particular schools. You can get information on these programs from the financial aid officer at your paralegal school or your high school guidance counselor.

Work-Study

The Federal Work-Study Program provides part-time jobs for students who need help in meeting educational costs. The program is designed to provide you, when possible, with work related to your field of study, or community service work. Most work-study jobs are on campus; however, some public agencies or private nonprofit groups have made arrangements to hire work-study students.

If you qualify for work-study, you will be "awarded" the total amount you may earn in a given period—for example, an academic year or a summer award. During the award period, you cannot collect more than your award; nor can you work more than twenty hours a week. Most work-study students are paid hourly, although some graduate students may be paid a salary. In order to receive a work-study job, you must apply and be hired as you would for any other job. The fact that you qualify for work-study doesn't guarantee you a job. The program really helps fund the jobs and determines which students qualify financially to be considered for them. After that, you are on your own.

If you do not qualify for federal work-study, check with the student employment office at your school anyway. There are often non-work-study jobs available for students. For example, in law school I sold bagels for the Student Bar Association. It was a great job, because most of the good gossip eventually made its way to my little counter. Of course, you can always work full- or part-time off campus too.

FINANCIAL AID CHECKLIST

There's a wide range of loans, grants, scholarships, and work-study sources. You do not have to have been accepted by a paralegal school to file a FAFSA; you should indicate the programs you are considering. Then your SAR will include COAs for the schools you listed, and you can see what your financial need will be. You can even have each school send you a financial award letter outlining your financial aid package and use that information to help you determine which school you will attend. You will not receive any aid until you have decided which school you will attend. Make sure you notify the financial aid office of any changes in your circumstances as they occur; for example, if you receive a grant or scholarship or your income estimates must be changed. If you keep good records and continually communicate with your financial aid officer, you should be able to locate all the financial aid you need. Use this checklist to keep yourself on track:

FAFSA

_____ Get a FAFSA from the financial aid office of the school you plan to attend or one of the schools you are considering. They are also available from public libraries, high school guidance offices, and the U.S. Department of Education.

_____ Create a financial aid file.

_____ Gather all the financial records you need—yours, your spouse's, and your parents'—and put them in your file.

_____ Fill out the FAFSA completely and accurately. Incomplete applications may be rejected.

_____ Sign and date the completed FAFSA. Do not date it before January 1.

_____ Make a copy of the FAFSA for your financial aid file.

_____ Mail the FAFSA to the appropriate processor as soon as possible after January 1. Don't put anything extra in the envelope when mailing the FAFSA.

State, School, and Private Applications

_____ Fill out all aid applications for state, institutional, and private financial aid. These should be available from your paralegal school's financial aid office, your high school counselor, public libraries, or the state agencies listed above.

_____ Make a copy of your completed state, institutional, and private aid applications for your financial aid file.

_____ File all the applications at the appropriate time.

SAR

_____ If you have not received your SAR within a month of filing your FAFSA, contact Federal Student Aid Programs, P.O. Box 4038, Washington, DC 52243-4038 or your financial aid office.

_____ When you receive your SAR, check for inaccuracies, correct any mistakes, and mail to the address indicated.

Verification Items

Some applications are selected for verification, either by the Department of Education or by the school you'll be attending. If yours is, you'll be notified that more information is being requested before any financial aid can be granted. You will receive a verification statement and may be required to provide (these should all be in your financial aid file):

_____ Tax returns: yours and your spouse's (if married) prior year's tax returns, including all schedules and attachments, if you're an independent applicant. If you are a dependent student, your parents' prior year's tax return, with all schedules and attachments.

_____ Alien Registration Card or other INS documents, if applicable

_____ Documentation of any untaxed income you reported

_____ Other documents as requested

Financial Aid Transcript (FAT)

_____ If you have recently attended another post-secondary school, your financial aid office may request a FAT for each previous school, even if you didn't receive financial aid at that school. If the financial aid office notifies you that they need a FAT, forms are available at the financial aid office. (Note: FATs are not academic transcripts!)

Updates

_____ Notify the financial aid office if your address, marital status, or name changes in the course of the financial aid application process.

_____ Notify the financial aid office if your financial situation changes or if you receive any aid from outside sources (such as grants or scholarships).

Financial Aid Awards

_____ Clarify any information on your financial aid package that you don't understand with the financial aid office.

_____ Compare financial aid awards, if you've been considering more than one school.

Show Me the Money

_____ Complete and file all necessary paperwork to receive your financial aid.

_____ Apply for work-study jobs, if applicable.

Finances should never keep you from furthering your education. There is money available, in the form of loans, scholarships, and grants. The financial aid office of your paralegal school is your best resource in the search for financial aid. They keep up on all the federal and state regulations and they know about all the local money sources. The process can be complicated and all the rules, regulations, and deadlines can be daunting, but mastering them is a small price to pay for your future in an exciting career.

*F*ree *A*pplication for *F*ederal *S*tudent *A*id
1997–98 School Year

WARNING: If you purposely give false or misleading information on this form, you may be fined $10,000, sent to prison, or both.

"You" and "your" on this form always mean the student who wants aid.

Form Approved
OMB No. 1840-0110
App. Exp. 6/30/98

U.S. Department of Education
Student Financial
Assistance Programs

Use dark ink. Make capital letters and numbers clear and legible.   `E X M 2 4`   *Fill in ovals completely. Only one oval per question.*   Correct ●   *Incorrect marks will be ignored.*   Incorrect ⊗ ✓

Section A: You (the student)

1–3. Your name

1. Last name   2. First name   3. M.I.

Your title (optional)   Mr. ○ ₁   Miss, Mrs., or Ms. ○ ₂

4–7. Your permanent mailing address
(All mail will be sent to this address. See Instructions, page 2 for state/country abbreviations.)

4. Number and street (Include apt. no.)

5. City   6. State   7. ZIP code

8. Your social security number (SSN) *(Don't leave blank. See Instructions, page 2.)*

9. Your date of birth   Month Day Year   `1 9`

10. Your permanent home telephone number   Area code

11. Your state of legal residence   State

12. Date you became a legal resident of the state in question 11 *(See Instructions, page 2.)*   Month Day Year   `1 9`

13–14. Your driver's license number *(Include the state abbreviation. If you don't have a license, write in "None.")*

State   License number

15–16. Are you a U.S. citizen? *(See Instructions, pages 2–3.)*

Yes, I am a U.S. citizen.   ○ ₁
No, but I am an eligible noncitizen.   ○ ₂
A
No, neither of the above.   ○ ₃

17. As of today, are you married? *(Fill in only one oval.)*

I am not married. (I am single, widowed, or divorced.)   ○ ₁
I am married.   ○ ₂
I am separated from my spouse.   ○ ₃

18. Date you were married, separated, divorced, or widowed. If divorced, use date of divorce or separation, whichever is earlier.
(If never married, leave blank.) Month   Year   `1 9`

19. Will you have your first bachelor's degree before July 1, 1997?   Yes ○ ₁   No ○ ₂

Section B: Education Background

20–21. Date that you (the student) received, or will receive, your high school diploma, either—
(Enter one date. Leave blank if the question does not apply to you.)

• by graduating from high school   **20.**   Month Year `1 9`

OR

• by earning a GED   **21.**   Month Year `1 9`

22–23. Highest educational level or grade level your father and your mother completed. *(Fill in one oval for each parent. See Instructions, page 3.)*

	22. Father	23. Mother
elementary school (K–8)	○ ₁	○ ₁
high school (9–12)	○ ₂	○ ₂
college or beyond	○ ₃	○ ₃
unknown	○ ₄	○ ₄

If you (and your family) have **unusual circumstances**, complete this form and then check with your financial aid administrator. Examples:

• tuition expenses at an elementary or secondary school,
• unusual medical or dental expenses not covered by insurance,

• a family member who recently became unemployed, or
• other unusual circumstances such as changes in income or assets that might affect your eligibility for student financial aid.

Page 2

Section C: Your Plans *Answer these questions about your college plans.*

24–28. Your expected enrollment status for the 1997–98 school year
(See Instructions, page 3.)

School term	Full time	3/4 time	1/2 time	Less than 1/2 time	Not enrolled
24. Summer term '97	○ 1	○ 2	○ 3	○ 4	○ 5
25. Fall semester/qtr. '97	○ 1	○ 2	○ 3	○ 4	○ 5
26. Winter quarter '97-98	○ 1	○ 2	○ 3	○ 4	○ 5
27. Spring semester/qtr. '98	○ 1	○ 2	○ 3	○ 4	○ 5
28. Summer term '98	○ 1	○ 2	○ 3	○ 4	○ 5

29. Your course of study *(See Instructions for code, page 3.)* Code ☐

30. College degree/certificate you expect to receive
(See Instructions for code, page 3.) ☐

31. Date you expect to receive
your degree/certificate Month Day Year ☐

32. Your grade level during the 1997–98 school year *(Fill in only one.)*

1st yr./never attended college ○ 1	5th year/other undergraduate ○ 6
1st yr./attended college before ○ 2	1st year graduate/professional ○ 7
2nd year/sophomore ○ 3	2nd year graduate/professional ○ 8
3rd year/junior ○ 4	3rd year graduate/professional ○ 9
4th year/senior ○ 5	Beyond 3rd year graduate/professional ○ 10

33–35. In addition to grants, what other types of financial aid are you (and your parents) interested in? *(See Instructions, page 3.)*

33. Student employment Yes ○ 1 No ○ 2

34. Student loans Yes ○ 1 No ○ 2

35. Parent loans for students Yes ○ 1 No ○ 2

36. If you are (or were) in college, do you plan to attend **that same college** in 1997–98? *(If this doesn't apply to you, leave blank.)* Yes ○ 1 No ○ 2

37. For how many dependents will you (the student) pay child care or elder care expenses in 1997–98? ☐

38–39. Veterans education benefits you expect to receive from July 1, 1997 through June 30, 1998

38. Amount per month $ ☐ .00

39. Number of months ☐

Section D: Student Status

40. Were you born **before** January 1, 1974? .... Yes ○ 1 No ○ 2

41. Are you a veteran of the U.S. Armed Forces? .... Yes ○ 1 No ○ 2

42. Will you be enrolled in a graduate or professional program (beyond a bachelor's degree) in 1997-98? .... Yes ○ 1 No ○ 2

43. Are you married? .... Yes ○ 1 No ○ 2

44. Are you an orphan or a ward of the court, or **were** you a ward of the court until age 18? .... Yes ○ 1 No ○ 2

45. Do you have legal dependents (**other than a spouse**) that fit the definition in Instructions, page 4? .... Yes ○ 1 No ○ 2

If you answered **"Yes"** to **any** question in Section D, go to Section E and fill out **both the GRAY and the WHITE** areas on the rest of this form.

If you answered **"No"** to **every** question in Section D, go to Section E and fill out **both the GREEN and the WHITE** areas on the rest of this form.

Section E: Household Information

Remember:
At least one "Yes" answer in Section D means fill out the GRAY and WHITE areas.

All "No" answers in Section D means fill out the GREEN and WHITE areas.

STUDENT (& SPOUSE)

46. Number in your household in 1997–98
(Include yourself and your spouse. Do not include your children and other people unless they meet the definition in Instructions, page 4.) ☐

47. Number of college students in household in 1997–98
(Of the number in 46, how many will be in college at least half-time in at least one term in an eligible program? Include yourself. See Instructions, page 4.) ☐

PARENT(S)

48. Your parent(s)' **current** marital status:

single ○ 1   separated ○ 3   widowed ○ 5

married ○ 2   divorced ○ 4   State ☐

49. Your parent(s)' state of legal residence ☐

50. Date your parent(s) became legal resident(s) of the state in question 49 *(See Instructions, page 5.)* Month Day Year 1 9

51. Number in your parent(s)' household in 1997–98
(Include yourself and your parents. Do not include your parents' other children and other people unless they meet the definition in Instructions, page 5.) ☐

52. Number of college students in household in 1997–98
(Of the number in 51, how many will be in college at least half-time in at least one term in an eligible program? Include yourself. See Instructions, page 5.) ☐

Section F: 1996 Income, Earnings, and Benefits *You must see Instructions, pages 5 and 6, for information about tax forms and tax filing status, especially if you are estimating taxes or filing electronically or by telephone. These instructions will tell you what income and benefits should be reported in this section.* *Page 3*

	STUDENT (& SPOUSE)	**PARENT(S)**
	Everyone must fill out this column.	

The following 1996 U.S. income tax figures are from: **53.** *(Fill in one oval.)*   **65.** *(Fill in one oval.)*

A—a completed 1996 IRS Form 1040A, 1040EZ, or 1040TEL .... ○ 1   A .... ○ 1

B—a completed 1996 IRS Form 1040 .... ○ 2   B .... ○ 2

C—an estimated 1996 IRS Form 1040A, 1040EZ, or 1040TEL .... ○ 3   C .... ○ 3

D—an estimated 1996 IRS Form 1040 .... ○ 4   D .... ○ 4

E—will not file a 1996 U.S. income tax return .... *(Skip to question 57.)* ○ 5   E *(Skip to 69.)* ○ 5

1996 Total number of exemptions (Form 1040–line 6d, or 1040A–line 6d; 1040EZ filers— *see Instructions, page 6.*)   **54.**   **66.**

1996 Adjusted Gross Income (AGI: Form 1040–line 31, 1040A–line 16, or 1040EZ–line 4— *see Instructions, page 6.*)   **55.** $ .00   **67.** $ .00

1996 U.S. income tax **paid** (Form 1040–line 44, 1040A–line 25, or 1040EZ–line 10   **56.** $ .00   **68.** $ .00

TAX FILERS ONLY

1996 Income earned from work   (Student) **57.** $ .00   (Father) **69.** $ .00

1996 Income earned from work   (Spouse) **58.** $ .00   (Mother) **70.** $ .00

1996 Untaxed income and benefits (yearly totals only):

Earned Income Credit (Form 1040–line 54, Form 1040A–line 29c, or Form 1040EZ–line 8)   **59.** $ .00   **71.** $ .00

Untaxed Social Security Benefits   **60.** $ .00   **72.** $ .00

Aid to Families with Dependent Children (AFDC/ADC)   **61.** $ .00   **73.** $ .00

Child support received for all children   **62.** $ .00   **74.** $ .00

Other untaxed income and benefits from Worksheet #2, page 11   **63.** $ .00   **75.** $ .00

1996 Amount from Line 5, Worksheet #3, page 12 *(See Instructions.)*   **64.** $ .00   **76.** $ .00

Section G: Asset Information   ATTENTION!

Fill out Worksheet A or Worksheet B in Instructions, page 7. *If you meet the tax filing and income conditions on Worksheets A and B, you do not have to complete Section G to apply for Federal student aid. Some states and colleges, however, require Section G information for their own aid programs. Check with your financial aid administrator and/or State Agency.*

Age of your older parent   **84.**

	STUDENT (& SPOUSE)	**PARENT(S)**

Cash, savings, and checking accounts   **77.** $ .00   **85.** $ .00

Other real estate and investments value *(Don't include the home.)*   **78.** $ .00   **86.** $ .00

Other real estate and investments debt *(Don't include the home.)*   **79.** $ .00   **87.** $ .00

Business value   **80.** $ .00   **88.** $ .00

Business debt   **81.** $ .00   **89.** $ .00

Investment farm value *(See Instructions, page 8.)* *(Don't include a family farm.)*   **82.** $ .00   **90.** $ .00

Investment farm debt *(See Instructions, page 8.)* *(Don't include a family farm.)*   **83.** $ .00   **91.** $ .00

Section H: Releases and Signatures

Page 4

92–103. What college(s) do you plan to attend in 1997–98?

(Note: The colleges you list below will have access to your application information. See Instructions, page 8.)

Housing codes	1—on-campus	3—with parent(s)
	2—off-campus	4—with relative(s) other than parent(s)

	Title IV School Code	College Name	College Street Address and City	State	Housing Code
XX.	0 5 4 3 2 1	EXAMPLE UNIVERSITY	14930 NORTH SOMEWHERE BLVD. ANYWHERE CITY	S T	XX. 2
92.					93.
94.					95.
96.					97.
98.					99.
100.					101.
102.					103.

104. The U.S. Department of Education will send information from this form to your state financial aid agency and the state agencies of the colleges listed above so they can consider you for state aid. Answer **"No"** if you **don't** want information released to the state. *(See Instructions, page 9 and "Deadlines for State Student Aid," page 10.)* .... **104.** No ◯ 2

105. Males not yet registered for Selective Service (SS): Do you want SS to register you? *(See Instructions, page 9.)* .... **105.** Yes ◯ 1

106–107. Read, Sign, and Date Below

All of the information provided by me or any other person on this form is true and complete to the best of my knowledge. I understand that this application is being filed jointly by all signatories. If asked by an authorized official, I agree to give proof of the information that I have given on this form. I realize that this proof may include a copy of my U.S. or state income tax return. I also realize that if I do not give proof when asked, the student may be denied aid.

Statement of Educational Purpose. I certify that I will use any Federal Title IV, HEA funds I receive during the award year covered by this application solely for expenses related to my attendance at the institution of higher education that determined or certified my eligibility for those funds.

Certification Statement on Overpayments and Defaults. I understand that I may not receive any Federal Title IV, HEA funds if I owe an overpayment on any Title IV educational grant or loan or am in default on a Title IV educational loan unless I have made satisfactory arrangements to repay or otherwise resolve the overpayment or default. I also understand that I must notify my school if I do owe an overpayment or am in default.

Everyone whose information is given on this form should sign below. The student (and at least one parent, if parental information is given) must sign below or this form will be returned unprocessed.

106. Signatures *(Sign in the boxes below.)*

1 Student

2 Student's Spouse

3 Father/Stepfather

4 Mother/Stepmother

107. Date completed

Month	Day	Year
		1997 ◯
		1998 ◯

Section I: Preparer's Use Only

For preparers other than student, spouse, and parent(s). Student, spouse, and parent(s), sign in question 106.

Preparer's name (last, first, MI)

Firm name

Firm or preparer's address (street, city, state, ZIP)

108. Employer identification number (EIN)

OR

109. Preparer's social security number

Certification: All of the information on this form is true and complete to the best of my knowledge.

110. Preparer's signature   **Date**

1

School Use Only

D/O ◯   Title IV Code

FAA Signature 1

MDE Use Only
Do not write in this box   Special handle

MAKE SURE THAT YOU HAVE COMPLETED, DATED, AND SIGNED THIS APPLICATION.
Mail the original application (NOT A PHOTOCOPY) to: Federal Student Aid Programs, P.O. Box 4008, Mt. Vernon, IL 62864-8608

Who:	Diane Austin
What:	Senior Corporate Paralegal
Where:	The Walt Disney Company, Burbank, California
How long:	Six years
Degree:	In-house training

Insider's Advice

I am an in-house paralegal; I do the work here at Disney. My day is very, very busy. I could put in ten hours a day or twelve hours a day and there still would be no end in sight. There are certain advantages to being in-house. Working in a corporate environment, versus working in law firm environment, I don't do billable hours. Which I think is a plus, because you're not having to track every phone call and every little thing that you do. It's Monday through Friday and if you do work Saturday and Sunday, that's your decision. I know that our litigation paralegals are very busy, all the time. I'm sure they work Saturdays and Sundays on occasion.

What I do is what would be considered corporate governance. I am responsible for setting up the corporations, qualifying the corporations to do business in other states, I register and maintain fictitious business names, I do dissolutions, mergers, and I also am responsible for filing annual reports. I don't do a lot of research or that type of thing unless it has particularly to do with qualifying in a state or incorporating in a state.

Insider's Take on the Future

I think that nowadays—for any paralegal—education is important because so many of the corporations require the paralegal certificate. They use that to review candidates—an advanced degree, a B.A. degree, helps even more.

CHAPTER | 5

Starting the hunt for your first job in a new field can be daunting. Especially if you are completely new to the legal profession, you may need some help identifying the places to begin and the ways to approach people. Every profession has its little quirks and tweaks; this chapter shows you what you can do to make landing your first job a little easier.

HOW TO LAND YOUR FIRST JOB

Hunting for a job usually involves three phases: You need to decide whom you are going to contact, you have to advertise yourself, and you have to sell yourself. Deciding whom to contact entails identifying potential employers and narrowing the field to those you think you would most like to work for and those most apt to hire you. Advertising yourself includes writing and sending out resumes and cover letters, but also networking and other methods of bringing your skills to the attention of the right people. Finally, selling yourself involves sitting down face-to-face with the person who has the authority to hire you and marketing yourself to convince that person you are right for the job.

BEFORE YOU BEGIN SEARCHING

What can you expect the paralegal job market to look like by the time you finish your training and are ready to launch your career? Expectations are that the market for paralegals will continue to grow over the next several years. According to the *Occupational Outlook Handbook, 1996,* published by the U.S. Department of Labor:

> Employment of paralegals is expected to grow much faster than the average for all occupations through the year 2005. Job opportunities are expected to expand as more employers become aware that paralegals are able to do many legal tasks for lower salaries than lawyers. Both law firms and other employers with legal staffs should continue to emphasize hiring paralegals so that the cost, availability, and efficiency of legal services can be improved.
>
> New jobs created by rapid employment growth will create most of the job openings for paralegals in the future. Other job openings will arise as people leave the occupation. Although the number of job openings for paralegals is expected to increase significantly through the year 2005, so will the number of people pursuing this career. Thus, keen competition for jobs should continue as the growing number of graduates from paralegal education programs keeps pace with employment growth.
>
> Private law firms will continue to be the largest employers of paralegals as a growing population demands additional legal services. The growth of prepaid legal plans should also contribute to the demand for the services of law firms. A growing array of other organizations, such as corporate legal departments, insurance companies, real estate and title insurance firms, and banks will also hire paralegals.
>
> Job opportunities for paralegals will expand even in the public sector. Community legal service programs—which provide assistance to the poor, aged, minorities, and middle-income families—operate on limited budgets. They will seek to employ additional paralegals in order to minimize expenses and serve the most people. Federal, state, and local government agencies, consumer organizations, and the courts should continue to hire paralegals in increasing numbers.

Things look good, then, for paralegals in the future, although, as this report notes, competition for paralegal jobs will increase as the number of jobs increases.

In this chapter, you'll find out what you can do to help make yourself a prime candidate for a top-notch paralegal job.

Internships

Internships give you valuable experience for your resume, and they often turn into permanent jobs. Law firms often use internships to hire their new lawyers; it's natural that they would rely on the same method to hire paralegals. It provides an opportunity for you to get a look at them and for them to get a look at you with very little obligation. However, if everybody likes what they see, it is to everyone's benefit to hire a former intern for a permanent position. Many internships turn into permanent jobs, so choose an internship that is the kind of work you think you want to do for the next several years.

Temporary Agencies

Some paralegals enjoy doing a variety of legal work and may work through temporary agencies for years. For others, it provides a passage to full-time work. Thus, it can be an excellent start to your career.

Temporary work gives you the opportunity to gain valuable experience. It also allows you to look over several different workplaces and get an idea of where you'd like to work permanently. And as with an internship, it gives employers a chance to get to know you. Many people gain permanent employment through temporary assignments. If, when you graduate from your program, you don't yet know for sure what kind of paralegal work you want to do, working for a temporary agency can be very valuable. If the perfect job doesn't seem to be forthcoming, temp work can lead you into it.

CONDUCTING YOUR SEARCH

Before you look for a job, you need to know what kind of job you are looking for. By that I mean not just *paralegal* but *criminal defense paralegal*, or *intellectual property paralegal*, or *real estate paralegal*. Or perhaps, for you, it's a paralegal in a small firm or a paralegal with a corporation or the government. I am a firm believer in looking for your dream job from the start. Of course, you should keep your feet on the ground; you probably aren't going to be hired right out of paralegal school to manage a legal assistant department and supervise several more-experienced paralegals. But it is worth spending some time pursuing the kind of job you think you would love.

One person you should definitely get to know as a paralegal student is the placement director. This is the person whose job it is to help you find a job when you graduate. A good placement office will have directories of law firms and other businesses in the local area, information about job fairs, and copies of any industry publications that list paralegal job openings. A top placement director also maintains contacts with the legal and business communities so that your school's placement office will be one of the first places to hear about a job opening and can give you valuable general information about the market in your area.

Researching the Field

Before you read this book, you probably assumed that all paralegals worked directly for lawyers. You now know this isn't true. However, most paralegals do work for law firms, so I'll start with how to find information on attorneys and law firms in your area or the area you are interested in moving to.

Law Firms

The *Martindale-Hubbell Law Directory* is a multivolume set that includes the names, addresses, and phone numbers of all lawyers and law firms in the U.S. This information is listed by attorney name, firm name, location, and specialty. The directory also lists lawyers employed by corporations and governments. If your placement office doesn't have a copy, check your nearest law library. You can also access Martindale-Hubbell on the Internet at http://www.martindale.com. West Publishing also maintains an Internet directory of attorneys, called *West's Legal Directory,* at http://www.wld.com. Another Internet directory is maintained by *Law Journal Extra!* at http://www.ljx.com.

Your state, county, or city bar association also compiles a directory of attorneys. In most cases, it will list the lawyers by name and by area of practice. And don't overlook something as obvious as the phone book. Many Yellow Pages have a section for "attorneys" or "lawyers" that includes lists by practice area as well as alphabetical lists. In addition, many of your professors probably are or were practicing attorneys, and they may know which firms in your area fit your picture of the ideal firm. There is a list of state bar associations in Appendix A of this book; to find a local bar, just look in the phone book under the name of the city or county "bar association."

Corporations

If you are considering work as a corporate paralegal, your placement office and public library should have a variety of directories to help you locate potential employers. If you are interested in a particular corporation, there are also directories like *Standard & Poor's Corporate Records* in which you can find the name of the company's chief legal officer and a wealth of other information about the company. Finally, for corporations, check general news indexes, such as the *Reader's Guide to Periodical Literature,* for articles about a corporation or industry in which you are particularly interested.

Nonprofit Organizations

There are a variety of regional directories of nonprofit organizations. One good national directory is Daniel Lauber's *Non-profits and Education Job Finder.* If you have been involved in a particular cause, as a paralegal or just as a citizen, ask around among the other volunteers and paid staff for ideas on locating organizations you might be interested in working for.

Government Agencies

Rules and regulations for finding and applying for federal government jobs are changing all the time. Your placement office should be on top of the changes when you begin job hunting, so check with them to verify the information that follows.

If you remember the days when, in order to get a federal civil service job, you had to get a rating and then get on the register and then wait for a call about an opening, you'll be happy to hear that times have changed. The whole process is much more decentralized, with most agencies doing their own hiring. In a majority of cases, the jobs are still "rated," but the rating is done by the personnel office of the individual agency, following guidelines administered throughout the government by the Office of Personnel Management. The point is, if you want to work for a particular department or agency of the federal government, you should start with that agency to find out if they have openings and to whom you should apply.

Many government agencies maintain a Web site that includes job openings. The Department of Justice, for example, is at http://www.doj.gov. Industry-specific periodicals, such as those listed later in this section, often list federal government job openings, as do national newspapers. If the federal job is in a local area, such as the local office of the Federal Bureau of Investigation, it may be listed in a local newspaper. In addition, each state has at least one Federal Employment Information Center. These centers post federal job openings in your area. Many of these centers are bare-bones, offering only a recording over the telephone or several job announcements posted on the wall, but they're a place to start. State Job Service offices usually list federal government openings, and generally you can call and talk to a live person.

Finally, Federal Reports, Inc., publishes a *Paralegal's Guide to U.S. Government Jobs.* Your placement office may have a copy of this book. If not, you can order it for $19.95 plus $2.50 shipping from Federal Reports, Inc., Suite 408, 1010 Vermont Ave. NW, Washington, DC 20005; the phone number is 202-393-3311.

If you are interested in working for state or local government, the state Job Service office is a good place to start as well. Your placement office also should be able to provide you with information about hiring procedures on the state level. In addition, most local (that is, city and county) governments post their openings in one or more central locations and advertise in local newspapers. Governments want to avoid the appearance of patronage—that is, giving someone a job in order to pay off a political favor. As a result, they usually advertise their openings pretty thoroughly.

Using Classified Ads

Conventional job hunting wisdom says you shouldn't depend too much on want ads for finding a job. While I wouldn't depend on them totally, there seem to be quite a few paralegal jobs advertised in the newspaper. For one thing, many law firms—especially smaller ones—see it as a relatively inexpensive way to fill positions. And even if you don't find a job through the classifieds, you can learn quite a lot about the market in your area. If you start paying attention to the ads well before you graduate, you'll be able to start a list of the places that hire paralegals. For example, a few months ago my hometown newspaper contained an ad from a local hospital for a paralegal. This was a market I had not considered before.

You can get other information from the classifieds, such as typical salaries and benefits in your area. One of the hardest questions to answer on an application or in an interview is "What is your desired salary?" If you've been watching the ads, you'll have an idea of the going rate. You can also get information about temporary and part-time jobs. In some areas, temporary and part-time jobs may be a common way for paralegals to begin their careers.

Online Resources

These days the World Wide Web is changing and growing so fast that it's dangerous to tell you about specific sites; they could be gone by the time you read this! But the major employment sites listed below look like they'll be around for a while. By the way, it's always worthwhile to start with your favorite search engine (such as Yahoo, Alta Vista, or Beatrice) to look for these and other employment sites.

Two good overview sites are The Law Engine, at http://www.fastsearch.com/law and Hieros Gamos, at http://www.hg.org/hg.html. Both contain links to all kinds of helpful legal information. Not only do they lead you to employment sites, but you also can follow the links to do legal research, find profiles of lawyers and firms, and even learn some new lawyer jokes.

Just as with classified advertisements, sometimes you will find job openings advertised on the Web that may be right for you, but there is also a wealth of information. Many Web sites contain legal and paralegal information; you should spend some time early in your student career visiting some of these areas. You can learn about salaries, job frustrations and pleasures, and various specialties that you may not have thought of, and you can even do some cyber-networking.

Networking

The play (made into a movie) *Six Degrees of Separation* is based on the premise that everyone in the world is separated by six degrees. That is, between any two people, there are only six other people separating them. (You may know a version of this called "Six Degrees of Kevin Bacon," in which the trick is to get from any actor to Kevin Bacon in less than six movies. For example, Winona Ryder to Kevin Bacon: Winona Ryder was in *Mermaids* with Cher, who was in *Silkwood* with Meryl Streep, who was in *The River Wild* with Kevin Bacon. That's an easy one.) The trick, of course, is to find the right six people. Although it may take you more than six people, it works the same way in networking. You want to get from you to an employer who is hiring by way of the people you know and the people they know.

While networking is about meeting people, it's also about much more than that. The point of networking is to use the relationships you have and new ones you make to help you find a job. A successful network continues to grow; it doesn't die once you get a job. As your network of acquaintances expands—one person leading you to the next and that person leading you to the next—eventually you will get to the person who is hiring.

Legal Employment Sites

Here is a list of legal employment sites that contain paralegal jobs. With a couple of exceptions, this index includes only legal employment sites. There are also a large number of general job sites on the Web; many of them probably include paralegal jobs. The following, though, are sites at which I've found paralegal jobs listed or that claim to list paralegal openings. Also, especially in the case of the nonprofit job lines, there may be situations where the job won't be listed as *paralegal* or *legal assistant* but will nonetheless be right for you.

America's Job Bank (The Public Employment Service) (http://www.ajb.dni.us)

CareerPath* (http://www.careerpath.com)

Emplawyernet (http://www.emplawyernet.com) (current charge is $9.95 per month)

Federal Job Announcements (http://www.fedworld.gov/jobs/jobsearch.html)

Law Journal Extra (http://www.ljx.com)

Law Match (lawmatch.com)

Legal Employ (http://www.legalemploy.com)

National Federation of Paralegal Associations

(http://www.paralegals.org/center/StateEmploy/home.html)

Nonprofit Job Resource Center (http://www.nonprofitcareer.com)

Public Service Jobs (includes some nonlawyer openings)

(http://www.umich.edu/academic/opsp/jobsalert)

The Seamless Website Legal Job Center (http://www.seamless.seamless.com:80/jobs)

*CareerPath lists ads from major newspapers, including the *Boston Globe, Chicago Tribune, Los Angeles Times, New York Times, San Jose Mercury News, Washington Post, Philadelphia Inquirer,* and *Southern Florida Sun-Sentinel.*

You should start your network with your family, friends, and classmates. The aim at this point is to get information. Chances are none of these people will be able to hire you, but they will know somebody, who knows somebody, who…. It's easier for most of us, especially when we are new networkers, to remember that the only favor we're asking for is information. You shouldn't expect Aunt Alice or the person who sits next to you in English composition class to hire you as a paralegal. But they just may know someone who can start you down the road that will end with a job.

In addition to family, friends, and classmates, be sure you remember your paralegal teachers as well. Many of them are or were practicing attorneys or paralegals, and they worked in law firms, corporations, the government, or nonprofit groups. They still know people there, and they may be able to lead you closer to your goal. Students sometimes feel a little intimidated by their professors and avoid getting to know them. This is a mistake; professors can be a wonderful job-hunting resource for you. It's unofficially part of their job to help students launch their careers, and they usually are enthusiastic about helping. But they are also quite busy, so you'll have to seek out their help. And, as mentioned earlier, make the placement officer part of your network early in your student career.

You can expand your circle of contacts by joining professional organizations while you're still a student. Both the National Association of Legal Assistants and the National Federation of Paralegal Associations have discounted student memberships; most professional organizations do. Be sure that you join both the national organization and the local chapter. Though the national organizations can give you valuable information, it's on the local level that you will be more effective at networking. Go to local meetings and ask questions—people almost always like to talk about their jobs—and volunteer for committees. I guarantee you that the members of the local paralegal group know about job openings before anyone else does.

Gayle Lund feels that as a group, paralegals are good at networking and supporting one another. "The ones I've known have networked quite a bit. In fact, they all keep lists of agencies at which you can get jobs, and they share them with each other. They call each other and tell each other about jobs, and they belong to the associations." She adds that many paralegals volunteer, "partly to learn and partly to network. If you're doing volunteer work, it looks good on your resume and you meet people. A lot of [paralegals] have gone on to get good jobs through the people they met" through volunteer work.

WRITING YOUR RESUME

Whether you are responding to an advertisement, following up on a networking opportunity, or making a cold contact, your resume usually is the first means by which a potential employer learns about you. Your resume is the advertisement you write to help sell yourself, and it helps to think of it that way. Think about ads you've seen in the newspaper or a magazine that made you want to go to a store and look at the item. Maybe you didn't end up buying it, but the ad made you consider it. That's what you want a resume to do for you.

A successful advertisement catches your attention by combining several elements: composition, clarity, content, and concentration. Falling short in any of these areas can cause a reader to pass over the ad; you want to make sure that a prospective employer will not be tempted to pass over *your* ad. There are many sources available to learn about writing resumes; my goal here is to address the specific issue of resumes for paralegals.

Even if you've written dozens of resumes in your day, it is probably worth your while to find a good resume-writing book or article to help you draft a resume for your new paralegal career. Your placement office may have a bank of former students' resumes that you can look at as well.

Once you have a rough draft, consider the four important elements of resume writing.

What Should A Resume Look Like?

If your resume doesn't look acceptable on a very basic level, it will probably get no more than a quick glance. You can find all kinds of advice about lengths of resumes, the kinds of paper they should be on, and what fonts you should use, as well as some suggestions for resumes that are real "eye catchers." When looking for a job in the legal field, keep in mind that it is a profession that is, in large part, defined by tradition and therefore fairly conservative. I certainly don't mean that in the political sense; nor do I mean to imply that you can't find a law firm where T-shirts are the preferred office attire. What I do mean is that much of what lawyers do every day has been done a million times before by other lawyers, and most lawyers take a certain comfort in tradition.

So I suggest you make conservative choices when it comes to your resume. Forgo the neon red paper; I'd even avoid parchment. Stick with something tried and true, such as white, cream or gray. Many larger law firms will want to scan your resume into their computer system to make it accessible to all the partners. Employment agencies will want to do this too. To help with the scanning process, send out originals of your resume, not photocopies. Light-colored, 8 1/2 x 11 paper, printed on one side only, will scan more easily. Try to avoid using tabs and any graphics or shadings. Don't use vertical or horizontal lines. Finally, don't staple the pages of your resume. If you stick to fairly conservative style, it should scan fine. There's more information on computers and resumes in the next section.

Don't use an off-the-wall font; would you want to read this whole page if it was printed like this?

Stick to more common computer fonts, such as Ariel, Courier, and Times New Roman. Ignore advice on how to make your resume stand out from all the rest. Especially avoid composing your resume so that it looks like a pamphlet or a pleading or a court decision. Like many other nontraditional tactics, it will send the message that you don't believe you can get an interview on your merits, so you've resorted to flashy advertising. Legal employers feel the same way about flashy resumes as the rest of us feel about that guy who comes on TV late at night screaming about stereos or used cars and causes us to dive for the remote's mute button.

Some resume advisers will tell you that you should never send out a resume that is more than one page long. I'm not convinced that is necessarily true. If, however, you have prior work experience and you draft a resume that is more than two pages, or you went straight from high school to paralegal training and you draft a resume that is more than one page, it probably means you are including irrelevant information or are being unnecessarily verbose. Read the rest of these suggestions and then try to cut it down. In the end, though, the content of your resume and how effectively you get it across to a prospective employer is what matters; if you need two or three pages to do that, use them.

Say It Clearly and Concisely

No matter how gorgeous your resume is, it won't do any good if a prospective employer finds it difficult to read. There is only one hard and fast rule of resume writing: Never send out a resume that contains mistakes. Proofread it several times and use your spell-check. For most people, writing a resume is an ongoing process, so remember to check it over every time you make a change. There is absolutely no excuse for sending out a resume with misspelled words or grammatical errors. After you proofread it, ask one or two friends to read it over too. If you are uncertain about a grammatical construction, for example, change it.

In addition to checking spelling and grammar, you want to make sure that your resume is well written. Resume writing is quite different from other kinds of writing, and it takes some practice. For one thing, most resumes don't use complete sentences. You'd rarely write, "As manager of the housewares department, I managed 14 employees and was in charge of ordering $2.5 million worth of merchandise annually." Instead you'd write, "Managed $2.5 million housewares department with 14 employees." Still, all the other rules of grammar apply to writing a resume. Tenses and numbers need to match, and double negatives and other awkward constructions are not acceptable. It is also important to be concise when writing a resume. It creates the impression that you are an efficient person.

The ability to communicate well is vital in the law field, and it is a skill that legal employers value highly. If they read something on your resume that causes them to say "Huh?" you won't look good. In addition to effective communication, paralegals need to demonstrate their talents in organization and analysis. These three skills can easily be reflected in your resume.

You demonstrate your communication abilities not only by making sure everything is spelled correctly and is grammatically accurate, but also by how well you write your resume. Word choice contributes to the clarity and persuasiveness of your resume. Experts have long recommended using verbs (action words) rather than nouns to promote yourself in a resume. For one thing, "*managed* $2.5 million housewares department with 14 employees" sounds more compelling than "manager of housewares department."

Using Keywords for Scannable Resumes

More and more job applicants are posting their resumes on the Internet, and many large firms are scanning resumes into their computer system, which allows people to call your resume up on their computers. Once your resume is on the Internet or in a computer system, potential employers will access it by searching for keywords. Keywords are simply words or phrases that indicate areas of expertise within an industry, in this case, the legal profession. They tend to be nouns, not verbs.

There is no way to know all of the possible keywords an employer might look for. If you are posting your resume on the Internet, look for the categories that Web site uses and make sure you use them too. Start with the obvious; make sure the word "paralegal" appears somewhere on your resume. I know that sounds silly, but it is possible to write an entire resume without it. Then make sure you use the accepted professional jargon. Don't, for example, write that you are interested in doing trial work. Someone scanning your resume will probably look for the word "litigation," so make sure that's the word you use.

For scanned resumes, "manager" is a better bet than "managed." And you can almost be sure that words like "initiated," "inspired," and "directed" won't be keywords. The good news is that as long as the system is working correctly, you only have to use a keyword once. So as long as you get "litigation paralegal" (or whatever) in there once, you can go on and talk about the things you initiated and directed. Also remember that keywords are often connected by "and" rather than "or." If an employer is looking for a person interested in being a litigation parale-gal in a criminal law firm, your resume won't come up if it only contains "litigation paralegal" and not "criminal." It can be helpful to look at some of the resumes posted on the Internet; think about the keywords you use to search for them. The successful hits you get will indicate the words you should be using.

What Goes In a Resume?

When you are just starting out, it is tempting to try to put everything you can think of in your resume to try to make it look more substantial. Don't. Stick to what's important and pertinent. Surrounding the important stuff with a lot of white space will make it stand out more, and that's good—it's a basic principle of advertising.

Don't include hobbies or interests. Quite frankly, a potential employer doesn't care whether you enjoy constructing card houses and practicing bird calls. Under no circumstances should you include personal information such as age, gender, religion, health or marital status, or number of children. For one thing, it's illegal for employers to ask about those things, and it's illegal for a reason: it has nothing to do with how well a person can do a job. The only personal information that belongs on your resume is your name, address, phone number, and fax number and email address if you have them. And by the way, your name should be on every page you send somebody, in case the pages get separated.

People often overlook or discount volunteer work when composing their resumes. Don't! For one thing, you gain skills and experience from these jobs just as you do from jobs you are paid for. Volunteering also indicates that you work well with others and that you are committed to your community. (Keep this in mind as you go through your paralegal training; if you are short on experience, you might think about volunteering.) Also make sure your resume includes any memberships and activities in professional organizations; they help demonstrate your commitment to the profession.

Another way to make yourself look more experienced is by including your internship. Some new graduates overlook this, considering it "just part of school." But for most newly graduated paralegals, it is their only legal experience and perhaps their only work experience. The point of an internship is to give you on-the-job training. You learned things on that internship that will help you on a new job; be sure to include them.

Make sure you don't overlook any previous experience. Applicants who are changing careers sometimes think the things they did in their previous work life don't apply to being a paralegal, but that's just not true. Any job you held taught you something that will make you a better legal assistant. At the very least it taught you the responsibility of showing up for work regularly and on time. No doubt you also learned about working with others and organizing your time. Beyond that, many jobs provide you with experience that will be highly valued by legal employers. Careers such as medicine, accounting, real estate, human resources, and insurance, as well as many others, will be considered hiring plusses by potential employers.

In addition to work experience, you may have life experience that should be emphasized for legal employers. Did you help a spouse in a business? Were you a candidate for public office? Any number of experiences can add to your attractiveness as a paralegal candidate. Especially if you don't have a great deal of work experience, be creative with other things you've done in your life. "Be creative" doesn't mean "lie." Just sit down and think about the things you've done; which have taught you lessons that are valuable for a paralegal to know? Find a way to include those experiences on your resume or in your cover letter.

How to Tailor Your Resume

Each time you send out a resume, whether in response to an ad, following up a networking lead, or even a cold contact, you should concentrate on tailoring your approach for the employer you are contacting. Earlier I said you should spend some time pursuing your dream job; well, it may be that you have a couple of dream jobs, and no doubt you will also be watching out for the close-to-dream-job opening. Let's say you're interested in being a civil litigation paralegal, but you're particularly interested in insurance litigation, because every summer in high school you worked in your mom's insurance office and you really enjoyed it. You'd probably also be willing to take a position in the human resources office of an insurance company or anywhere in a large firm that does insurance work, just to get your foot in the door. Insurance litigation is your dream job; the others are your close-to-dream jobs. And if enough time passes, you'll be happy to take any litigation position in any kind of office. Right there, you need at least four resumes.

The resume for the insurance litigation job stresses the work you did in your mom's office, the litigation skills you learned at your internship, and how well you did in civil procedure in paralegal school. Although it depends on what format you are using, you may very well stress them in that order. For a litigation position in a large firm that handles insurance, you'd probably stress your internship and education—but make sure your insurance experience stands out too. For the human resources job, you'd emphasize your insurance experience and any employment law classes or experience. Finally, for the basic entry-level job, you'd want to construct your resume to show that you are a generalist.

Most books that tell you how to write a resume include advice about the information you should gather before you start. If you keep all of that information at hand, it won't be that difficult to construct a resume that targets a particular job—that concentrates your information so that a prospective employer will see that you are a likely candidate for this opening. In many cases, a few changes to a basic resume are enough to make it appropriate for a particular job opening. One good way to approach tailoring your resume for a particular opening is to sit for a minute and imagine what you think the job would be like. Imagine, based on the description of the job, the major things you will be expected to do day to day. Then look at your experience and education and decide how to present your information so that the employer will know that you are capable of doing those tasks.

Finally, make sure you get your resume to the appropriate person in the appropriate way. If you got the person's name through a networking contact, your contact may deliver it or suggest that you deliver it in person; most likely, though, you should mail it. If you are making a cold contact—that is, if you are contacting a firm that you found through your research but that is not actively looking to fill a position—make sure you find out the name of the hiring partner or head of the paralegal department and send your resume to that person. If you are responding to an ad, make sure you do what the ad says. If it directs you to fax your resume, fax it. If it indicates you should send a writing sample, make sure you include one. (If you are using a sample you wrote on a job or internship, you must black out all names and any other identifying information.) Demonstrate your ability to attend to detail.

Following are two sample resumes. The first is for an applicant who wants to highlight both previous experience as a tax preparer and educational background. The second is for an applicant who has more education than experience.

PAT PARALEGAL
1234 Broadway
Mytown, ST 00000
Phone and fax: 007-555-5678
Email: pat89@online.com

OBJECTIVE: To work as a paralegal in a position that allows me to utilize and enhance my specialized computer skills and tax preparation experience.

EXPERIENCE
September–December 1996
Paralegal Intern, Zelda County Attorney's Office, 180 West Bubba Street, Mytown, ST 00000; 007-555-3456
>   ***DUTIES***
>   Answered multiline telephones
>   Greeted the public
>   Assisted with scheduling meetings, events, and appointments
>   Assisted with filing of pleadings
>   Performed legal research on CD-ROM, online, and in the library
>   Wrote legal memoranda
>   Shepardized cases
>   Filed documents

January 1992–April 1995
Tax Consultant, H & R BLOCK, 1440 Ivy Road, Mytown, ST 00000; 007-555-1040
>   ***DUTIES***
>   Interviewed clients
>   Prepared individual income tax returns, including out-of-state returns
>   Researched and applied IRS rules and regulations

January 1991–Present
Volunteer, Dogs and Cats Shelter, RR 1, Mytown, ST 00000, 007-555-9876
>   ***DUTIES***
>   Interview adopters
>   Write column for newsletter

EDUCATION
Associate of Art, Paralegal Studies, May 1997
Paralegal College, 7890 Troubadour Street, Mytown, ST 00000

Associates of Science, Computer Technology, December 1995
Community College, Eli Hills Campus, Mytown, ST 00000

SKILLS
Fluent in Spanish

PAT PARALEGAL
1234 Broadway ◆ Mytown, ST 00000
Phone and fax: 007-555-5678 ◆ Email: pat89@online.com

OBJECTIVE: Entry-level paralegal position that allows me to utilize and enhance my specialized computer skills and paralegal education.

EDUCATION
Associate of Art, Paralegal Studies, May 1997, Paralegal College, 7890 Troubadour Street, Mytown, ST 00000
Associate of Science, Computer Technology, December 1995, Community College, Eli Hills Campus, Mytown, ST 00000

RELEVANT COURSES

PARALEGAL	COMPUTER TECHNOLOGY
Legal Research and Writing	Lotus 123r4
Business Law	QBASIC
Litigation	DBASE IV
Family Law	WordPerfect
Criminal Law	QUICKBOOKS QUICKPAY

EXPERIENCE
September–December 1996 Paralegal Intern, Zelda County Attorney's Office, 180 West Bubba Street, Mytown, ST 00000, 007-555-3456
   DUTIES
   Answered multiline telephones
   Greeted the public
   Assisted with scheduling meetings, events, and appointments
   Assisted with filing of pleadings
   Performed legal research on CD-ROM, online, and in the library
   Wrote legal memorandum
   Shepardized cases
   Filed documents
   Updated Web site

September 1994–August 1995 Sales Associate, The Store, 345 Route 66, Mytown, ST 00000, 007-555-6543
   DUTIES
   Operated cash register
   Stocked shelves
   Assisted customers

January 1993–present Volunteer, Dogs and Cats Shelter, RR 1, Mytown, ST 00000, 007-555-9876
   DUTIES
   Interview adopters
   Write column for newsletter
   Bathe dogs

SKILLS: Fluent in Spanish

WRITING A COVER LETTER

You should never send out a resume without a cover letter. The cover letter aims your resume directly at the available job; your resume, in turn, describes in detail why you are the person for the job. If your cover letter is a failure, your resume will get only a cursory glance at best. Your cover letter should give the impression that you are a good candidate for the job.

Most people seem to feel that writing cover letters is a real pain. You should view it, however, as another opportunity to demonstrate your writing skills, as well as your ability to organize and analyze. Although you tailor your resume to some degree for different job openings, employers expect that you will send the same resume to several potential employers. The cover letter, on the other hand, should be personalized and directed to the particular job opening.

How to Format Your Cover Letter

Your cover letter needs to grab the attention of the reader, but not because it's so bizarre that it will be posted on the office bulletin board for everyone to laugh at. As with your resume, avoid fancy fonts and stationery; choose something that matches or coordinates with your resume. Your cover letter should always be typed (printed) on good paper, and I recommend using letterhead with your name, address, phone and fax numbers, and email address. You don't have to spend a lot of money to have letterhead stationery printed; you can make it on your computer.

A cover letter should be composed in the same way as a business letter. It should include your address (preferably in the letterhead), the date, the name and address of the person the letter is to be sent to, and a salutation. At the end of the body of the letter, you should include a closing (such as "Sincerely"), your signature, and your name typed out below. Other formatting choices are up to you—for example, whether you prefer block paragraphs or indented paragraphs and whether you write "enc." at the bottom, indicating there is material (your resume) enclosed with the letter.

Rarely do you need a cover letter that is more than one page. On occasion, an advertisement for a job will ask for a resume and a detailed statement of interest (or words to that effect). Sometimes ads will even ask you to address specific questions or issues in your letter, such as your goals, what you can contribute to the organization, et cetera. In such cases, you may need to write a letter that is more than one page. Normally, however, your letter should be contained on one page.

Write Clearly and Concisely

You should never send out a cover letter with a grammatical or spelling error. Even when you are pressed for time and rushing to get a letter out, make sure to spell-check it and proofread it carefully. If writing letters doesn't come naturally to you—and writing cover letters doesn't come naturally to most of us—have someone read it over. It should be accurate, clear, and concise. It serves as a letter of introduction, an extension of your advertisement. Your cover letter needs to convince a prospective employer that *you* are one of the people who should be interviewed for this position.

Your cover letter should begin with some sort of introduction, followed by an explanation of why you are right for this job and a closing paragraph. As with your resume, it is vital that your cover letter be well written; however, it requires a different writing style. Sentence fragments don't work in a cover letter. In addition, a resume offers a somewhat formal presentation of your background, but a cover letter should let a bit of your personality come through. It should be written in an almost conversational tone. It shouldn't be quite as informal as the tone of this book—for example, I don't suggest using contractions in a cover letter—but you should view it as your first chance to "chat" with a prospective employer. The resume tells employers what you know and what you can do; the cover letter should tell them a little bit about who you are.

What to Include In Your Cover Letter

Much more than a resume, a cover letter is targeted to a particular job. The concentration on a particular job opening is the major component of a cover letter. A cover letter should never read like a form letter; the best way to avoid that is by writing a new letter for every job you apply for. A cover letter does more than just repeat the information in your resume. It tells the prospective employer why you are the one for a particular job.

In the first paragraph, you should indicate why you are writing this letter at this time. You may write something like

- "I would like to apply for the litigation paralegal position advertised in the *Sunday Post*."
- "I am writing in response to your ad in the *Sunday Times*."
- "I am interested in obtaining an entry-level paralegal position with your firm."

- "If you are looking for a legal assistant with insurance experience and top-notch paralegal training, you will be interested in talking to me."
- "We met last July at the NALA Convention. I will be graduating from my paralegal program in May."

The first paragraph also usually indicates that your resume is enclosed for consideration, although this may also be in the closing paragraph.

In the body of the cover letter, you want to explain why your training and experience make you the right person for the job. The cover letter provides you with the opportunity to include something that is not on your resume. For example, life experience can be difficult to incorporate into a resume, but it is much easier to talk about in a letter. Also, the body of the letter should highlight and summarize the information in your resume. You have to assume that the employer is going to read your resume, so don't just repeat things. For example, instead of writing, "Before paralegal school, I worked at The Store for two years, and before that at The Shop for three years," try something like, "I have five years of retail experience in which I interacted with the public on a daily basis." The body of the letter is your opportunity to explain why the employer should care about your experience and training.

In the body of the letter, you can also include information about how soon you are available for employment or why (if it's the case) you are applying for a job out of town. You may also include specifics that you are looking for in a job—if they are either nonnegotiable or flattering to the employer. You should definitely make some direct reference to the specific position and organization. Here are some examples:

- "I will graduate on May 16 and will be available for employment immediately. A position with your firm appeals to me because I understand you do a great deal of plaintiff employment work, and this is a field I am very interested in. Employment law was one of the electives I chose as a student. In addition, at this time I am looking for part-time employment and I believe you currently have a part-time opening."
- "Although my internship was with the County Attorney's Office, I have come to realize that while that work was intensely interesting, I would prefer a position in the private sector that will afford me the opportunity to call on my real estate experience and my paralegal training. I believe your firm is the place for me and I am certain I would be an asset to you."

- "As you look at my resume, you will notice that although I am just now finishing my paralegal training, I offer a background in administration and problem solving. Since your company has recently undergone a major expansion, I believe you would find me a valuable addition to your staff."

Finally, the last paragraph (some people prefer it to be two short paragraphs) should thank the person, make a reference to future contact, and offer to provide further information.

- "Thank you for your consideration. Please contact me at the address or phone number above if you need any further information."
- "I look forward to meeting you to discuss this job opening."
- "Thank you and I look forward to speaking with you in person."
- "I would welcome the opportunity to discuss the match between my skills and your needs in more detail. You can contact me at the address or phone number above, except for the week of the 27th, when I will be out of town. Thank you for your time."

A cover letter provides the opportunity for you to sell yourself for a particular job, and it should be tailored that way. The letter should indicate some knowledge about what makes this job better than all the other jobs and what makes you a better candidate than all the other candidates.

SURVIVING YOUR INTERVIEW

When I'm job hunting, I send out carefully worded resumes and cover letters. But some of the time—okay, as is true of most job hunters, most of the time—I either get a polite brush-off or no response at all. After a while, I get really whiny. "It's not fair," I whimper. "They should at least *talk* to me!" Then, miracle of miracles, someone wants to interview me, and I immediately revive my dream of fleeing the country to aid rebels trying to overthrow the corrupt government of some small nation.

More than anything, we want to get an interview. When we get one, though, we'd rather do almost anything else—go to the dentist, give the cat a bath, clean the oven, *anything*. I can't promise to make your next interview painless, but you can get through it and come out a winner.

Preparing for Your Interview

When you study the law, you hear judges and lawyers talk about a "level playing field." As you know, this means that two parties are equal in contract negotiations or applying for a job or whatever. Generally, in the law, we think a level playing field is a good thing, although it can be tough to achieve. If you prepare for your interview adequately, you'll go a long way toward leveling the field between you and the big bad interviewer. As with writing resumes and cover letters, there are many fine sources of information about job interviews; I will go over some things that are specific to paralegal job hunting, especially when you're after your first job in the field.

Most interviewers will ask, "Why do you want to come to work here?" Sometimes the true answer to that question is, "I don't necessarily want to work here; I'd be just as happy down the street, but you've got the opening." This is not a good answer. I'm ashamed to admit the number of times I've been surprised by that question in an interview. Every time you get an interview, you should prepare an answer to it.

If you managed to get an interview without researching the firm ahead of time, do so now. (If, as you should have, you researched the firm before you applied, make sure you saved everything so you can use it now.) Keep researching until you find something that makes you excited about working there. I know sometimes that can be difficult, but there will be something. Don't forget to keep an eye on the newspapers; if you read about an interesting local case and they mention an attorney, find out where that lawyer works; someday that may provide you with a reason you want to work at this firm.

Even if you're not asked why you want to work at a firm, find an opportunity to let your interviewer know you've done your research. Is it a fairly new firm or has it been around forever? Is it the largest or one of the smallest firms in town? Did it just win (or lose) a big case?

Of course, before your interview you'll check the exact address and find out how to get there and where to park. You'll try on your interview outfit and make sure it's comfortable for both walking and sitting. The night before, make sure you'll be armed with everything you need by reviewing the following list.

- Bring your resume (a few copies) and a list of references. I suggest carrying them in a decent, but not expensive, briefcase. Remember, it's called a briefcase because it's for carrying briefs; it's a legal thing.

- Make sure you have a decent-looking pen that works and a legal pad, in case you want to take notes.
- Also, I would suggest having a writing sample with you, even if no one has mentioned it specifically.
- You should also have copies of your transcripts in your briefcase.
- Bring an extra pair of pantyhose; men, of course, may prefer to have an extra tie.
- I also bring a handkerchief, although, I am proud to say, I've never begun sobbing until the interview was officially over.

Answering Tough Questions

My law school friend Ann Tomkins gave me some great advice as I finished law school and began job hunting. Ann spent several years in—as she calls it—corporate America before she went to law school. She told me the two important things to keep in mind while job hunting. One is that even if you apply and interview for a job, you don't have to take it; and the other is that good interviewers will be trying to sell *you* on coming to work for *them*.

I found these two ideas very calming. Understanding that you aren't required to take a job just because it's offered makes the interview seem less like a life-or-death situation and more like an opportunity to get to know at least one person at this firm. There are other jobs out there, and although job hunting isn't much fun, you *will* find a job. Realizing that interviewers should be trying to sell you on coming to work for them is helpful too. Although conducting job interviews is a skill that some people never master, good interviewers want to find a good person to fill the job opening. They already think you're a possibility; even though they may end up hiring someone else, during the interview they should be convincing you that you would be very happy working there.

Neither of these points takes away from the fact that you have to sell yourself. But in preparing for the interview, keep in mind that you have certain requirements of your own and that you are meeting these potential employers to find out if the two of you are a match.

The world won't end if you stumble or don't know how to answer a question or forget your phone number, but that doesn't mean you shouldn't prepare. At a minimum, get out your resume and look at it and think about what you would want to know about this person. For example, you may be asked why you want to be a paralegal. You'll probably be asked which areas of the law you like best and least. And once you answer, you may be asked, "Why?" If you are changing careers, you may be asked why you're changing and what you liked and didn't like about your former career. Spend some time thinking about and practicing ways to answer these questions.

As you look at your resume, note any "unusual" aspects that might elicit questions. For example, I once worked as a cab driver; as long as that was on my resume, I *always* got asked about it. I was relieved when this experience was more than ten years old and I could leave it off and start talking about other things. If you have a gap in your work history, be prepared to explain why. Be prepared to talk about the kinds of legal computer software you are familiar with, as well as the kinds of work you've done in an internship or a previous job.

If you are not fresh out of paralegal school but are leaving one position for another, you will no doubt be asked why. You will probably be asked about your billable hours at your previous paralegal job, and you may be expected to discuss what went well or poorly at that job, how you handled difficult clients or attorneys, and what you hope will be different about your new job.

The toughest of the tough questions that you will have to deal with are the illegal ones—and, yes, attorneys sometimes ask them. A potential employer is not allowed to ask you about your marital status, whether you have kids or plan to, your age, your religion, or your race (these kinds of questions *may* be asked on anonymous affirmative action forms). Nor can an interviewer employ sneaky techniques to find out. (Such as, "I bet your husband and kids are really proud of you!") If someone does ask you such a question, you can say, "It's illegal for you to ask me that" and then sit silently until the interviewer says something. Or try to get a handle on why they are asking, and address that. So the answer to "Do you have children?" becomes "If you're asking if I can travel and work overtime, that's generally not a problem." Or you can say something like, "I don't understand the question; what is it you want to know?"

Remember that illegal questions aren't always obvious. Most interviewers know enough not to say, "How old are you, anyway?" But they might say, "Will it bother you if your supervisor is younger than you?" If you encounter this kind of situation, think long and hard before you accept a position with this firm. Also, if you were referred to this interview through an employment agency or your school's placement office, notify that source that you believe you were asked illegal questions.

Asking Questions

When we think about the kinds of questions an interviewee should ask in an interview, we often concentrate on what kinds of questions we think we are expected to ask. But the main goal is to ask the things you really want to know. One exception is that you should probably save questions about salary and benefits for a second interview; a first interview is an opportunity to learn more about the firm.

Beyond that, ask about almost anything. You may want to know about the kinds of assignments you can expect, whether you will be able to follow cases from start to finish, whether you'll have the opportunity to specialize, who manages paralegals and determines their assignments. These are all legitimate questions. You may also have questions about the resources of the firm, such as the computers and library. The number of billable hours you will be expected to produce is certainly something you will want to know.

If the firm is large, you can ask about its structure. For example, is there a paralegal department or are paralegals assigned to attorneys? Do paralegals have secretarial support? Is there a paralegal training program in place? If the firm is small, you may ask how long it has employed paralegals, whether it plans to hire more in the future, and whether paralegals are expected to do significant clerical work. In any size firm, you can ask about chances for promotion.

Once when I was being interviewed by a committee, I asked one of the committee members (who would be a colleague if I got the job) what he liked about working there and what he didn't like. I think he found it an intriguing question; it also gave me a break, because he had to stop and think about the answer and it reminded me that they didn't hold *all* the cards. If there is no paralegal sitting in your interview, ask what a typical day for a paralegal at this firm is like. Imagine you have been offered this job and another. Think about what you would like to know about this job that would help you decide which one to take.

By the way, you don't need to wait to be asked, "Do you have any questions?" It is perfectly appropriate to ask them when they fit into the interview. For example, if the interviewer tells you that each paralegal and attorney has a computer, it's a good time to ask what software they use and whether the firm subscribes to an online service.

Follow-Up Procedures

You should follow up your interview with a letter. There is some disagreement about the form this letter should take. When I was in law school, we were told that we should send handwritten thank-you letters to everyone we met in an interview. That's the tradition many of the lawyers who interview you will be used to. On the other hand, a typed (printed) letter on letterhead looks more professional. If your handwriting is not easily decipherable, you should definitely type your thank-you letters. Other than that, check with your placement office and fellow paralegal job hunters to determine the tradition in your area. Generally speaking, I like to use a handwritten note when I have interviewed with only one or two people and it was fairly informal—if we went to lunch, for example. Otherwise, I prefer the professionalism of a typed letter. You should do what is commonly accepted in your area and makes you feel most comfortable. Note that there may be times when you have no choice but to handwrite a letter; if you are out of town or at a professional conference, for example.

Whatever your letter looks like, it should include a warm thank you for the interviewer's time and should reiterate your enthusiasm for the job. You should also say something specific to your interview to give it a personal touch. Thank-you letters are generally quite short. Here are a few examples.

- ♦ "I enjoyed meeting with you yesterday to discuss the paralegal position at Barrister, Counselor, and Solicitor. In addition to providing a good deal of information, you made me very enthusiastic about the position. I was very pleased to have the opportunity to meet Mr. Law; I can see that he will be difficult to replace. I am gratified to be considered for the position."
- ♦ "Thank you so much for the time you spent with me yesterday. I really appreciated the tour of the office and the information you shared about the paralegal position. By the way, I double-checked when I got home, and the case I was trying to think of was *Marbury v. Madison*."
- ♦ "The legal assistant position we discussed yesterday certainly sounds like a challenging one. After reviewing the information you gave me about your needs for this job, I am convinced that I am the right person for the position. Thank you for the time and consideration you gave me. I look forward to hearing from you again soon."

Basically, a follow-up letter serves to remind employers who you are and make you stand out from the crowd, to clarify (but only if necessary) anything that you were unable to make clear in the interview, and to let employers know that you really want this job.

As you begin your job hunt, keep in mind that you are not just looking for a job; you're looking for a good job, one you will enjoy and feel challenged by. At each stage of the hunt—researching the market, sending out resumes and cover letters, having interviews, and accepting or rejecting offers—keep in mind the principles of job hunting. You need to decide who you are going to contact, you have to advertise yourself, and you have to sell yourself. Remember that each of these involves particular activities and particular ways of thinking about yourself and what you want, as well as marketing yourself to appeal to employers. Once you've finished paralegal school and an internship, you have a lot to offer to any legal employer. Keep that in mind throughout the process: You're not begging for a job; you're trying to find an employer who will be a match for your skills and talents.

Who:	Kayne Larimer, CLA
What:	Paralegal
Where:	Palmer Law Firm, Sioux Falls, South Dakota
How long:	Three and one-half years
Degree:	Bachelor's degree in business, paralegal certificate

Insider's Advice

[You should do] anything you can to distinguish yourself from other applicants. I do think a post-baccalaureate or bachelor's degree program is looked at a little bit higher than the associate degree programs. I guess a bachelor's degree plus the paralegal studies or including the paralegal program does seem to help more. What I got out of the college degree that would come across here would be communication, writing skills, and certainly a degree of problem solving and analysis. That's helped.

To be honest, I think in some respects, being a male versus a female can make it just a little bit easier, in some offices. I know there's not as many in the [paralegal] industry, but I think in the legal field there's still a male bias; in some parts of the country it's changing, but in other areas it may not be. I think that I'm treated by other attorneys in a different way than they would treat a female paralegal. At least that's been my experience, I don't know how far that goes. It doesn't have so much to do with actually getting the job, but I know some female paralegals that have basically been put in a secretary position. They see me come in and watch me type an awesome forty words per minute, they know I'm not going to be a secretary.

Insider's Take on the Future

In January of 1995 I took and passed the CLA [Certified Legal Assistant] exam. What I found out is different chapters of the state legal assistants groups are chartered under either the NALA [National Association of Legal Assistants] or the NFPA [National Federation of Paralegal Associations]. South Dakota is under the

NALA; they're the ones who started the CLA and really push that. So what's interesting in South Dakota, even though there's probably five percent of the paralegals there are in Minnesota, is the CLA does help here, whereas in Minnesota there's just a handful of people that actually have that. So, that's one thing I did as soon as I got here and realized that there were a few in this state that were doing that; in a case like that, it would help to get your CLA.

Being able to focus in one area, I think that's going to become more important. I think a strong computer background, which I'm still trying to learn, is going to be helpful. South Dakota's a small enough state—I think the largest firm in the state has about twenty-five attorneys—so there's not a large base of attorneys, and there's not a lot of paralegals or legal assistants in the state. I think it will be the groups of three or four attorneys, not the solo practitioners, hiring a paralegal—that's what I've seen across the state.

CHAPTER | 6

The key to success in any new endeavor is understanding what the people around you expect of you, what you can expect of them, and how those expectations can be made to work together so that you will not only succeed but be comfortable and maybe even enjoy yourself as well. In this chapter you'll find tips on fitting into the legal work environment as well as resources from which you can get general information about fitting into your working environment and dealing with difficult people.

HOW TO SUCCEED ONCE YOU'VE LANDED THE JOB

The first thing you need to know is that the law as a profession in the U.S. has undergone tremendous change in the last half of this century. The civil rights movement, which began in the 1960s, and the women's movement, which began in the 1970s, caused societal upheavals that affected the legal community. Within the legal profession, two developments in the 1970s led to great changes as well: the plain-language movement and the poverty law movement, which led to the establishment of the Legal Services Corporation.

Prior to these changes, the law was often a profession for well-off young men who needed a career but didn't want to be bankers. Not surprisingly, most of their clients were well-off, too. Some of them used legal training as a springboard into politics, and there have certainly been various crusading lawyers throughout history. But before these new developments, the majority of people went through their whole lives without consulting an attorney, except, perhaps, to write a will.

The various social movements of the last half of the twentieth century opened the legal profession to women, people of color, and poor people and resulted in a lot of changes in the legal culture. However, the law as a profession was deeply infused with tradition and, to some extent, these new people applied these traditions to themselves. So there have been some major changes and some mere adaptations.

The plain-language movement and Legal Services have had a greater and, I believe, more lasting impact. The plain-language movement suggested that the written product of lawyers did not have to be full of "heretofore" and "party of the first part" and other overblown language whose only purpose was to obfuscate the plain meaning of a document and make people feel that they had to have lawyers to handle even routine matters. The purpose of the plain-language movement was to get lawyers to begin writing documents in plain language that any average person can understand.

Legal Services Corporation is a nonprofit corporation established by Congress in 1974 to address the needs of poor people who did not have access to legal advice when they needed it, thus leaving themselves vulnerable to those who could afford a lawyer. Legal Services deals with big discrimination cases but also represents tenants and spouses who would otherwise be unrepresented in legal proceedings. The paralegal profession grew directly out of Legal Services (and other privately funded poverty law organizations). To provide more people with legal services for less money, paralegals began doing some of the tasks that lawyers had done in the past.

Fitting Into the Workplace Culture

Two results of all these changes have direct impact on paralegals and the way they fit into various legal cultures. People who have entered the legal profession in the last several decades have introduced new ways of doing things. Many of the old traditions have remained but have been adapted. For example, it would be difficult for a law firm today to state that "all partners and associates must wear ties," because many partners and associates are now women. However, in most law firms, both men and women dress conservatively. Until you find out otherwise, you should dress and behave on your new job in accordance with the idea that you are working in an old, established profession.

Of course, if you go to work for the legal services/environmental law/nonprofit crowd, you will find a much less conservative, much more casual work culture. In offices like these, except on days when you go to court, jeans and T-shirts may be appropriate attire. Somewhere between the old established firms and the politically active organizations are the small firms and solo practitioners, where style is determined much more by the individuals in the firm than anything else. The safest thing is to take your cue from those around you. You may not meet any other paralegals in the interview and hiring process, but if you do, dress according to their style for your first couple of days. If you're uncertain at first, wear businesslike attire. Once you've worked in a place for a while, you'll know what's acceptable.

Fitting into the workplace culture is about a lot more than what you wear, however. Law firms have very well established traditions, and it will be to your benefit to figure them out. There may, for example, be unspoken rules about who works for whom and when you drop everything to do a particular partner's bidding. In particularly traditional firms, you may be expected to call the attorneys Mr. or Ms. Or maybe that's only required for the partners, not the associates. In a legal services office, the attorneys are probably known by their first names.

There are two ways to ensure that you will fit into your workplace culture. Realize that there *is* a culture and that you may not know what it is. Then keep your eyes open and act the way other people act. If no one brings a sack lunch and eats it in the law library, don't immediately take it upon yourself to start a new trend. The other way to learn the ropes is to get yourself a mentor as soon as possible. See the section entitled Finding a Mentor.

Power in Numbers

In addition to the changes to the profession that resulted from the influx of new attorneys, the poverty law movement and the plain-language movement led directly to a greater number of paralegals. These movements empowered legal consumers so that they realized they didn't always need to hire an attorney to accomplish a legal objective. With some information, people who have not been to law school can write divorce decrees, articles of incorporation, and bankruptcy petitions. However, most people still feel unsure about doing these things on their own, and paralegals fill the gap. Either within a legal organization or on their own, paralegals can assist their clients with many of the rudimentary legal activities. What they cannot do—as you know by now—is practice law. Once legal decisions are made, however, they can take over most aspects of a case. They also can tell you when you do need to consult an attorney.

An unfortunate result of this growth of the paralegal profession is that some attorneys are suspicious of paralegals. The number is shrinking all the time; nonetheless, the tension still exists. The concern among attorneys is that paralegals can easily slip over the line and begin practicing law. As you go through your paralegal studies, you'll see that this can be a difficult line to draw. Especially as you become a more experienced paralegal, you'll be tempted to answer when your client says, "Do you think I should do X or Y?" But legally, you can't answer those questions.

Lawyers aren't just worried about losing business to paralegals—although, frankly, I think that was a large part of it in the beginning—they're worried that people will receive bad legal advice. Over the years, though, paralegals have conducted themselves in such a professional manner and have been so conscientious about understanding their role that lawyers are, for the most part, now welcoming paralegals into the legal culture.

But as a result of this tradition of tension, you may encounter (particularly in a large organization) an attorney who, at best, doesn't understand what paralegals do, or, at worst, is openly hostile to paralegals. The ones who don't understand may just need to be gently reminded that you are not a legal secretary—that other, very competent and talented people in the firm do *that* job. The hostile ones, obviously, are more difficult. I'll talk about this in more depth in the next section.

In the end, you will fit in on your first paralegal job the same way you have any time you went to a new school or did something for the first time. You'll watch people around you and behave as they do, and when you can't figure something out, you'll ask somebody. And you will find that lawyers aren't necessarily scary.

MANAGING WORK RELATIONSHIPS
Lawyers

Most of us spend more waking hours with the people we work with than with our families and friends. It's to everyone's advantage to find ways to get along. One of the most difficult people to work with is the attorney who doesn't believe paralegals should exist. Fortunately, the number of lawyers who feel that way is shrinking, if for no other reason than that paralegals have been around for quite a while and most attorneys have worked with at least one paralegal and had a positive experience. If you do run into an anti-paralegal lawyer, the best way to handle the relationship is to do your job very well. It is also imperative that you never, ever, do anything that this individual can interpret as practicing law.

Lawyers are often accused of being a little overloaded on ego. You may be able to exploit that. If you have to deal with an anti-paralegal lawyer, maybe you can make that person your expert on helping you understand and define the practice of law. In the process, that attorney may learn that many of the things a lawyer does are not, strictly, the practice of law, and that a paralegal can take them over with no harm done. Then again, the lawyer may be one of those people who doesn't like change and will never get used to working with paralegals. The good news is you will probably only find this person in a large organization; a single anti-paralegal attorney in a small firm would probably have enough power to keep paralegals from being hired at all.

Sexual Harassment

In the last chapter, in the section on interviewing, I noted that sometimes attorneys break the law (remember Watergate?). It's worth noting again, but this time I'm referring to sexual harassment. The courts generally define sexual harassment based on the way the recipient feels about the behavior. If something is making you uncomfortable, it is probably inappropriate and you should report it. Most firms have a policy about sexual harassment in place, and that policy should include the way you are expected to report it. And remember, men can be the victims of sexual harassment and women can be the perpetrators.

Coworkers

You're apt to run into other kinds of difficult coworkers. Any number of books can give you advice about coworkers who backstab, undercut, or short-circuit you. In general, the best advice is to learn about the personnel structure of the firm you are working in. There may be a paralegal manager, or perhaps you work under the supervision of a particular partner. Make sure you know whom to talk to if problems with your coworkers reach that level of seriousness.

The Client Relationship

In a great many paralegal jobs, more of your time will be spent with clients than with coworkers. Often, when people come to see a lawyer, it is because they are facing a crisis. Perhaps they have been arrested or threatened, are getting divorced, or are contemplating death. They need legal representation to defend themselves, protect their rights, negotiate a settlement, or write a will. None of these are things most of us look forward to doing. Even in corporate law, your clients may be facing crises involving hostile takeovers or product liability suits. For most of us, when things get bad enough that we hire a lawyer, we want the lawyer to wave a magic legal wand and make all the bad go away. Unfortunately, that's not how it works.

Many attorneys have little training in client counseling—and it's too rarely part of the paralegal curriculum. Remember, the operative word is *counseling*. If at all possible, a client should leave a meeting with a lawyer or paralegal feeling better than before. That can be tricky for you, because when you interview a client, you are forcing thoughts to the surface that most people would rather keep tucked away. Imagine how you would feel if someone asked you questions like these:

- And after he threatened your life, what did he do?
- Tell me about all your debts and assets.
- Did the police read you your rights?
- Are you afraid your ex-spouse will harm your child?

A situation that leads to such questions is probably one clients would rather not think about. And there you are, making them think about it. It can be harrowing.

You need great counseling and communication skills to handle these kinds of situations. If these don't come naturally to you, you are well advised to get as much training as you can and learn as much on your own as you can. In addition to reading books, watch the people you work with who seem to be good at counseling and follow their example. Always remember that your clients probably wish they didn't have to be seeing you; but it's nothing personal.

Your clients probably have little knowledge about what paralegals are and what they do. As a result, clients may either not want to talk to you, feeling you are somehow a poor substitute for a lawyer, or they may pressure you for legal opinions. In the first instance, a professional demeanor on your part will go a long way toward gaining a reluctant client's confidence. You may sometimes have to say, "Your lawyer trusts me to handle this matter. Please give me a chance to show you that trust is justified." In the second instance, remember that engaging in the unauthorized practice of law could jeopardize your job and your career. Don't do it; explain, kindly, that it's not your place to give legal advice and that the client should ask the attorney, or you can pass the question along. That doesn't mean you can never answer a question; of course you will and should exercise your independent judgment. Just don't let a weeping client convince you that just this time it's okay to suggest which bankruptcy chapter to file.

Managing Your Time

Effective time management is crucial to a law practice. A great deal of a lawyer's—and therefore a paralegal's—schedule is determined by someone else. If you have twenty days to respond to a complaint, its due date is determined by the date the complaint was filed. Even when your client is initiating the action, you have to wait for the client to come to you with a problem. The stereotype of ambulance-chasing lawyers aside, attorneys really don't sit around thinking, "Gee, maybe I can talk someone into getting divorced; I haven't done a good divorce decree in a while!" In addition to courts and clients, government agencies determine when documents need to be filed. In some cases, a judge or other hearing officer then tells you when the hearing will be. Of course, they try to accommodate everyone's schedule, but ultimately the judge decides when the trial will be.

If you miss any such deadlines, it can mean an ethical violation for the attorney you work for and even a malpractice suit. And you can bet that of all the work lawyers want to give up to paralegals, calendaring is at the top of the list. Very often it will be up to you to let your boss know that something is due to be filed.

Computer programs have come a long way, even since I started in the law in 1990. Then, the advice I received was to run a "tickler" to organize my time. (Sorry, I have no idea why it's called a tickler!) My tickler was a little recipe box with 3 x 5 cards and a divider for every day of the month. When I took on a new project, I made up several cards, the exact number depending on how much lead time I had. One might read "X v Y appeal brief due one month from today." If the final brief was due on January 4, that card would be filed under December 7. Then, on December 21, the card would read "X v Y appeal brief due two weeks from today," and so on. As the work progressed, I added other cards reminding me what was done and what was left; the card for a certain day might read, for example, "complete standing research and check on statute of limitations." The whole point of a tickler is to make sure that you are never surprised by a due date. Have you ever written something on your calendar, in the first week of the month, and then completely forgotten it until you turned the page over? That's the kind of "yikes!" a tickler is supposed to eliminate.

The bad news is that as a paralegal, the tickler may well be your responsibility. The good news is that now there are a variety of computer programs to do the trick. The best advice I can give you is never, ever, think you'll remember something without writing it down. In large firms, there may be one person whose job is doing the entire calendar; in other firms, you will be responsible, but only for particular attorneys or certain cases. However it is handled, the information has to get to the right place; a computer program doesn't know you have a response due next week unless you tell it so. Make sure you come up with some surefire method for doing your part of the calendaring.

Budgeting Time for Projects

Remember that most of a law office's schedule is determined by someone else. Then remember that you will probably be working for more than one attorney. Now picture several attorneys handing you projects that take three days and are all due tomorrow. Suddenly, finals week doesn't look so bad, does it?

Relax. Just because somebody says something is due tomorrow doesn't mean it really is. Often it just makes people feel important to say, "I need this right away!" Also, no matter how much you want to please your bosses, you can't take on more than one three-day project and have them done tomorrow (whether you can do one is questionable as well). Deep down in most every lawyer is a reasonable person who knows that. You're not going to be fired if you say, "I can't do that" to the second and third requests. Finally, just because someone asked you first doesn't mean that person's task is more urgent. The key to working these things out is to get everybody together (as much as possible) and figure out which project really has to be done tomorrow and which can wait or be done by someone else. You'll save yourself some time if you get that kind of information at the outset; don't wait until you're swamped. Then, when one attorney says, "You have to do this first! It's due next week!" you can say, "Yes, but this is due tomorrow."

The main points of organization are communication and knowledge. Find out as much as you can about each assignment, and keep your bosses informed about your progress. For your own sanity, bear in mind that people who like crises seem to be drawn to the law. Some people believe—whether it's true or not—that they are more productive when they work in "crisis mode." An unusually high number of these people seem to become lawyers. If you are one of those types, you'll fit right in; if not, you'll quickly become valued as "the rock," the calm, organized person everyone else can count on.

FINDING A MENTOR

A mentor is a person who is almost as dedicated to advancing your career as you are. In addition, a mentor needs to have the knowledge and experience to help you advance. The typical mentor is an attorney or a senior paralegal at the firm where you work. But a mentor also can be a professor or someone you met through a professional organization. Mentors can be invaluable in helping you succeed in your career—and I mean "succeed" in the broadest sense, not just as in getting a promotion. A good mentor not only advises and helps you advance in your career, but also is interested in helping you fit in at your job and listening when you need to talk out a problem. A mentor is a combination of friend and teacher.

By now, you're probably thinking, "Sounds good; how do I find one of them?" That, of course, is the difficult part. Aggressively seeking out a mentor may lead to a very insincere—and, therefore, uncomfortable—relationship. Instead, just keep the idea of a mentor in the back of your mind. If the paralegal in the next office, who's worked at the firm for several years, asks you to lunch, go. Then ask a lot of questions. Ask what is best and worst about working there, ask about interesting cases from the past, ask how the paralegal department has evolved. In other words, demonstrate that you are interested and that you believe this person has a lot of answers. No matter how well you seem to hit it off the first time, try a couple of more times. Next time, ask the other paralegal out to lunch. If you hit it off, you may have found yourself a mentor. If you don't, you've gained a lot of useful information about the firm, including, maybe, some ideas about other people you can try out as mentors.

Never become so single-minded in your search for a mentor that you forget to keep your eyes open for friends. They can come in quite handy too. Be aware, too, that older, more traditional firms may be quite hierarchical, and approaching an attorney to be your mentor may be a faux pas. However, an attorney can make a great mentor, especially because paralegals sometimes decide they want to become attorneys.

Becoming A Mentor

You should also strive to *be* a mentor, as much as you can. When you are fresh out of paralegal school and on your new job, it may be hard to imagine that you can be much help to anybody else. Although you probably can't help much with information about the job, you may know other helpful things, such as the best place to get a haircut, or who makes the best pizza in town, or where the best parking spaces are. If you open up that way to others, they are likely to open up to you. Over time, you will have enough knowledge about the job to be a paralegal mentor; in the meantime, do what you can to create relationships.

It's a mistake to think of mentoring as a one-way process in which the senior person is helping the junior person along. Mentoring is multidirectional; it works best when those involved aim to advance themselves while looking out for each other. If a senior paralegal is mentoring you and you hear about a job opening that is exactly what your mentor is looking for, you pass on that information. And the person mentoring you will be pleased to see you mentoring others. The plain truth is, nobody gets ahead without some help. Mentoring is just a way of acknowledging that.

PROMOTING YOURSELF

The paralegal profession is new enough that there are still quite a few people out there who aren't sure just what a paralegal does. If you end up working for one of those people, you may find that your job feels quite dead-end after a while. When some attorneys first get a paralegal, they are told, "Oh, paralegals are great; they can do all your research!" So your first assignment is to do some research, and you do a good job, so your next assignment is to do some more research, and pretty soon you realize that's all you ever do. Now every time this attorney gives you a research assignment, you sigh and think, "I do have other skills, you know." A better response is to offer something concrete that you can do. "After I finish, I can draft the complaint for you. I can have that done by next Thursday." That makes the attorney think, "Paralegals do more than research?" Most attorneys are swamped enough that they'll be willing to let you try something new.

In addition, keep your ears open for the litany that every lawyer spouts on a fairly regular basis. It goes something like this: "I am so busy. I have a telephone hearing at 11 and a deposition this afternoon, and I have to finish an answer to a complaint by the filing deadline tomorrow!" At this point, you can say, "I can draft the answer for you and have it first thing in the morning. You can see if there need to be any changes, and then I can file it before the end of the business day." You have just volunteered your way into more responsibility and a chance to show off your writing skills.

No matter how well you work with others and how organized you are, in the end you will be judged by the product you put out. You want to develop a reputation as someone who gets an assignment, does it right, and does it on time. To accomplish this, whenever someone gives you a task, make sure you know exactly what is expected of you. When an attorney tells you to do research for a memo, ask him or her if you are to draft the memo, or whether the research should be organized in a particular way. And when the attorney tells you the research is needed "next week," find out if there is an appointment with the client and whether it is on Monday or Friday. If you don't have this kind of information, you may manage to do the assignment, but the attorney may be disappointed in the end result. It never hurts to get things in writing, either.

Maintain a Record of Your Work

As your career progresses, find a way to keep track of the work you do. Please note that you should never make unauthorized copies of work and sock it away in your own file; to do so could lead to breaches in client confidentiality. But you can keep a record of the work you do. On your calendar or elsewhere, write down when assignments were given and just what they were, as well as when and if they were modified and when you completed them. That way, when your performance is reviewed and some attorney says, "I think you were late on the X research last month," you can look at your records and point out that you were told to put that work aside when another, more pressing, matter came up. It also allows you to chart, both for yourself and your bosses, the path your career has taken at the firm.

Some larger firms use forms for requesting in-house paralegal services. The information on these forms and their degree of detail varies a great deal, but in essence, their purpose is to outline the tasks required of the paralegal department. When you are the only paralegal working on a case, that request form will be given to you; when several paralegals will work on the case, each will be given a copy indicating which tasks are assigned to which person. If you keep a file of copies of these request forms—and make any notes on them about verbal instructions you received—you'll be well on your way to having a complete record of the work you've done.

Handle Criticism in a Positive Way

When you do receive criticism about your job performance—and we all do, sometimes—try to remain calm and listen carefully to what is being said. First, pay attention to positive comments. Most of us tend to zero in on the one bad thing and discount all the good. Let's say your critique is something like "Your research and organization on this memo are excellent; I do think you need to work a bit on your writing skills, however." Most of us walk away thinking, "My writing stinks!" So make sure you hear the part about your excellent research and organization.

Second, ask for concrete help to rectify the situation. Don't say, "Thanks. I'll work on my writing." Instead, ask for specific information. Is the problem spelling, grammar, legal-ese? Too wordy, too terse? Ask for suggestions. There are books on legal writing; or maybe it's just a question of remembering to use the spell-check on the final copy. Then follow the advice you are given, and ask the person for help in the future. See if you can find a time when things aren't so busy to go over your brief and make specific suggestions for changes; maybe this attorney would be willing to read some earlier drafts in the future and give you feedback.

Good Luck

As I've said throughout this book, the paralegal profession is growing, and it doesn't look likely to slow down anytime soon. Not only are there more and more paralegals, but paralegals also are moving in many new directions. The paralegal career pays quite well, is well respected, and affords you opportunities for advancement. But the best thing about working in the legal profession, no matter what area you're in and no matter how routine your work may be, every once in a while you make a huge difference in someone's life, whether it be in a big area such as tobacco or breast-implant litigation or a small one such as getting the used car dealer to take back the lemon and refund the money. Or getting a sign-language interpreter for a deaf student. Or stopping the hostile takeover of a small corporation. These are only small victories in the grand scheme of things; to your client, they mean everything. And you helped make it happen. Pretty cool.

THE INSIDE TRACK

Who:	Audrey Manteufel
What:	Paralegal
Where:	Legal Aid Society of Minneapolis, Minneapolis, Minnesota
How long:	Four years; ten years at Legal Aid (originally as a secretary)
Degree:	Paralegal certificate

Insider's Advice

I've been here a long time. The starting salaries [in Legal Aid] are below the median. But I've worked almost exclusively for non-profits throughout my career, so I think it's kind of a mind-set. The gratification is worth it. And, there are some other benefits that make the lower salary worthwhile. For example, except when meeting with clients, there's a more casual atmosphere, not the sort of stodgy corporate law firm.

I pretty much do family law. In the Legal Aid Society of Minneapolis there's family law, government benefits, and housing. Those are the main areas; there's a lot of people doing work on the welfare reform stuff and also housing—landlord/tenant cases. In the downtown office, I'm the only paralegal. I have a lot of client contact. I do a lot of interviews, rough drafting of documents, and some research. It has to do with the attorneys that you work with; some just prefer to do [research] on their own. If they have the time, they like to do it. Whereas others would rather not have to deal with it. I don't do a lot of it, but I do some. It really just depends on the attorney.

The nice thing is a lot of times there's a lot of younger attorneys who haven't quite decided if they are going to specialize or what that specialty will be, so they come [to work at Legal Aid] right after having passed the bar. That's always fun, to work with young, motivated people, who are gung-ho to wage justice.

Insider's Take on the Future

Getting formal training is really important and valuable. I actually was hired to do the paralegal work before I started at the [Minnesota Paralegal] Institute, because

I'd been a secretary in my particular unit for a long time prior to that. Getting a formal education really broadened my horizons and was really helpful in terms of exposure to other areas of law.

APPENDIX A

In addition to contact information for national organizations and state bar associations, this appendix lists the affiliated organizations of the National Federation of Paralegal Associations. You'll also find a state-by-state listing of higher education agencies.

PROFESSIONAL ASSOCIATIONS

This appendix contains a list of professional associations that can offer you relevant information related to employment or training as a paralegal.

National Organizations

American Association for Paralegal Education (AAFPE)
P.O. Box 40244
Overland Park, KS 66204
913-381-4458; FAX: 913-381-9308
http://www.aafpe.org

American Bar Association (ABA)
Standing Committee on Legal Assistants
750 North Lake Shore Dr.
Chicago, IL 60611
312-988-5000
http://www.abanet.org

Association of Legal Administrators
175 East Hawthorn Pkwy., Suite 325
Vernon Hills, IL 60061-1428
708-816-1212
http://www.alanet.org

Legal Assistant Management Association
638 Prospect Ave.
Hartford, CT 06105-4298
203-232-4825

National Association of Legal Assistants
(NALA)
1516 Boston Ave., Suite 200
Tulsa, OK 74119
918-587-6828; FAX: 918-582-6772
http://www.nala.org
Contact the NALA for a complete listing of affiliated associations.

National Federation of Paralegal Associations (NFPA)
P.O. Box 33108
Kansas City, MO 64114
816-941-4000; FAX: 816-941-2725
http://www.paralegals.org

State Bar Associations

Alabama Bar Association
415 Dexter Ave.
P.O. Box 671
Montgomery, AL 36104
334-269-1515

Alaska Bar Association
507 L St., Suite 602
Anchorage, AK 99501
907-272-7469

State Bar of Arizona
111 West Monroe, Suite 1800
Phoenix, AZ 85003
602-252-4804

Arkansas Bar Association
400 W. Markham
Little Rock, AR 72201
507-375-4606

State Bar of California
555 Franklin St.
San Francisco, CA 94102
415-561-8200

Colorado Bar Association
1900 Grant St., 9th Fl.
Denver, CO 80203
303-860-1115

Connecticut Bar Association
101 Corporate Pl.
Rocky Hill, CT 06067
860-721-0025

Delaware State Bar Association
1201 Orange St., Suite 1100
Wilmington, DE 19801
302-658-5279

Bar Association of D.C.
1819 H St. NW, 12th Fl.
Washington, DC 20006
202-223-6600

The Florida Bar
650 Apalachee Pkwy.
Tallahassee, FL 32399
850-561-5808

State Bar of Georgia
800 The Hurt Bldg.
50 Hurt Plaza
Atlanta, GA 30303
404-527-8700

Hawaii State Bar Association
1136 Union Mall, PH 1
Honolulu, HI 96813
808-537-1868

Idaho State Bar Association
525 West Jefferson St.
P.O. Box 895
Boise, ID 83701
208-334-4500

Illinois State Bar Association
Illlinois Bar Center
424 South 2nd St.
Springfield, IL 62701
217-525-1760

Indiana State Bar Association
Indiana Bar Center
230 East Ohio St.

Indianapolis, IN 46204
317-639-5465

Iowa State Bar Association
521 East Locust St., Fl. 3
Des Moines, IA 50309
515-243-3179

Kansas Bar Association
1200 Harrison St.
Topeka, KS 66601
785-234-5696

Kentucky Bar Association
514 West Main St.
Frankfort, KY 40601
502-564-3795

Louisiana State Bar Association
601 St. Charles Ave.
New Orleans, LA 70130
504-566-1600

Maine State Bar Association
124 State St.
P.O. Box 788
Augusta, ME 04332
207-622-7523

Maryland State Bar Association, Inc.
Maryland Bar Center
Baltimore, MD 21201
410-685-7878

Massachusetts Bar Association
20 West St.
Boston, MA 02111-1218
617-338-0530

State Bar of Michigan
The Michael Franck Bldg.
306 Townsend St.
Lansing, MI 48933
517-346-6300

Minnesota State Bar Association
514 Nicollet Mall, Suite 300
Minneapolis, MN 55402
612-333-1183

The Mississippi Bar
643 North State St.
P.O. Box 2168
Jackson, MS 39225
601-948-4471

The Missouri Bar
P.O. Box 119
Jefferson City, MO 65102
573-635-4128

State Bar of Montana
46 Last Chance Gulch #2A
P.O. Box 577
Helena, MT 59624
406-442-7660

Nebraska State Bar Association
635 South 14th St.
P.O. Box 81809
Lincoln, NE 68501
402-475-7091

The Nevada State Bar
201 Las Vegas Blvd. S., Suite 200
Las Vegas, NV 89101
702-382-2200

New Hampshire Bar Association
112 Pleasant St.
Concord, NH 03301-2931
603-224-6942

New Jersey State Bar Association
1 Constitution Square
New Brunswick, NJ 08901
732-249-5000

State Bar of New Mexico
Springer Square
121 Tijeras Ave., NE
Albuquerque, NM 87124
505-842-6132

New York State Bar Association
1 Elk St.
Albany, NY 12207
518-463-3200

North Carolina Bar Association
P.O. Box 3688
Cary, NC 27519
919-677-0561

State Bar Association of North Dakota
515 East Broadway, Suite 101
P.O. Box 2136
Bismarck, ND 58502
701-255-1404

Ohio State Bar Association
P.O. Box 16562
Columbus, OH 43216
614-487-2050

Oklahoma Bar Association
1901 N. Lincoln
P.O. Box 53036
Oklahoma City, OK 73152
405-524-2365

Oregon State Bar
5200 SW Meadows Rd.
P.O. Box 1689
Lake Oswego, OR 97035
503-620-0222

Pennsylvania Bar Association
100 South St., P.O. Box 186
Harrisburg, PA 17108
717-238-6715

Rhode Island Bar Association
115 Cedar St.
Providence, RI 02903
401-421-5740

South Carolina Bar Association
950 Taylor St.
P.O. Box 608
Columbia, SC 29202
803-799-6653

State Bar of South Dakota
222 East Capitol Ave.
Pierre, SD 57501
605-224-7554

Tennessee Bar Association
3622 West End Ave.
Nashville, TN 37205
615-383-7421

State Bar of Texas
1414 Colorado St., Suite 501
Austin, TX 78701
512-463-1463

Utah State Bar
Utah Law & Justice Center
645 South 200 E.
Salt Lake City, UT 84111
801-531-9077

Vermont Bar Association
35-37 Court St.
P.O. Box 100
Montpelier, VT 05601
802-223-2020

Virginia State Bar
707 East Main St., Suite 1500
Richmond, VA 23219
804-775-0501

Washington State Bar Association
2101 Fourth Ave., 4th Fl.
Seattle, WA 98121
206-727-8200

West Virginia State Bar
2006 Kanawha Blvd. E.
Charleston, WV 25311
304-558-2456

State Bar of Wisconsin
402 West Wilson St.
P.O. Box 7158
Madison, WI 53707
800-444-9404

Wyoming State Bar
500 Randall Ave.
Cheyenne, WY 82001
307-632-9061

NFPA-Affiliated Organizations

ALASKA

Alaska Association of Legal Assistants
P.O. Box 101956
Anchorage 99510-1956
907-566-2001
Alaska@paralegals.org

ARIZONA

Arizona Association of Professional
Paralegals, Inc.
P.O. Box 430
Phoenix 85001
Arizona@paralegals.org

CALIFORNIA

California Association of Independent
Paralegals
39120 Argonaut Way, #114
Fremont 94538
800-780-2247
CAIndependent@paralegals.org

Sacramento Association of Legal Assistants
P.O. Box 453
Sacramento 95812-0453
916-763-7851
Sacramento@paralegals.org

San Diego Association of Legal Assistants
P.O. Box 87449
San Diego 92138-7449
619-491-1994
SanDiego@paralegals.org

San Francisco Association of Legal
Assistants
P.O. Box 2110
San Francisco 94126-2110
415-777-2390; FAX: 415-586-6606
SanFrancisco@paralegals.org

West Coast Association of Paralegals
P.O. Box 32242
Long Beach 90832-2242
310-460-2939
WestCoast@paralegals.org

COLORADO

Rocky Mountain Paralegal Association
P.O. Box 481864
Denver   80248-1834
303-369-1606
RockyMountain@paralegals.org

CONNECTICUT

Central Connecticut Paralegal Association, Inc.
P.O. Box 230594
Hartford 06123-0594
CentralConnecticut@paralegals.org

Connecticut Association of Paralegals, Inc.
P.O. Box 134
Bridgeport 06601-0134
Connecticut@paralegals.org

New Haven County Association
of Paralegals, Inc.
P.O. Box 862
New Haven 06504-0862

DELAWARE

Delaware Paralegal Association
P.O. Box 1362
Wilmington 19899
302-426-1362
Delaware@paralegals.org

DISTRICT OF COLUMBIA

National Capital Area Paralegal Association
P.O. Box 86171
Gaithersburg 20886-6171
202-659-0243; FAX: 202-659-0243
NationalCapital@paralegals.org

GEORGIA

Georgia Association of Paralegals, Inc.
1199 Euclid Ave., NE
Atlanta 30307
404-522-1457; FAX: 404-522-0132
Georgia@paralegals.org

HAWAII

Hawaii Association of Legal Assistants
P.O. Box 674
Honolulu 96809
Hawaii@paralegals.org

ILLINOIS

Illinois Paralegal Association
P.O. Box 8089
Bartlett 60103-8089
630-837-8088; FAX: 630-837-8096
Illinois@paralegals.org

INDIANA

Indiana Paralegal Association
Federal Station, P.O. Box 44518
Indianapolis 46204
317-767-7798
Indiana@paralegals.org

Michiana Paralegal Association
P.O. Box 11458
South Bend 46634
219-237-1237
Michiana@paralegals.org

Northeast Indiana Paralegal Association, Inc.
P.O. Box 13646
Fort Wayne 46865
219-455-4506
NortheastIndiana@paralegals.org

KANSAS

Kansas City Paralegal Association
8826 Santa Fe Dr. , Suite 208
Overland Park 66212
913-381-4458; FAX: 913-381-9308
KansasCity@paralegals.org

Kansas Paralegal Association
P.O. Box 1675
Topeka 66601
785-296-5322
Kansas@paralegals.org

KENTUCKY

Greater Lexington Paralegal Association, Inc.
P.O. Box 574
Lexington 40586
Lexington@paralegals.org

LOUISIANA

New Orleans Paralegal Association
P.O. Box 30604
New Orleans 70190
504-467-3136
NewOrleans@paralegals.org

MARYLAND

Maryland Association of Paralegals
P.O. Box 13244
Baltimore 21203
410-576-2252
Maryland@paralegals.org

National Capital Area Paralegal Association
P.O. Box 86171
Gaithersburg 20886-6171
202-659-0243; FAX: 202-659-0243
NationalCapital@paralegals.org

MASSACHUSETTS

Central Massachusetts Paralegal Association
P.O. Box 444
Worcester 01614
CentralMassachusetts@paralegals.org

Massachusetts Paralegal Association
19 Harrison St.
Framingham 01702
508-879-4001
Massachusetts@paralegals.org

Western Massachusetts Paralegal Association
ciation
P.O. Box 30005
Springfield 01103

MINNESOTA
Minnesota Paralegal Association
1711 W. County Rd. B, #300N
Roseville 55113
612-633-2778; FAX: 612-635-0307
Minnesota@paralegals.org

NEW JERSEY
Prudential Insurance Company
of America-Paralegal Council
751 Broad St.
Newark 07102

South Jersey Paralegal Association
P.O. Box 355
Haddonfield 08033
SouthJersey@paralegals.org

New York
Long Island Paralegal Association
877 Bly Rd.
East Meadow 11554-1158

Manhattan Paralegal Association, Inc.
521 Fifth Ave., 17th Fl.
New York 10175
212-330-8213
Manhattan@paralegals.org

Paralegal Association of Rochester
P.O. Box 40567
Rochester 14604
716-234-5923
Rochester@paralegals.org

Southern Tier Association of Paralegals
P.O. Box 2555
Binghamton 13902
SouthernTier@paralegals.org

West/Rock Paralegal Association
P.O. Box 668
New City 10956
914-786-6184
WestRock@paralegals.org

Western New York Paralegal Association
tion
P.O. Box 207, Niagara Square Station
Buffalo 14202
716-635-8250
WesternNewYork@paralegals.org

OHIO
Cincinnati Paralegal Association
P.O. Box 1515
Cincinnati 45201
513-244-1266
Cincinnati@paralegals.org

Cleveland Association of Paralegals
P.O. Box 5496
Cleveland 44101
216- 902-7035

Greater Dayton Paralegal Association
P.O. Box 515, Mid-City Station
Dayton 45402
Dayton@paralegals.org

Northeastern Ohio Paralegal Association
P.O. Box 80068
Akron 44308-0068
NEOhio@paralegals.org

Paralegal Association of Central Ohio
P.O. Box 15182
Columbus 43215-0182
614-224-9700
CentralOhio@paralegals.org

OREGON
Oregon Paralegal Association
P.O. Box 8523
Portland 97207
503-796-1671
Oregon@paralegals.org

PENNSYLVANIA
Central Pennsylvania Paralegal Association
P.O. Box 11814
Harrisburg 17108

Chester County Paralegal Association
P.O. Box 295
West Chester 19381-0295

Lycoming County Paralegal Association
P.O. Box 991
Williamsport 17701

Philadelphia Association of Paralegals
P.O. Box 177
Lafayette 19144
610-825-6504
Philadelphia@paralegals.org

Pittsburgh Paralegal Association
P.O. Box 2845
Pittsburgh 15230
412-344-3904
Pittsburgh@paralegals.org

RHODE ISLAND
Rhode Island Paralegal Association
P.O. Box 1003
Providence 02901

SOUTH CAROLINA
Palmetto Paralegal Association
P.O. Box 11634
Columbia 29211-1634
803-252-0460

TENNESSEE
Memphis Paralegal Association
P.O. Box 3646
Memphis 38173-0646
Memphis@paralegals.org

TEXAS

Dallas Area Paralegal Association
P.O. Box 12533
Dallas 75225-0533
972-991-0853
Dallas@paralegals.org

VERMONT

Vermont Paralegal Organization
P.O. Box 6238
Rutland 05702

WASHINGTON

Washington State Paralegal Association
P.O. Box 48153
Seattle 98148
253-813-9499; 800-288-WSPA (in-state); FAX: 253-813-9779
Washington@paralegals.org

WISCONSIN

Paralegal Association of Wisconsin, Inc.
P.O. Box 92882
Milwaukee 53202
414-272-7168
Wisconsin@paralegals.org

State Higher Education Agencies

Alabama Commission on Higher
Education
Suite 205
3465 Norman Bridge Rd.
Montgomery, AL 36105-2310
334-281-1998
or

State Department of Education
Gordon Persons Office Bldg.
50 N. Ripley St.
Montgomery, AL 36130-3901
205-242-8082
http://www.alsde.edu/

Alaska Commission on Postsecondary
Education
3030 Vintage Blvd.
Juneau, AK 99801-7109
907-465-2962
http://sygov.swadm.alaska.edu/BOR/
or
State Department of Education
Goldbelt Pl., 801 West 10th St., Suite 200
Juneau, AK 99801-1894
907-465-8715
http://www.educ.state.ak.us

Arizona Commission for Postsecondary
Education
2020 N. Central Ave., Suite 275
Phoenix, AZ 85004-4503
602-229-2531
http://www.abor.asu.edu/
or
State Department of Education
1535 W. Jefferson
Phoenix, AZ 85007
602-542-2147
http://www.ade.state.az.us/

Arkansas Department of Higher
Education
114 E. Capitol
Little Rock, AR 72201-3818
501-324-9300
or
Arkansas Department of Education
4 State Capitol Mall, Rm. 304A
Little Rock, AR 72201-1071
(501) 682-4474
 ref HYPERLINK http://www
 http://arkedu.k12.ar.us/

California Student Aid Commission
P.O. Box 510845
Sacramento, CA 94245-0845
916-445-0880
http://www.ucop.edu/ucophome/system
/regents.html
or
1515 South St., North Bldg.
Suite 500, P.O. Box 510845
Sacramento, CA 94245-0621
916-322-2294
or
California Department of Education
721 Capitol Mall
Sacramento, CA 95814
916-657-2451
http://goldmine.cde.ca.gov/

Colorado Commission on Higher
Education
Colorado Heritage Center
1300 Broadway, 2nd Fl.
Denver, CO 80203
303-866-2723
http://www.state.co.us/edu_dir/state_hre
du_dept.html
or
State Department of Education
201 E. Colfax Ave.
Denver, CO 80203-1705
303-866-6779
http://www.cde.state.co.us/

Connecticut Department of Higher
Education
61 Woodland St.
Hartford, CT 06105-2391
203-566-3910
http://www.lib.uconn.edu/ConnState/
HigherEd/dhe.htm
or
Connecticut Department of Education
165 Capitol Ave.
P.O. Box 2219
Hartford, CT 06106-1630
800-667-2000
http://www.aces.k12.ct.us/csde/

Delaware Higher Education
Commission
Carvel State Office Bldg., 4th Fl.
820 North French St.
Wilmington, DE 19801
302-577-3240
http://www.state.de.us/high-ed/commiss
/webpage.htm
or
State Department of Public Instruction
Townsend Bldg., #279
Federal and Lockerman Sts., P.O. Box
1402
Dover, DE 19903-1402
302-739-4583
http://www.dpi.state.de.us/dpi/dpi/dpi.h
tml

Department of Human Services
Office of Postsecondary Education,
Research, and Assistance
2100 Martin Luther King Jr. Ave. SE,
Suite 401
Washington, DC 20020
202-727-3685
or
District of Columbia Public Schools
Division of Student Services
4501 Lee St. NE
Washington, DC 20019
202-724-4934
http://www.k12.dc.us/DCPSHP.html

Florida Department of Education
Office of Student Financial Assistance
1344 Florida Education Center
325 W. Gaines St.
Tallahassee, FL 32399-0400
904-487-0649
http://www.nwrdc.fsu.edu/bor/

Georgia Student Finance Authority
State Loans and Grants Division
Suite 245, 2082 E. Exchange Pl.
Tucker, GA 30084
404-414-3000
http://www.peachnet.edu/BORWEB/
or
State Department of Education
2054 Twin Towers E., 205 Butler St.
Atlanta, GA 30334-5040
404-656-5812
http://www.doe.state.ga.us/

Hawaii State Postsecondary Education
Commission
2444 Dole St., Rm. 202
Honolulu, HI 96822-2394
808-956-8213
http://www.hern.hawaii.edu/hern/
or
Hawaii Department of Education
2530 10th Ave., Rm. A12
Honolulu, HI 96816
808-733-9103
http://www.doe.hawaii.edu/

Idaho Board of Education
P.O. Box 83720
Boise, ID 83720-0037
208-334-2270
or
State Department of Education
650 West State St.
Boise, ID 83720
208-334-2113
http://www.sde.state.id.us/

Illinois Student Assistance Commission
1755 Lake Cook Rd.
Deerfield, IL 60015-5209
708-948-8500

State Student Assistance Commission of
Indiana
Suite 500, 150 W. Market St.
Indianapolis, IN 46204-2811
317-232-2350
http://www.ai.org/ssaci/
or
Indiana Department of Education
Rm. 229, State House
Center for Schools Improvement and
Performance
Indianapolis, IN 46204-2798
317-232-2305
http://ideanet.doe.state.in.us:80/

Iowa College Student Aid Commission
914 Grand Ave., Suite 201
Des Moines, IA 50309-2824
800-383-4222
http://www.state.ia.us/government/icsac/
index.htm

Iowa Department of Education
http://www.state.ia.us/educate/

Kansas Board of Regents
700 SW Harrison, Suite 1410
Topeka, KS 66603-3760
913-296-3517
or
State Department of Education
Kansas State Education Bldg.
120 E. 10th St.
Topeka, KS 66612-1103
913-296-4876

Kentucky Higher Education Assistance
Authority
Suite 102, 1050 U.S. 127 S.
Frankfort, KY 40601-4323
800-928-8926
or
State Department of Education
500 Mero St.
1919 Capital Plaza Tower
Frankfort, KY 40601
502-564-3421
http://www.kde.state.ky.us/

Louisiana Student Financial Assistance
Commission
Office of Student Financial Assistance
P.O. Box 91202
Baton Rouge, LA 70821-9202
800-259-5626
or

State Department of Education
P.O. Box 94064
626 N. 4th St., 12th Fl.
Baton Rouge, LA 70804-9064
504-342-2098
http://www.doe.state.la.us/

Finance Authority of Maine
P.O. Box 949
Augusta, ME 04333-0949
207-287-3263
http://www.maine.edu
or
Maine Department of Education
23 State House Station
Augusta, ME 04333-0023
207-287-5800; hearing impaired: 207-
287-2550; FAX: 207-287-5900
http://www.state.me.us/education/home
page.htm

Maryland Higher Education
Commission
Jeffrey Bldg., 16 Francis St.
Annapolis, MD 21401-1781
410-974-2971
http://www.ubalt.edu/www/mhec/
or
Maryland State Department of
Education
200 W. Baltimore St.
Baltimore, MD 21201-2595
410-767-0480
http://www.maryland.umd.edu/
mde.html

Massachusetts Board of Higher
Education
330 Stuart St.
Boston, MA 02116
617-727-9420
or
State Department of Education
350 Main St.
Malden, MA 02148-5023
617-388-3300
http://www.doe.mass.edu/
or
Massachusetts Higher Education
Information Center
666 Boylston St.
Boston, MA 02116
617-536-0200 x4719
http://www.heic.org/

Michigan Higher Education Assistance
Authority
Office of Scholarships and Grants
P.O. Box 30462
Lansing, MI 48909-7962
517-373-3394
or
Michigan Department of Education
608 W. Allegan St.
Hannah Bldg.
Lansing, MI 48909
517-373-3324
http://web.mde.state.mi.us

Minnesota Higher Education Services
Office
Suite 400, Capitol Square Bldg.
550 Cedar St.
St. Paul, MN 55101-2292
800-657-3866
gopher://gopher.hecb.state.mn.us/
or
Department of Children, Families, and
Learning
712 Capitol Square Bldg.
550 Cedar St.
St. Paul, MN 55101
612-296-6104
gopher://gopher.educ.state.mn.us/HOM
E.HTM

Mississippi Postsecondary Education
Financial Assistance Board
3825 Ridgewood Rd.
Jackson, MS 39211-6453
601-982-6663
or
State Department of Education
P.O. Box 771
Jackson, MS 39205-0771
601-359-3768
http://mdek12.state.ms.us/

Missouri Coordinating Board for
Higher Education
3515 Amazonas Dr.
Jefferson City, MO 65109-5717
314-751-2361
gopher://dp.mocbhe.gov/
or

Missouri State Department of
Elementary and Secondary Education
P.O. Box 480
205 Jefferson St., Sixth Fl.
Jefferson City, MO 65102-0480
314-751-2931
http://services.dese.state.mo.us/

Montana University System
2500 Broadway
Helena, MT 59620-3103
406-444-6570
http://www.montana.edu/~aircj/manual
/bor/
or
State Office of Public Instruction
State Capitol, Rm. 106
Helena, MT 59620
406-444-4422
http://161.7.114.15/OPI/opi.html

Coordinating Commission for
Postsecondary Education
P.O. Box 95005
Lincoln, NE 68509-5005
402-471-2847
or
Nebraska Department of Education
P.O. Box 94987
301 Centennial Mall S.
Lincoln, NE 68509-4987
402-471-2784
http://www.nde.state.ne.us/

Nevada Department of Education
400 W. King St., Capitol Complex
Carson City, NV 89710
702-687-5915
http://nsn.scs.unr.edu/nvdoe/

New Hampshire Postsecondary
Education Commission
2 Industrial Park Dr.
Concord, NH 03301-8512
603-271-2555
or
State Department of Education
State Office Park S.
101 Pleasant St.
Concord, NH 03301
603-271-2632
http://www.state.nh.us/doe/education.
html

State of New Jersey
Office of Student Financial Assistance
4 Quakerbridge Plaza, CN 540
Trenton, NJ 08625
800-792-8670
http://ww.state.nj.us/highereducation/
or
State Department of Education
225 West State St.
Trenton, NJ 08625-0500
609-984-6409
http://www.state.nj.us/education/

New Mexico Commission on Higher
Education
1068 Cerrillos Rd.
Santa Fe, NM 87501-4925
505-827-7383
http://www.nmche.org/index.html
or
State Department of Education
Education Bldg.
300 Don Gaspar
Santa Fe, NM 87501-2786
505-827-6648
http://sde.state.nm.us/

New York State Higher Education
Services Corporation
One Commerce Plaza
Albany, NY 12255
518-474-5642
http://hesc.state.ny.us
or
State Education Department
111 Education Bldg., Washington Ave.
Albany, NY 12234
518-474-5705
http://www.nysed.gov/

North Carolina State Education
Assistance Authority
P.O. Box 2688
Chapel Hill, NC 27515-2688
919-821-4771
or

State Department of Public Instruction
Education Bldg., Division of Teacher
Education
116 W. Edenton St.
Raleigh, NC 27603-1712
919-733-0701
http://www.dpi.state.nc.us/

North Dakota University System
North Dakota Student Financial
Assistance Program
600 E. Boulevard Ave.
Bismarck, ND 58505-0230
701-224-4114
or
State Department of Public Instruction
State Capitol Bldg., 11th Fl.
600 E. Boulevard Ave.
Bismarck, ND 58505-0164
701-224-2271
http://www.sendit.nodak.edu/dpi/

Ohio Student Aid Commission
P.O. Box 182452
309 S. 4th St.
Columbus, OH 43218-2452
800-837-6752
http://www.bor.ohio.gov
or
State Department of Education
65 S. Front St., Rm. 1005
Columbus, OH 43266-0308
614-466-2761
http://www.ode.ohio.gov/

Oklahoma State Regents for Higher
Education
http://www.osrhe.edu/

Oklahoma Guaranteed Student Loan
Program
P.O. Box 3000
Oklahoma City, OK 73101-3000
405-858-4300; 800-247-0420
http://www.ogslp.org
or
State Department of Education
Oliver Hodge Memorial Education Bldg.
2500 N. Lincoln Blvd.
Oklahoma City, OK 73105-4599
405-521-4122
gopher://gopher.osrhe.edu/

Oregon State Scholarship Commission
Suite 100, 1500 Valley River Dr.
Eugene, OR 97401-2130
503-687-7400
http://www.teleport.com/~ossc/home.
htm
or
Oregon State System of Higher
Education
700 Pringle Pkwy. SE
Salem, OR 97310-0290
503-378-5585
http://www.osshe.edu/
or
Oregon Department of Education
255 Capitol St. NE
Salem, OR 97310-0203
503-378-3825
http://www.ode.state.or.us/

Pennsylvania Higher Education
Assistance Agency
1200 N. 7th St.
Harrisburg, PA 17102-1444
717-720-2800
http://www.pheaa.org

Council on Higher Education
Box 23305, UPR Station
Rio Piedras, PR 00931
809-758-3350
or
Department of Education
P.O. Box 759
Hato Rey, PR 00919
809-753-2200

Rhode Island Board of Governors for
Higher Education
Rhode Island Office of Higher
Education
301 Promenade St.
Providence, RI 02908-5720
401-277-6560; FAX: 401-277-6111
http://www.ids.net/ribog/index.htm
Email: RIBOG@uriacc.uri.edu
or
Rhode Island Higher Education
Assistance Authority
560 Jefferson Blvd.
Warwick, RI 02886
800-922-9855
or

State Department of Education
22 Hayes St.
Providence, RI 02908
401-277-3126
http://www.ri.net/RIDE

South Carolina Higher Education
Tuition Grants Commission
1310 Lady St., Suite 811
P.O. Box 12159
Columbia, SC 29201
803-734-1200
http://che400.state.sc.us
or
State Department of Education
803-a Rutledge Bldg.
1429 Senate St.
Columbia, SC 29201
803-734-8364
http://www.state.sc.us/sde/

Department of Education and Cultural
Affairs
Office of the Secretary
700 Governors Dr.
Pierre, SD 57501-2291
605-773-3134
http://www.state.sd.us/state/executive/de
ca/deca.html
or
South Dakota Board of Regents
http://www.ris.sdbor.edu

Tennessee Higher Education
Commission
404 James Robertson Pkwy., Suite 1900
Nashville, TN 37243-0820
615-741-3605
http://www.TBR.state.tn.us
or
State Department of Education
100 Cordell Hull Bldg.
Nashville, TN 37219-5335
615-741-1346; 800-342-1663 (in-state)
http://www.state.tn.us/other/sde/homep
age.htm

Texas Higher Education Coordinating
Board
P.O. Box 12788, Capitol Station
Austin, TX 78711
800-242-3062
http://www.texas.gov/agency/781.html

Utah State Board of Regents
Utah System of Higher Education
355 W. North Temple
#3 Triad Ctr., Suite 550
Salt Lake City, UT 84180-1205
801-321-7205
http://www.gv.ex.state.ut.us/highered.
htm
or
http://www.usoe.k12.ut.us/
Utah State Office of Education
250 East 500 S.
Salt Lake City, UT 84111
801-538-7779

Vermont Student Assistance
Corporation
Champlain Mill
P.O. Box 2000
Winooski, VT 05404-2601
800-642-3177
http://www.vsac.org
or
Vermont Department of Education
120 State St.
Montpelier, VT 05620-2501
802-828-3147; FAX: 802-828-3140
http://www.state.vt.us/educ/

State Council of Higher Education for
Virginia
James Monroe Bldg.
101 N. 14th St.
Richmond, VA 23219
804-786-1690
http://www.schev.edu
or
State Department of Education
P.O. Box 2120
James Monroe Bldg.
14th and Franklin Sts.
Richmond, VA 23216-2120
804-225-2072
http://pen1.pen.k12.va.us:80/Anthology/
VDOE/

Washington State Higher Education
Coordinating Board
P.O. Box 43430, 917 Lakeridge Way SW
Olympia, WA 98504-3430
206-753-7850
or

State Department of Public Instruction
Old Capitol Bldg., P.O. Box FG 11
Olympia, WA 98504-3211
206-753-2858
http://www.ospi.wednet.edu/

State Department of Education
1900 Washington St.
Bldg. B, Rm. 358
Charleston, WV 25305
304-588-2691
or
State College & University Systems of
West Virginia Central Office
1018 Kanawha Blvd. East, Suite 700
Charleston, WV 25301-2827
304-558-4016
http://www.scusco.wvnet.edu/

Higher Educational Aids Board
P.O. Box 7885
Madison, WI 53707-7885
608-267-2206
http://www.uwsa.edu/
or

State Department of Public Instruction
125 S. Wester St., P.O. Box 7841
Madison, WI 53707-7814
608-266-2364
http://www.state.wi.us/agencies/dpi/

Wyoming State Department of
Education
Hathaway Bldg.
2300 Capitol Ave., 2nd Fl.
Cheyenne, WY 82002-0050
307-777-6265
http://www.k12.wy.us/wdehome.html
or
Wyoming Community College
Commission
2020 Carey Ave., 8th Fl.
Cheyenne, WY 82002
307-777-7763

APPENDIX B

Now that you have a good idea of what steps you need to take to accomplish your goals, look through this appendix for titles that will give you more specific advice on the areas with which you need help.

ADDITIONAL RESOURCES

For additional information on the topics discussed in this book, refer to the following reading lists organized by subject.

GENERAL INFORMATION

Paralegals in American Law: Introduction to Paralegalism, Delmar Publishing, 1994.

Bernardo, Barbara. *Paralegal: An Insider's Guide to One of the Fastest-Growing Occupations of the 1990s.* Peterson's Guides, 1997.

Estrin, Chere B. *Everything You Need to Know About Being a Paralegal.* Delmar Publishing, 1995.

FINDING A JOB

Lauber, Daniel. *Government Job Finder: 1997–2000.* Planning /Communications, 1997.

Lauber, Daniel. *Non-Profits and Education Job Finder*. Planning /Communications, 1997.

Secol, Dorothy. *Starting and Managing Your Own Business: A Freelancing Guide for Paralegals*. Wiley Law Publications, 1994 (*1997 Cumulative Supplement*, 1996).

Treffinger, Karen. *Life Outside the Law Firm: Non-Traditional Careers for Paralegals*. Delmar Publishing, 1995.

Wagner, Andrea. *How to Land Your First Paralegal Job: An Insider's Guide to the Fastest-Growing Profession of the Next Millennium*. Prentice Hall, 1997.

ON THE JOB

The Bluebook: A Uniform System of Citation, Harvard Law Review Association, 1996 (Updated as appropriate).

Albrecht, Steve and Steve Albright. *The Paralegal's Desk Reference*. Macmillan, 1993.

Black, Henry Campbell, Joseph R. Nolan, and Jacqueline M. Nolan-Haley. *Black's Law Dictionary*. West Publishing Co., 1991.

Burton, William C. *Legal Thesaurus*. Macmillan, 1992.

Faulk, Martha and Irving Mehler. *The Elements of Legal Writing: A Guide to the Principles of Writing Clear, Concise, and Persuasive Legal Documents*. Macmillan, 1994.

LeClercq, Terri. *Expert Legal Writing*. University of Texas Press, 1995.

ASSOCIATION PUBLICATIONS
Publications from the National Association of Legal Assistants, Inc. (NALA):

Facts & Findings, NALA's quarterly journal, which contains educational articles for paralegals. Subscription is part of NALA membership.

Membership Newsletter, published at least quarterly to update NALA members on activities all across the U.S., including legislative and bar activities. Subscription is part of NALA membership.

The Career Chronicle (published by NALA annually) and *The National Utilization and Compensation Survey Report* (published by NALA biannually), which provide current information on the state of the paralegal profession.

Publications from the National Federation of Paralegal Associations, Inc. (NFPA):

PACE Candidates Handbook, with sample test questions and an application.

PACE Study Manual

Review Course for PACE Video

Directory of NFPA Pro Bono Programs, with information on how individuals and associations can get involved in pro bono ("for the good"—legal services performed free of charge) causes.

NFPA Paralegal Compensation And Benefits Report, the results of an annual survey on salaries and benefits for paralegals. Also contains information on education, experience, and practice areas of paralegals.

Paralegal Responsibilities, a booklet that summarizes the typical duties of paralegals in a variety of specialties.

National Paralegal Reporter, a quarterly publication provided to NFPA members. Past issues may be viewed on the NFPA web site. (http://www.paralegals.org/Reporter/)

Publications from the American Association for Paralegal Education (AAfPE):

Sidebar, a quarterly publication containing information on the activities of AAfPE and paralegal education in general.

Paralegal Educator, a quarterly magazine that features material on paralegal education, the paralegal profession, and AAfPE news.

The Journal for Paralegal Education and Practice, a scholarly journal with articles by educators, legal assistants, and attorneys on issues affecting paralegal education and the paralegal profession.

Order Form

CALIFORNIA EXAMS

___ @ $35.00   CA Police Officer
___ @ $35.00   CA State Police
___ @ $35.00   CA Corrections Officer
___ @ $20.00   CA Law Enforcement Career Guide
___ @ $35.00   CA Firefighter
___ @ $30.00   CA Postal Worker
___ @ $35.00   CA Allied Health

NEW JERSEY EXAMS

___ @ $35.00   NJ Police Officer
___ @ $35.00   NJ State Police
___ @ $35.00   NJ Corrections Officer
___ @ $20.00   NJ Law Enforcement Career Guide
___ @ $35.00   NJ Firefighter
___ @ $30.00   NJ Postal Worker
___ @ $35.00   NJ Allied Health

TEXAS EXAMS

___ @ $35.00   TX Police Officer
___ @ $30.00   TX State Police
___ @ $35.00   TX Corrections Officer
___ @ $20.00   TX Law Enforcement Career Guide
___ @ $35.00   TX Firefighter
___ @ $30.00   TX Postal Worker
___ @ $32.50   TX Allied Health

NEW YORK EXAMS

___ @ $30.00   NYC/Nassau County Police Officer
___ @ $30.00   Suffolk County Police Officer
___ @ $30.00   New York City Firefighter
___ @ $35.00   NY State Police
___ @ $35.00   NY Corrections Officer
___ @ $20.00   NY Law Enforcement Career Guide
___ @ $35.00   NY Firefighter
___ @ $30.00   NY Postal Worker
___ @ $35.00   NY Allied Health
___ @ $30.00   NY Postal Worker

MASSACHUSETTS EXAMS

___ @ $30.00   MA Police Officer
___ @ $30.00   MA State Police Exam
___ @ $30.00   MA Allied Health

FLORIDA EXAMS

___ @ $35.00   FL Police Officer
___ @ $35.00   FL Corrections Officer
___ @ $20.00   FL Law Enforcement Career Guide
___ @ $30.00   FL Postal Worker
___ @ $32.50   FL Allied Health

ILLINOIS EXAMS

___ @ $25.00   Chicago Police Officer
___ @ $25.00   Illinois Allied Health

The MIDWEST EXAMS

(Illinois, Indiana, Michigan, Minnesota, Ohio, and Wisconsin)

___ @ $30.00   Midwest Police Officer Exam
___ @ $30.00   Midwest Firefighter Exam

The SOUTH EXAMS

(Alabama, Arkansas, Georgia, Louisiana, Mississippi, North Carolina, South Carolina, and Virginia)

___ @ $25.00   The South Police Officer Exam
___ @ $25.00   The South Firefighter Exam

NATIONAL EDITIONS

___ @ $14.95   ASVAB (Armed Services Vocational Aptitude Battery)
___ @ $12.95   U.S. Postal Worker Exam
___ @ $15.00   Federal Clerical Worker Exam
___ @ $12.95   Bus Operator Exam
___ @ $12.95   Sanitation Worker Exam
___ @ $20.00   Allied Health Entrance Exams

NATIONAL CERTIFICATION EXAM

___ @ $20.00   Home Health Aide Certification Exam
___ @ $20.00   Nursing Assistant Certification Exam
___ @ $20.00   EMT-Basic Certification Exam

CAREER STARTERS

___ @ $14.95   Computer Technician
___ @ $14.95   Health Care
___ @ $14.95   Paralegal
___ @ $14.95   Administrative Assistant/Secretary
___ @ $14.00   Civil Service

To Order, Call TOLL-FREE: **1-888-551-JOBS, Dept. A040**

Or, mail this order form with your check or money order* to:
LearningExpress, Dept. A040, 20 Academy Street, Norwalk, CT 0685

Please allow at least 2-4 weeks for delivery. Prices subject to change without notice   **NY, CT, & MD residents add appropriate sales t*